Motorcycle Safety and Dynamics Volume Two

How to Survive the Experience Throughout Your Riding Career

First published in 2011 by The Master Strategy Group, Houston, Texas.

Copyright © 2011 The Master Strategy Group

All rights reserved. With the exception of quoting brief passages for the purposes of review, no part of this publication may be reproduced without prior written permission from the Master Strategy Group.

The information in this book is true and complete to the best of our knowledge. All recommendations are made without any guarantee on the part of the authors or the Master Strategy Group, who also disclaim any liability incurred in connection with the use of this data or specific details.

We recognize, further, that some words, model names, and designations mentioned herein are the property of the trademark holder. We use them for identification purposes only. This is not an official publication.

ISBN 978-1-257-96309-6

Manufactured in the United States of America
First United States Edition

Table of Contents

INTRODUCTION	6
PHASE 2	10
I. COMPETENCE	10
A. Braking skills	10
B. Aggressive swerve or aggressive stop?	24
C. Safety margin	26
D. Endurance is part of a "safety margin"	31
E. The value of planning	32
F. Extraordinary parking lot practice	39
G. It may be true – they don't see you	41
H. Traction and weight management	42
I. Maintenance and how the bike works	45
J. Attention	50
K. Conspicuity	52
II. GROUP RIDING	53
A. Group riding: why?	53
B. Group riding: why not?	54
C. Rules: who needs them?	54
D. Common group riding terms	54
E. Preparing for a group ride	57
F. Pre-ride briefing	58
G. The "Prime Directive"	58
H. Normal group riding maneuvers	59
I. "Caution / Warning / Danger" Signal	63
J. Joining a group	64
K. Size matters – the "rubber band effect"	65
L. Closing the gap after a rider leaves	66
M. "Closing the door"	67
N. Groups of two	67
O. Super-Groups	68
P. What to do with the impaired rider	69
Q. Responsibilities of other riders	70
R. "Odd Duck" in the group	71
S. "Rules" don't outweigh safety	72
T. Guidelines for street bikes	73
III. CARRYING A PASSENGER	74
A. Six months later, you're still not ready	74
B. Passenger's pre-ride briefing	75
C. Restrictions to enforce obsessively	75
D. Communications	76
E. Experienced passengers add value	76
IV. CAMPING	77

V. CONFIDENCE 80

A. Belief rather than fact 80
B. Survival is a better goal than a gauge 81
C. Your guard may go down 81

VI. SELF-INDUCED NEW THREATS 82

A. More powerful and faster motorcycles 82
B. 1,000 miles in 24 hours 83
C. Advanced or performance training 84
D. Efforts to improve and compete 86

VII. LIMITED UNDERSTANDING 87

A. Weight Transfer 88
B. Path Traveled 95
C. Neutral Steering 97
D. Braking in a curve is counter-steering 101
E. Tire pressure is temperature-sensitive 101
F. Slow-speed counter-steering? No way! 102
G. Spreadsheets and other tools 104

PHASE 3 117

I. MATURE 117

A. It's a matter of exposure 117
B. Aging and disabilities 118
C. Trikes, sidecars, lighter motorcycles, scooters, and modifications 121

II. CONSTRUCTIVE CONTRIBUTIONS 122

A. Mentoring 122
B. Becoming a RiderCoach or instructor 124
C. Safety officer 126
D. Writing 126
E. Ambassadorial influence 126

GLOSSARY 128

APPENDIX A – ENGINE GUARDS 146

APPENDIX B – PATH OF TRAVEL 147

APPENDIX C – SLIP ANGLES 150

APPENDIX D – SPEED ADVISORY SIGNS 152

APPENDIX E – PULLING A TRAILER 156

APPENDIX F – PASSENGERS ARE NOT HELPLESS 158

APPENDIX G – HOW THE DRAG AND LIFT MODEL WORKS 159

APPENDIX H – AN EQUIPMENT AND CAMPING CHECKLIST 161

1. For everyday rides 161
2. For Camping – additional personal items and equipment 162
3. For Camping – additional items for cooking and picnicking 162
4. For Camping – extra clothing, information, and entertainment-related items 163

APPENDIX I – TWENTY-THREE STUDIES DOCUMENTING INEFFECTIVENESS OF TRAINING	**163**
INDEX	**169**
TABLE OF FIGURES	**172**
LIST OF TABLES	**174**

Introduction

In their early days of touring by motorcycle, the two authors of this book, Cash and Jim, were part of a group from the Houston area making a tour of Oklahoma and Arkansas, where they had ridden the "Tali-Mena Trail," which runs across 57 miles of mountaintop twisties stretching from Talihina, OK to Mena, AR. After three days of riding without incident, the group began its return trip, following a route through east Texas.

One of the riders in the group, Evelyn Cline, was riding an older model Honda Gold Wing that had been recently given to her by an employer who knew she would love the sport. She had taken her bike into a Houston dealership for service just before the trip to check it out.

Riding through Tyler late on that warm summer morning, Evelyn experienced a terrific scare as she braked on a shimmering, white-painted stripe in a left-turn lane at a signal light that controlled a major six-lane intersection. Her bike failed to slow down for the red light, and she skidded into the intersection just as the light changed to permit cross-traffic to move.

Horrified, the other riders watched her bike pass the lead bike, barely missing its rear fender, and fishtail repeatedly, dipping and swerving until she was able to regain traction, make a controlled left turn, and stop. Fortunately, all the other drivers at the intersection stayed in their positions until she was clear of their path.

The rest of the riders made their turn and stopped with Evelyn (who literally kissed the pavement with gratitude that she'd been able to make the turn and hadn't been hit). We all parked and went into a fast-food restaurant nearby to allow her to collect herself. Trying to figure out what had gone wrong, we believed that the reflective beads on the surface of the white painted stripe had become extremely slick, possibly from an earlier rain shower or with a skim of oil, before Evelyn started braking for the light.

In other words, it could have happened to any of us; and the more experienced riders felt that few, if any, of us could have done any better than she did in maintaining her balance and regaining control. Evelyn was understandably shaken, though, so we all rested and ate ice cream until she regained her confidence.

Meanwhile, two of the most experienced riders in the group, both of whom had mechanical skills, inspected her motorcycle, even though there had been no impact. They saw nothing wrong with it, but they did notice a "hot" smell from the rear brake area. By the time she was ready to ride again, the odor had dissipated.

While the riders were eating their ice cream, Cash and Jim decided that, when they reached a convenient point, they would switch motorcycles, for fun. They made the other riders aware of their intentions. Thus, everyone knew they were expecting to make another stop before long.

The group took off again toward Houston with Evelyn riding in the second, "slot" position. Cash was on a cruiser in the third position, Jim was behind Cash on his Gold Wing, and another friend was riding drag.

Not far from Tyler's southern city limits, the group was traveling at about 50-55 MPH when the lead rider signaled for a right turn into a parking lot to allow Cash and Jim to make the swap.

When Evelyn applied her front and rear brakes to slow for the turn, her rear brake locked up.

She attempted to control the ensuing skid by turning the front wheel into it, correctly, but she couldn't recover her path of travel and straighten the bike. Her Gold Wing's rear tire laid a long skid mark as the other riders held their breath and watched, helpless. Then suddenly it regained traction, and the skidding stopped with a chirp. Evelyn's Gold Wing, an 850-pound machine loaded for touring, launched itself and Evelyn high into the air!

She had had experience, as many Texas women have, with riding unpredictable horses and being thrown off them; and as the bike twisted mid-air, she was thrown again. Later she said she had tried to launch herself as far from it as she could when she came off; and after hitting the hot pavement, she rolled over and over. The Gold Wing came crashing down on its handlebar and top box, literally exploded into flying parts, flipped back into the air and landed on its right side, then flipped into the air one last time before landing on its left side, ending up only a foot from where Evelyn lay unconscious. The bike had "high-sided."

The other riders traveling with Evelyn were able to perform their emergency stops without hitting her or her bike; and everyone dismounted immediately to try to assist her. Drivers who witnessed the crash site stopped at once to render first aid and call 911 for help.

When she reached the East Texas Medical Center by ambulance, Evelyn was conscious again. Though she had been wearing appropriate safety gear, she had sustained a concussion and broken bones in one hand; but she was amazingly intact after such a vicious crash. Many high-sides are fatal because the bike lands on the rider.

As we waited to hear her prognosis, the group speculated about what could have caused the bike's rear brake to lock. Though Gold Wings have an interlocked braking system, we all felt certain that Evelyn didn't "grab a handful of brake" when there was no unexpected threat that required it, nor did she stomp on her rear brake so soon after experiencing a skid and near-miss in Tyler. If anything, we felt she would have been quite reluctant to brake aggressively.

The hot smell, we believed in retrospect, indicated that the rear brake had probably been involved in the first incident, too, causing a skid that had been exacerbated by the reflective beads in the white paint. Reluctantly, the rest of the group rode home late that night through the pitch-dark countryside, the sight of our friend's accident replaying in our heads again and again.

Days later, when the remains of the motorcycle had been towed from Tyler to her home, an independent mechanic who examined Evelyn's bike felt he had found the answer to our question: "What caused the rear brake to stick so?"

Part of the brake line on her Gold Wing consisted of a rubber tube that conveyed brake fluid from the master cylinder to the slave cylinder when the rear brake pedal was depressed, which in turn moved the pads against the brake rotor.

This mechanic believed that a small piece of that rubber tubing had eroded and finally broken off into the brake fluid. When Evelyn depressed the rear-brake pedal, the fluid forced the brake pads to move against the rotor, but that piece of debris then kept them there. The fluid was blocked and couldn't flow back up the line to allow her to moderate that pressure after the brake was initially applied.

This mechanic believed that either the shop which had serviced the bike before the trip had not flushed the brake fluid, though the service department had represented to her that they had; or the service technicians had failed to perceive that the old rubber brake line might be faulty and should be replaced before she started her tour with us.

Fortunately, Evelyn's injuries did not keep her from riding again. The fact that she had been wearing all her safety gear prevented a more serious outcome, and in fact, she purchased another Gold Wing and still tours the United States with friends. Still, the sight of a large motorcycle whirling in the air was unforgettable to those of us who witnessed the crash. It triggered many talks about "high-side" accidents and how and when they can occur; and whether there's any response to such a situation that makes it more survivable.

Jim set about examining the physics and rider behavior involved in Evelyn's accident, while Cash sought (and continues to seek) the best motorcycle mechanics she could find to service her bike and Jim's. Witnessing a subsequent accident (described in MOTORCYCLE SAFETY AND DYNAMICS, Vol. One) reinforced the need for these inquiries.

Given that Jim had been riding for 35 years at the time, attaining nearly half a million miles of experience without any accidents or even a ticket, he came to believe that he could have a significant impact on other riders on issues of motorcycle safety. Cash had confidence that this was so, for he had been her first motorcycle riding instructor. Avoiding a "high-side", a "low-side", or any other kind of crash became even more imperative as she and Jim began to plan longer and longer trips for their riding groups. It was clear that tour riders could expect to encounter all kinds of unknown and unexpected threats on the road, as well as close to home.

Jim decided to become actively involved in teaching riders how to avoid any similar disaster and became a certified Motorcycle Safety Foundation (MSF) instructor soon thereafter, with Cash working as his Range Aide.

Eventually Jim realized that he could reach only about 12 students per week teaching for the MSF. He decided he wanted to reach a million riders, not a few hundred.

To do so, he created a web site, Motorcycle Tips & Techniques, (www.msgroup.org) with a discussion forum called All Things Motorcycle, where he could write and publish detailed articles exploring motorcycle safety and dynamics. In the years the site has been active it has reached over 20 million visitors with over 60 million hits.

As of the writing of this book, Jim's mileage has increased to well over half a million miles during over 50 years of riding, while he remains accident-free and ticket-free. Cash has joined him for most of those miles during the last 23 years.

Over time the number of articles Jim and Cash wrote, and the other material Jim published on his website, grew so voluminous that it would take a new visitor to the site literally days to read it all.

We received many requests to publish the articles in an organized manner in book form. Riders wanted a reference book that they could read and consult off-line.

That was the genesis of this book and the previous volume. The ultimate objective for us in teaching and writing about motorcycling is to help motorcyclists survive their experiences by minimizing the risks of injury and death, and making the experience enjoyable for many miles.

Riding a motorcycle is undeniably fraught with risk. Given today's transportation system and the huge variety of vehicles and drivers on the public roads, inevitably motorcycle casualties result; but in most cases these are neither necessary nor certain.

It's true that you can be extremely safety-conscious, well educated, well-defended with the best safety gear, and riding what you think is well maintained equipment—and still become a casualty of the road. Despite your best efforts, you'll encounter drivers who are distracted by chatting on their phones, or drivers who are drunk or under the influence of illegal drugs or prescription medications, or deer or stray pets that jump into the roadway ahead of you, or drivers who attempt a sudden U-turn, or mechanics who misrepresent their work, and much, much more.

But the reality is that these are **minor** causes of motorcycle accidents compared to the number of accidents that are caused, or not avoided, by the motorcyclist. Although Evelyn's accident may have been the result of inept service or an undiagnosed mechanical problem, in fact most motorcycle casualties are **primarily** the result of rider error.

The material in Volume Two is designed to help you avoid becoming a casualty not by teaching you how to ride, but by discussing how to ride intelligently, and with understanding; and how to deal with the unexpected incidents that really shouldn't be unexpected at all.

Along the way, we debunk a number of myths, and readers will have a chance to learn the how's and why's of motorcycle and rider behaviors (dynamics) in all kinds of situations and environments. And while we recognize that entertainment value can be important, we're primarily interested in conveying practical and useful facts that you can assimilate into a safety mindset that will serve you every time you put a leg over your saddle.

We ask that you have patience and make a commitment to learn from this material. There's more here than most readers can absorb in one reading. Indeed, we invite you to go through this book at a pace that satisfies your curiosity—the first time—and then to come back and read closely each and every "lesson" presented here. Depending on your experience level, you might already know as much as 95% of what you read here; but it is the other 5% that can save your life. For example, you'll discover that when you slow down while moving in a turn at speeds in excess of about 10 MPH, your motorcycle will try to "fall up" instead of "fall down". And you'll understand why.

We believe that there are three phases in the riding career of most motorcyclists. We refer to them as Phases 1 through 3. They are essentially characterized in terms of **risk categories**, not competence or skill levels.

Phase 1 is when the rider is known as a newbie. He's usually hurt or killed as a result of mistakes he makes that are the result of lack of experience or knowledge.

Phase 2 is when the rider has gained enough experience that he or she has become a competent rider. This rider thinks he's able to deal with almost any "unexpected incident" that presents itself. He's usually hurt or killed as a result of doing something stupid because he has become **over**-confident. In other words, he takes chances that he **thinks** he can handle instead of **knowing** that he can, or he simply fails to pay attention to what he's doing and to his environment. Why? Because he's been there, done that, and cannot conceive of the fact that his experience so far, and the good habits he's adopted, still do not protect him from reality.

Phase 3 is when a rider has amassed a substantial number of miles of riding experience. He or she has an established "safety mindset" and behaves <u>abnormally</u>. This rider understands that in order to beat the odds, he **must not behave** like the rest of the riding population. He does **not** occasionally drink and drive, he **always** wears his safety gear, he **avoids**

risks instead of testing limits, and he **never** loses control of his bike or **himself**! He's usually hurt or killed as a result of **exposure**—to normal unavoidable risks. The material in Volume Two discusses these risks and how to anticipate and prepare for them.

For the reality is, there's a limit on how competent a rider can be! A rider in Phase 3 is that competent, almost always. But he keeps riding and exposing himself to those who are not so competent in their driving / riding skills, and those unexpected events take their toll. In other words, a Phase 3 rider has reduced the odds of having a self-caused accident to almost zero, but he or she continues to be exposed to vehicles driven by the man holding a cell phone to his ear or to that deer that crosses the road in front of him. But this rider is better prepared for such incidents and as a result, he almost always turns those experiences into near-misses—but not always.

There's actually one more phase—**Phase 0**—which describes the risks confronting a person who's not yet riding but who has made the decision that he or she wants to ride and join the family of motorcyclists. This is a person who, failing to approach the hobby intelligently, can get hurt or killed within only minutes of putting a leg over a motorcycle saddle. This person simply has no idea what he or she is doing, what protection is necessary, nor how to gain the experience and education needed to survive.

A careful reader will recognize that these phases are fluid in nature. Riders who have attained Phase 2 in their motorcycling lives might step away from riding for a dozen years as they focus, instead, on a new family or career and then return to the hobby–once again in Phase 1. Indeed, the simple act of beginning to ride a new, larger or faster motorcycle from the one a rider has developed a high level of competence on means that a rider immediately reverts from Phase 3 back to Phase 1. The learning curves are shorter with these reversions, but they still happen.

What you read here won't teach you how to ride or justify your decision to enter or remain in the world of motorcycling. Instead, it will attempt to provide you information and perspectives that will allow you to survive the motorcycle riding experience for many years undamaged.

If you have any preconceived notion that riding motorcycles can be ever considered safe or made safe, even after thousands of miles of experience, you should reconsider wanting to ride—because you are absolutely wrong. You cannot reduce the risk of having an accident to near zero. What you can do is reduce risks to the point where an accident, if it should happen to you, is **not your fault**. The vast majority of motorcycle accident-related injuries or deaths result **primarily** from the motorcyclist's mistakes. This material is meant to help you avoid making those rider errors.

Safety is the theme throughout this material. Our writing style, however, may sometimes sound like a couple of curmudgeons. We talk straight, just as we don't allow our behavior or that of anyone around us in the motorcycle world to be less than as safe and **controlled** as possible.

Another characteristic of this material is that the conclusions can usually be defended with math and science, not merely Cash's or Jim's opinions.

Occasionally riders will say that the scientific reasoning here is "all very well" or "just theory," but they prefer to deal with "the real world of riding." We wonder what other reality they think science, engineering, and mathematics describe?

You don't have to know all the equations, but you should be able to understand that when a statement says proof, it means proof. The equations in this material are drawn from standard math and engineering texts, the tips have been peer-reviewed, and the drawings, while not always to scale, illustrate mathematically correct conclusions.

We are much more concerned with a rider's demonstrated level of maturity than we are chronological age: when we meet a 23-year-old new father who has decided it's time to begin riding a motorcycle, he gets our scrutiny faster than a 16-year-old who wants to ride dirt bikes with the rest of his family on the farm.

Writing this material has absorbed thousands of hours of intense research and study, as well as practical observation. Many fine authors write about various aspects of motorcycling, including Pat Hahn, David L. Hough, Ken Condon, and Keith Code, who write about riding; and Vittole Cossalter and Gaetano Cocco, who write about the very technical aspects of motorcycle dynamics. We acknowledge their contributions with gratitude. However, Cash and Jim are responsible for this material, and any mistakes are entirely our own.

James R. Davis
Cash Anthony

Phase 2

Volume One of MOTORCYCLE SAFETY AND DYNAMICS opened with this statement: **There is one "rule" that, if followed faithfully, makes the riding of a motorcycle relatively less risky for you: never lose control of your motorcycle—or yourself!**

That admonition for Phase 1 riders is repeated here at the beginning of this volume, because it remains the key to your survival throughout your motorcycling career.

While you were a newbie or just becoming a competent rider, your risks were primarily associated with lack of knowledge and lack of experience.

During **Phase 2** of your riding career, however, your risks will primarily result from losing control of yourself or failing to plan. That is, from over-estimating your capabilities, or deciding to push the envelope, or electing to engage in riskier behaviors in order to satisfy a desire to experience a little more of the thrill of riding that may have been lost for you, because riding has become routine.

Your competence causes you to focus on what you know and how well you handle your motorcycle, to the extent that you fail to see the larger picture and to plan for unexpected consequences.

Only when you get past this state of mind and become the mature rider of phase 3 will your reactions and behaviors cease to be the primary source of threat to yourself. Never forget this first rule.

I. Competence

You are no longer a newbie. That's not because other riders have stopping thinking of you as being relatively new to riding, but because you have survived the learning experiences of dealing with all the varied threats you encountered as a new rider.

Along the way, you became a believer in maintaining a safety mindset. You behave abnormally at your level, in ways that minimize the odds you'll encounter threats or that you won't be able to handle them effectively. You are a competent rider because, with experience and practice, **nothing** about how your motorcycle behaves is a mystery to you now.

You may never have taken your motorcycle to its performance limits, but you know quite well what those limits are and can easily recognize when you are approaching them.

You have developed certain skills, especially braking skills, to the point that you can use them appropriately if called upon to do so; and it takes you absolutely no time to decide how or what to do when faced with a threat, because you've practiced and maintained your skill levels so that they're now reactive in nature.

As a competent rider, your odds of being in an accident that was caused by something you did or did not do are now extremely low.

So is that all there is to it? Have you "made it"? Why is there yet another phase past Phase 1? This section will answer those questions and offer suggestions about surviving this particular phase.

A. Braking skills

In discussing braking as a new rider in Phase 1, we stated that a motorcyclist is not qualified to ride on public roads unless he or she is capable of consistently achieving a deceleration rate of at least 0.7g's. A rider who has taken a basic rider course has had minimal experience with this.

For that reason, we provided a parking lot practice exercise to help riders improve their braking skills until they consistently achieve a deceleration rate of 0.8g's. Until a rider can do this, he or she is not a competent rider.

If you now believe yourself to be a competent rider, it follows that you have managed to improve your braking skills so that you can consistently achieve a deceleration rate of 0.8g's.

Assuming you followed our earlier suggestions, your practice involved stopping from a speed of 20 MPH. Now you should expand your experience and practice stopping from a somewhat greater speed.

Braking skill practice should never be done at speeds greater than 30 MPH, however, because there's nothing to gain from doing so, and your risks increase substantially.

Speed	Distance	Deceleration Rate	Time
20 MPH	16.7 feet	0.8g's	1.1 seconds
25 MPH	26.0 feet	0.8g's	1.4 seconds
30 MPH	37.5 feet	0.8g's	1.7 seconds

Table 1: Stopping measurements

On the other hand, a competent rider should gain the experience of practicing quick stops from 30 MPH, because there's actually something important to learn from that experience. To be specific, it's far easier to attain a given deceleration rate starting at a higher speed than when starting at a lower speed. Notice the rates and times in Table 1.

What you are about to learn will probably make you feel pretty good about your braking performance so far: It was not easy for you to achieve the ability consistently to reach a deceleration rate of 0.8g's at lower speeds.

As it turns out, it was difficult because **you were actually achieving a rate of somewhere between 0.9g's and 1.0g's**.

1. Measured deceleration rate as an average

If you can bring your motorcycle to a complete stop from 20 MPH within approximately 17 feet, you have achieved an **average** deceleration rate of 0.8g's while braking.

When you begin your braking effort, until you reach your maximum deceleration rate (maximum squeeze pressure), your deceleration rate is obviously less than the average. Clearly, then, in order to average a deceleration rate of 0.8g's, for some period of time your actual deceleration rate must be higher than 0.8g's.

It takes only 1.1 seconds to bring a bike moving 20 MPH to come to a stop if it's decelerating at a rate of 0.8g's.

2. How long does weight transfer take?

You may have heard otherwise knowledgeable riders and even MSF RiderCoaches suggest that you should squeeze your front brake hard, then squeeze harder, then harder still until you've achieved your maximum deceleration rate. In other words, they suggested you take some time before you reach your maximum braking pressure.

The reasoning that accompanied those suggestions was that you need to allow weight transfer to occur in order to increase the traction provided by your front tire, so that you don't "overdo it" and lock up the front brake.

As to how long it should take to reach that maximum, you may have heard suggestions such as "about one second".

Though the advice about allowing for weight transfer is correct, the reasoning's flawed.

Weight transfer happens **instantly**. It's the effects of weight transfer that take time. Your front shocks begin compressing the moment you start applying your brakes. The process is not that they compress first, and then weight transfer occurs.

As your shocks compress, more and more weight is felt on the tire's contact patch--increasing traction. Braking force can grow faster than the effects of weight transfer and can exceed available traction in as little as 0.2 seconds.

Thus, applying too much brake during those 0.2 seconds can exceed the traction the tire provides during that time. As a result, the tire will skid.

It makes sense, then, to take **more than 0.2 seconds** to reach maximum braking pressure on the front-brake lever.

But anyone who suggests that it takes "about one second" for your shocks to compress simply doesn't understand motorcycle dynamics.

3. Grabbing a handful – what does it mean?

It should never take you as long as 0.7 seconds to reach maximum squeeze pressure on your front-brake lever when you are trying to stop aggressively. In fact, most people can easily hit their maximum squeeze pressure in 0.5 seconds, and with practice you should be able to reach maximum in about 0.3 seconds.

Thus, there's a huge difference between reality and the well-intentioned suggestion of "about one second". And if it takes you as long as 0.7 seconds to reach maximum squeeze pressure on your front brake lever, the odds are very high that you will skid the front tire if you manage to stop within 17 feet starting at 20 MPH.

Look at the case represented in Figure 1 below, where a rider attempts a 0.8g stop starting at 20 MPH. Assume it takes the rider a full half-second to increase his braking pressure until he's reached his maximum.

During that first 0.5 seconds, he has achieved an average deceleration rate of approximately half his maximum rate of **1.04g's**. For the remaining 0.6 seconds, he will maintain an average deceleration rate of 1.04g's.

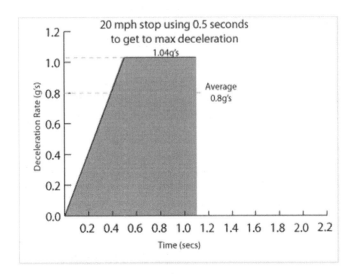

Figure 1: Using 0.5 second squeeze time

The calculations are easy. An average deceleration rate of 0.8g's for a period of 1.1 seconds is a total deceleration-rate-time of 0.88g seconds. To find the maximum rate (X) during the stop, we solve this simple formula:

Time to get to max rate * ½ of max rate + time during max rate * max rate = deceleration-rate-time

$$(0.5 * 0.5 * X) + 0.6 * X = 0.88$$
$$0.25X + 0.6X = 0.88$$
$$0.85X = 0.88$$
$$X = 1.04g's$$

If the rider takes a full half-second to get to maximum squeeze pressure on the front-brake lever, he must achieve an actual deceleration rate of 1.04g's in order to average 0.8g's for the entire braking duration.

Now look at Figure 2, which shows the rider attempting an unrealistic braking effort: here, he takes a full 0.7 seconds to reach maximum squeeze pressure.

A rider would have to achieve a deceleration rate of 1.17g's in order to average 0.8g's. That's beyond the capabilities of most riders and even beyond the capabilities of most bikes on good concrete, let alone asphalt.

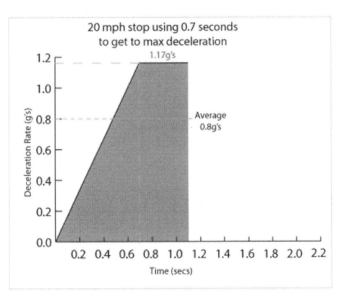

Figure 2: Using 0.7 second squeeze time

But since we know that we can take as little as 0.3 seconds to reach maximum braking pressure without inducing a skid, let's see what that looks like.

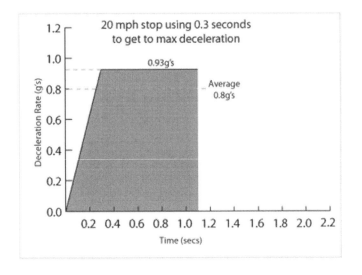

Figure 3: Using 0.3 second squeeze time

There should be no doubt about what this means.

The faster a rider can reach maximum braking pressure on the front-brake lever, the easier it will be to achieve his desired average deceleration rate.

'Grabbing a handful" means reaching your maximum braking pressure in less time than it takes for the effects of weight transfer to occur; in other words, in less than 0.2 seconds.

A competent rider, from a braking skills point of view, does a "quick squeeze" instead of grabbing that handful.

4. How dangerous is a quick squeeze time?

A rider simply must be concerned that a quicker squeeze time to reach maximum brake pressure invites locking the front brake. Consider the dynamics occurring during a quick stop. When you decelerate, the front end of your motorcycle dips as a result of weight transfer. It takes time for your shocks to compress.

Remember, on the other hand, that it takes **no time** for weight transfer to occur. That is, weight transfer is instantaneous relative to the bike's deceleration rate.

But for that transferred weight to be felt on the front tire's contact patch in order to increase traction, the front shocks must compress.

That means that although weight transfer is immediate, it takes some amount of time before you can make full use of it in the form of increased braking force. When a motorcycle is braked with near optimum efficiency, it takes just over 0.35 seconds for the front shocks to compress half the distance that they will ultimately compress.[1]

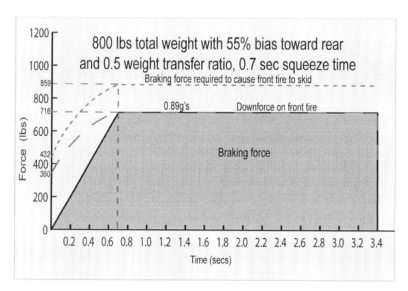

Figure 4: Braking force using 0.7 second squeeze time

On public roads, a quick stop is more likely to occur at speeds closer to 60 MPH than at 20 to 30 MPH.

---

[1] From a braking test series presented in *TASK ANALYSIS FOR INTENSIVE BRAKING IN A STRAIGHT LINE* (2004), developed by the PROMOCYCLE Foundation for the Federation Motorcycliste du Quebec, p. 12. This article is available at http://www.fmq.qc.ca/pdf/amorce-freinage_eng.pdf.

Assuming that a motorcyclist achieves a competent level of braking as reflected by a 0.8g deceleration rate, stopping from 60 MPH will take only 3.4 seconds.

The typical weight distribution of a motorcycle with rider is close to 55% on the rear tire when the rider's not accelerating or decelerating. The Weight Transfer Ratio (the height of the bike's Center of Gravity divided by the length of the bike's wheelbase) is typically near 0.5. [Recall that a Center of Gravity (CG) is that point within the mass where an equal amount of mass is above that point as is below, an equal amount is in front of that point as is behind it, and an equal amount is to the left as to the right.]

Thus, before braking, an 800-pound motorcycle (including the rider) will have 440 pounds of weight on its rear tire and only 360 pounds on its front tire.

If it takes 0.7 seconds to reach maximum braking squeeze pressure, then in order to achieve an **average** 0.8g rate of deceleration, then a rider must reach and maintain a maximum deceleration rate of 0.89g's. The amount of weight transferred from the rear tire to the front tire as a result of a 0.89g deceleration rate would be 356 lbs.[2] Thus, when the front shocks have compressed fully, 716 pounds will be on the front tire's contact patch.

Since a good tire on a good clean asphalt surface won't skid until it has reached a deceleration rate of approximately 1.2g's, that means that after 0.7 seconds of braking effort, the front tire would support a braking force of 859 pounds.

The solid black line in Figure 4 represents the total braking force provided by both brakes in order to achieve the 0.89g deceleration rate. The long-dash line represents the total downforce (weight) on the front tire over time. The short-dash line represents the amount of braking force from the front tire that will result in a skid. From inspecting the short-dash line, it's clear that before deceleration begins, the front tire could support a braking force of 432 pounds without a skid, and as much as 859 pounds at the maximum deceleration rate of 0.89g's. At no time does the braking force imposed on the front tire approach that which would result in a skid.

---

[2] 0.89 deceleration rate * 0.5 wt. transfer ratio * 800 lbs. = 356lbs.

This discussion will assume that all of the braking force is coming from the front brake. Insofar as any of it comes from the rear brake, the risk of skidding the front tire is less.

Now let's look at a faster squeeze time of 0.5 seconds.

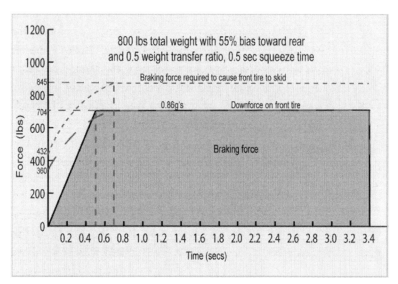

Figure 5: Using 0.5 second squeeze time

Because the rider reaches maximum braking pressure more quickly, he needs only to achieve a maximum deceleration rate of 0.86g's in order to average a deceleration rate of 0.8g's throughout the stop.

In other words, it's easier to achieve a stop in the same distance than when taking a full 0.7 seconds to reach maximum squeeze pressure.

Also notice that from about 0.45 seconds until 0.7 seconds into the effort, the braking force exceeds the weight on the front tire. Since again the bike doesn't approach the short-dash line, the rider's in no danger of a front tire skid.

He gets close to a skid, however, when he shortens that squeeze time to only 0.3 seconds. Figure 6 shows this scenario.

Now you can see why you always want to use some rear brake pressure to augment front brake pressure during an aggressive stop.

A competent rider will always use both brakes whenever attempting an aggressive stop.

This assures the shortest distance, the least time to come to a stop, and it provides some anti-yaw force that helps keep the bike's rear end in-line with the front of the bike.

And, for every bit of braking force that's provided by the rear tire, less braking force is required from the front tire. Figure 7 on the next page shows a distribution of braking forces when 90% of the braking force comes from the front tire.

From this we can see that the solid black line (braking force from the front tire) is significantly lowered as compared to the short-dash line (braking force at which skidding will occur).

Since it's when the solid black line (not the gray area) crosses the short-dash line that skidding occurs, clearly when the rider uses both brakes, this reduces the odds of a front tire skid.

There's one more important, though relatively small, dynamic that helps prevent a skid in this situation. Because your front shocks are compressing, the wheelbase is shortening.

That change increases the weight transfer ratio and, as a result, causes more weight transfer to occur than shown.

This dynamic means that the front tire actually provides more traction than Figure 5 and Figure 6 suggest, because it raises both the short-dash and long-dash lines, but it doesn't raise the solid black line.

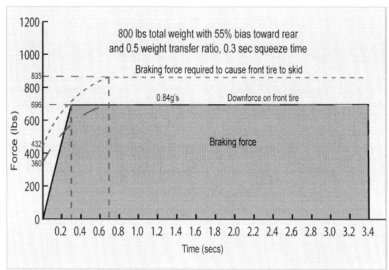

Figure 6: Using 0.3 second squeeze time

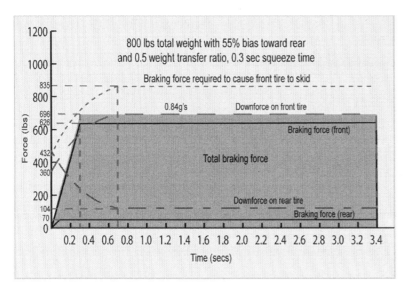

Figure 7: Using 0.3 seconds with 90% front brake

5. What do you learn practicing at 30 MPH?

The most important thing you learn is that the faster you are moving, the easier it is to achieve a given average deceleration rate.

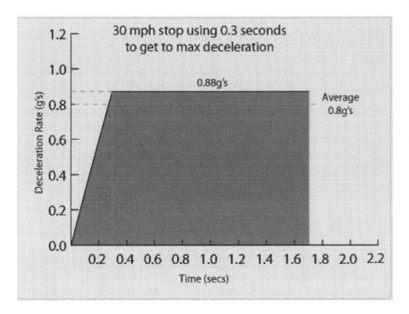

Figure 8: 0.3 second squeeze at 30 MPH

Assume the rider takes 0.3 seconds to reach maximum braking pressure starting at 30 MPH.

Further, assume the rider achieves an average deceleration rate of 0.8g's.

It takes 1.7 seconds to come to a complete stop from 30 MPH at an average deceleration rate of 0.8g's. Figure 8 shows that the rider only had to achieve a maximum deceleration rate of 0.88g's to accomplish that from 30 MPH, while it took a maximum of 0.93g's from 20 MPH.

Some instructors will state that the reason it's easier to stop quickly at a faster starting speed is because you have more time after you reach your maximum declaration rate to "properly modulate your brakes" at the higher speeds. Rubbish! There's absolutely no "modulating" or "moderating" your brakes once you reach maximum deceleration. You merely maintain the same braking pressure.

So congratulations! You've been achieving deceleration rates of in excess of 0.9g's since you became competent and didn't even know it. Recognize that this means that you can, if you wish, continue to achieve those higher deceleration rates and drive up your average rates as a result. You've been threshold braking since you became competent.

While you may think that the advantage of practicing quick stops at 30 MPH instead of 20 MPH is that it's easier to achieve your target deceleration rates, the more significant message here, by far, is that you are learning that when you do a quick stop at speeds greater than 30 MPH with exactly the same braking effort, your deceleration rates will be higher than your 20 MPH "scores".

If you can achieve a 0.8g deceleration rate when practicing at 20 MPH, you will achieve a deceleration rate in excess of 0.9g's when stopping at any speed in excess of 30 MPH. And that improvement comes at no cost—it's free!

6. Exaggerations and consequences

There have been reports of quick stop test runs from 20 MPH suggesting that some highly skilled riders have achieved an average deceleration rate of 1.2g's and better. While no one reporting those results has intentionally misrepresented the data, these results are suspicious and probably the result of faulty test methods or "rounding errors" or possibly data recording errors. Here's what such a result, if true, implies.

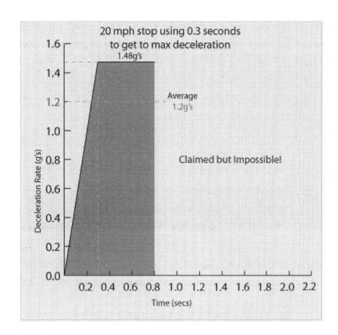

Figure 9: Impossible, but claimed stopping rate

If the rider took longer than 0.3 seconds to achieve his maximum deceleration rate, then his maximum deceleration rate had to have been greater than 1.5g's.

No motorcycle has ever achieved a deceleration rate even close to 1.48g's, let alone greater than that.

Remember, at deceleration rates greater than about 1.1g's, a motorcycle is very likely to do a stoppie. (Some sportbikes will do a stoppie with deceleration rates below 1.0g's.) It's simply not possible for a motorcycle to achieve a deceleration rate as high as 1.48g's.

Further, the rolling Coefficient of Friction, even on the best concrete surface, does not exceed about 1.3g's, so when a deceleration rate exceeds 1.3g's, the motorcycle's front tire will lose traction, and a skid will begin.

It can take a motorcycle **less than one-half second** to fall down when the front tire loses traction. Since it would take longer than that to come to a stop after reaching its maximum deceleration rate if that motorcycle had not performed an end-over, it would with extremely high odds have ended up on its side before coming to a stop.

7. Going for a world-record test result

Some riders believe that they can always get better, no matter how good they are, and they place themselves in grave danger as a result.

Figure 10 closely approximates what will happen to a motorcycle whose rider elects to try for world-record quick stop performance and attains a deceleration rate of about 1.3g's in the effort (assuming there's a sliding coefficient of 0.86). Two assumptions are made in this graph.

First, it's assumed that this motorcycle can attain a deceleration rate of 1.3g's without having lifted its rear wheel off the ground. This would not be a reasonable assumption in the case of a sportbike. Second, it's assumed that the rider of this motorcycle ignores the fact that he's skidding and elects to try to complete the quick stop run, instead of simply releasing the front brake lever and aborting the effort.

A competent rider will always elect to abort the test by easing off the front brake lever pressure and stopping the skid the moment it started.

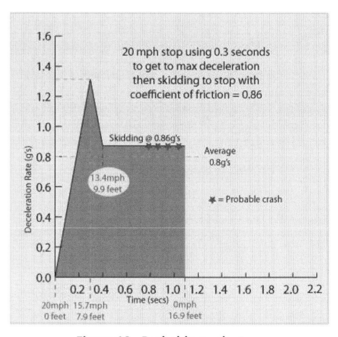

Figure 10: Probable crash stop

If the motorcycle can do a stoppie, it will happen long before it reaches a deceleration rate of 1.3g's. Sportbikes can do one with a deceleration rate of just under 1.0g's, and some other bikes can achieve a rate as high as 1.2g's before their rear wheels lift off the ground. Obviously these bikes do not skid the front tire. (A bike will either skid or do a stoppie when it reaches its maximum deceleration rate, not both.)

Figure 11 below shows a best-effort quick stop attempt by a rider whose bike does a stoppie when it reaches a deceleration rate of 1.2g's. Here the rider **must** (absolutely must) reduce his front brake pressure as soon as the stoppie begins, because as the rear-end rises, the bike's Center of Gravity is rising and its wheelbase is shortening.

Thus, more and more weight transfer occurs even if the deceleration rate remains constant—which means that the motorcycle will do an end-over unless it's reduced.

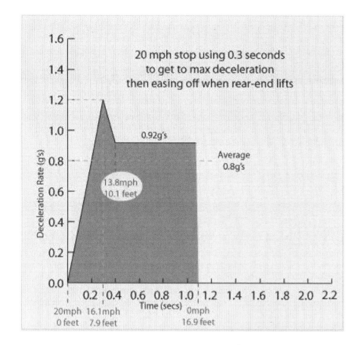

Figure 11: Rear end lift during stop

Feeling the rear wheel lift off the ground, a competent rider immediately eases off the front brake and settles that tire back on the ground.

Even with this awful start, this bike can still achieve an average 0.8g deceleration rate. But there's nothing <u>safe</u> about trying for world records when developing your braking skills.

A competent rider should maintain the ability consistently to achieve a quick stop from 20 MPH at a 0.8g average deceleration rate, but not more than that.

8. The faster you go, the less you weigh

That's not a typo—it's true. There's an aerodynamic lift force that varies as a function of speed.[3]

---

[3] An excellent discussion of this can be found starting on p.145 of Gaetano Cocco's book, **MOTORCYCLE DESIGN AND TECHNOLOGY**, Giorgio NADA Editore (1999). ISBN 88-7911-189-2.

If you were to measure how much your motorcycle (and you) weigh at a dead stop and then while you are moving at, say, 80+ MPH, there would be a meaningful difference.

This happens because the faster you travel through the air, the stronger the turbulence and, thus, the lift that the relatively low pressure of turbulence creates. Turbulence below the bike is trivial by comparison to that above it. If instead of sitting straight up, you are leaned forward, then your back creates an airfoil that creates an even greater lift.

If the combined weight of your body and the bike, when at a dead stop, is about 800 pounds, then when you are moving at speeds of 80+ MPH that combined weight will be closer to 760 pounds, or less. And the faster you go, the lower that total will be.

For comparison purposes, a 1970 Chevelle weighed in at 3820 pounds standing still and was found to weigh 321 pounds less (8%) at 100 MPH. Your bike, however, will probably not lose more than 6% of its weight at that speed (or for example, at a more commonly seen speed of 80 MPH with a 20 MPH headwind), because it does not have quite the horizontal profile of an automobile.

Now, you might think the lift would be evenly distributed fore and aft. Wrong. Far more of the aerodynamic lift is on the front wheel than the rear.

The reason this is important is that, as weight on the front end is reduced, there's a corresponding reduction in traction. Stabilization from the restoring force is reduced, too. (A discussion of the restoring force appears later in this book.)

At very high speeds your motorcycle will feel unresponsive and "light" in the front end—so much so that you won't trust it (nor should you) to hold onto the ground in your turns.

While there's always a net lift caused by airflow with speed, the effect on the rear end of your bike could well be to increase its weight. Just as the amount of weight transfer that acceleration generates is determined by how high the Center of Gravity is as compared to the wheelbase, wind resistance creates a downforce in the rear proportional to how high the center of wind resistance is to that wheelbase.

[All wind resistance is **above** the ground while all forward motion forces are **at** ground level. That automatically creates a torque which tries to lift the front and lower the rear.]

Downforce on the rear wheel can be less than, equal to, or greater than the lift generated by turbulence. That's largely determined by how high the center of wind resistance point is relative to the wheelbase. The taller you sit, the more "baggy" your clothing, the "wider" you are, the bigger your windscreen, and the faster you move, the lighter your front end will get; and the more likely the bike's rear will get heavier rather than lighter.

Lest you think this is academic, the reason for the short, seemingly useless windscreens on sportbikes is to diminish turbulence behind the rider, so that lift on the bike at speed doesn't badly compromise the rider's control. These are small so that they don't increase downforce from wind resistance that would simultaneously lighten the front end even more. Tour riders take note: your windscreen lightens your front end dramatically!

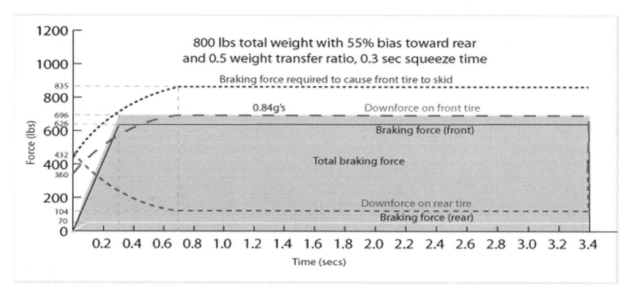

Figure 12: 0.3 second squeeze, 90% front brake

Given enough horsepower and proper gearing, your maximum possible speed becomes limited to that which results in insufficient front wheel traction to steer the motorcycle.

Since we've focused most of this section on braking, consider how such a speed-related change in weight affects your ability to make a rapid stop from excessive speeds. Look at Figure 12 above, which you've seen earlier.

It demonstrates how quickly squeezing your front brake at the start of an emergency stop while moving at moderate speeds affects a particular bike.

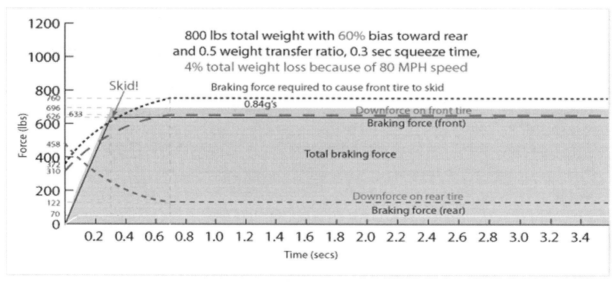

Figure 13: Effect of high speed on downforce and lift

When traveling at a speed of about 80 MPH with a 20 MPH headwind, the bike will lose about 4% of its total weight, or about 32 pounds.

However, that will not be evenly distributed weight loss. The front end of the bike will **lose about 50 pounds** while the rear end will **gain about 18 pounds**.

Thus, the weight bias of the bike will change from 55% to 60% toward the rear. If you used the **same braking force** at this speed as you did at more moderate speed, **the front tire will skid**.

Compare this to Figure 13 above. It should be obvious that as the bike slows down, the downforce on the front tire will increase, and the downforce on the rear tire will decrease.

9. Maintaining your braking skills

An interval of 4.5 seconds isn't a lot of time—but it could be the rest of your life.

That 4.5 second interval is about how long it **should** take you to stop your motorcycle after applying your brakes while moving at 60 MPH.

Stopping a motorcycle as fast as possible requires that you master only a few fundamentals:

- **Alertness** - No matter how fast your reflexes are or how skillful you are with your brakes, if you don't see the need to stop, you won't;

- **Reflexes** - First you need time to recognize a threat and decide to react to it, then your fast reflexes take over and make the difference; and

- **Skill** - Under-utilizing your brakes is just as dangerous as over-doing it.

Let's get a feel for magnitudes.

It usually takes about 0.7 seconds to recognize a threat. A person with normal reflexes takes about 0.3 seconds to start braking from the moment he realizes he has to do so. Combined, that's about one full second from the time a threat presents itself to you and when you begin to slow down. (This is called PDR or Perception, Decision, and Reaction time.) At 60 MPH, you travel **88 feet** in one second.

That it takes you about 0.7 seconds to recognize the threat is a mental reality. But it does not necessarily take 0.3 seconds to react to it.

The simple practice of always covering your front brake can shave a full tenth of a second (one third!) of that time away. **That's almost nine feet**!

As a competent rider, you have a good idea about how to use your brakes. Here's some data that should give you a sense of magnitude associated with the skill part of braking.

Traffic Engineers have developed rules-of-thumb. For example, they've found that if the street surface is dry, the average driver can safely decelerate an automobile at the rate of 15 feet per second per second (ft/sec^2).

That is, an average driver can slow down at this rate without any real likelihood that he will lose control in the process, and he will attain an average deceleration rate of only about 0.45g's.

If the surface is wet, the engineers assume that a deceleration rate of 10 ft/sec^2 (0.3g's) is safely attainable by almost any driver qualified to be behind the wheel.

Let's assume a wet street surface, and that this driver is moving at 60 MPH. At a 10 ft/sec^2 deceleration rate, it will take him 8.8 seconds to stop after he begins applying his brakes. (This means a total of 9.8 seconds from the time the threat presents itself, given PDR.)

The distance an average driver would travel before coming to a complete stop is 475 feet.

If, however, the road's dry, it would take this driver only a total of 6.9 seconds to stop (including the one second of PDR delay), and the distance traveled until he comes to rest would be 346 feet.

Clearly, the more effective your braking is, the less time it takes to stop, and the less distance traveled.

Most riders know that a motorcycle can stop more quickly than most automobiles. Indeed, a professional motorcycle racer can achieve a deceleration rate of 1.0g or better on his motorcycle.

Even beginner riders should easily be able to achieve deceleration rates in excess of 19 ft/sec^2 (0.6g's).

A competent rider can consistently attain deceleration rates of about 29 ft/sec^2 (0.9g's) starting at 60 MPH.

What does that mean in our example threat scenario?

It means that even a newly trained motorcyclist can stop his motorcycle in a total of 5.5 seconds (including the one second PDR delay). His total stopping distance would be 288 feet. But a competent rider can stop his motorcycle in 4.0 seconds with a total stopping distance of 221 feet.

By maintaining your enhanced braking skills with practice, you can shave off 67 feet and 1.5 seconds compared to the newly trained rider's results.

And you could shave off another nearly 9 feet just by covering your brakes. That brings the distance traveled before stopping down by about 76 feet. **That's at about four car-lengths!**

The message is clear: You only hit that car if you don't **quite** stop in time. You might not hit it at all if you cover your brakes and maintain your braking skills.

You achieve a deceleration rate of 0.9g's whenever you stop from speeds in excess of 30 MPH so long as you are capable of consistently achieving an average deceleration rate of 0.8g's on a parking lot **from 20 MPH**.

10. Rear tire "chirps" when braking hard

Some riders have experienced their rear tire skidding or squalling whenever they do hard braking. Some have decided that they should replace their rear tires with wider rear tires in an attempt to minimize this phenomenon.

Though it will certainly help to have a larger tire (in terms of mass) on the rear in order to minimize the skid and squall mentioned, it won't eliminate that problem. That's not its source. And this is not the same as the situation where a rear tire is lifted off the ground during a stoppie, discussed above.

Let's look at what's actually causing this problem.

When accelerating, a motorcycle's back-end **rises**, not falls. This is true for virtually any bike. It's the result of the location of the pivot point of the bike's swing arm for shaft driven bikes, or the intersection of the lines defined by your swing arm and the top of your chain (or belt).

A line drawn from the rear contact patch to that point defines the "chain angle" of a bike. This is shown as "c1" and "c2" in Figures 14 1nd 15.

In the diagrams, "wt" is the weight transfer angle for the bike, which is the height of your Center of Gravity divided by the length your wheelbase.

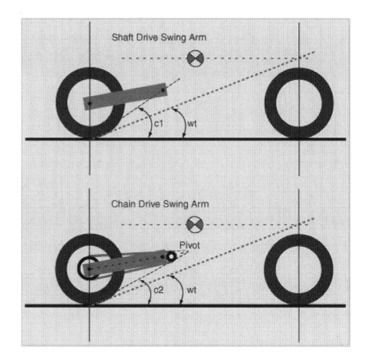

Figure 14: Comparing weight transfer and chain angles

The chain angle is larger than the weight transfer angle. Thus, when a rider accelerates, he decompresses the rear suspension. The reverse is equally true: when he brakes, he compresses the rear suspension.

Because the mass of the motorcycle body is so much larger than the mass of the rear wheel, when a rider brakes hard with the rear brake, the wheel will be lifted instead of the bike's squatting onto it.

That reduces traction, resulting in a "chirping" of the tire, or skidding and squalling.

Figure 15 below shows the forces that account for this behavior. The dark arrow is the vectored braking force that removes weight from the rear wheel. The grey arrow is the vectored braking force that removes weight from the rear of the motorcycle as a result of weight transfer. Note that the rear wheel has lost more weight than the rear-end.

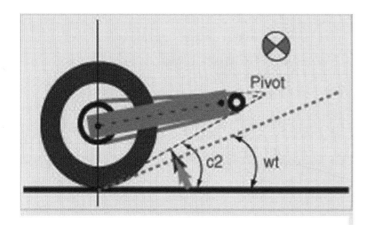

Figure 15: Rear-end compression forces

In other words, the wheel will rise farther and will compress the rear suspension as a result.

Unless a substantially larger rear tire (in terms of mass) is added, it's not possible to overcome the tendency of the rear tire to be pulled up off the ground by the rear suspension during hard braking using the rear brake. The real issue is "hard braking using the rear brake", not that the rear tire chirps when doing so.

It's never, never—not once in your lifetime—appropriate to use your rear brake aggressively.

The dynamics of your motorcycle make it foolish to do so, as that immediately limits the amount of braking you can do (leaving a great deal of stopping power unusable) because of lost traction. Worse, of course, it leads to **yaw** of the rear-end and that, in turn, leads to high-sides.

If you use the engine to slow down, the pivot point mentioned earlier is defined by the intersection of the swing arm with the **bottom** of the chain instead of its top; but the result is the same, though diminished in magnitude.

But this explains why it's so easy to skid your rear tire if you downshift and release the clutch too quickly or have a significant mismatch in engine speed and tire rotation speed.

The rear brake is the most dangerous control you have on a motorcycle.

Thinking that you can make it work better by increasing the size of the rear tire is simply asking for trouble if you don't change your braking methods.

11. Sometimes it's better to use no brakes

Despite the attention we've devoted to the development and maintenance of braking skills, **a competent rider understands that there are times when it's far safer to use absolutely no brakes at all when confronted by a threat, even if it's directly ahead of you.**

A couple of years ago two riders were riding two-up on a freeway at highway speed at about 75 MPH in the fast lane. Out of nowhere, a three-foot square cardboard box blew into the lane directly in front of the motorcycle.

The rider who was handling the bike first experienced a mas-**sive** adrenalin surge! Thinking increased to an unimaginable speed. His thought process went something like this:

Sh*t!

He began an aggressive braking effort.

Can we aggressively stop before hitting it? **No!**

Can we swerve and avoid it?

The box was moving to the left, so the rider swerved to the

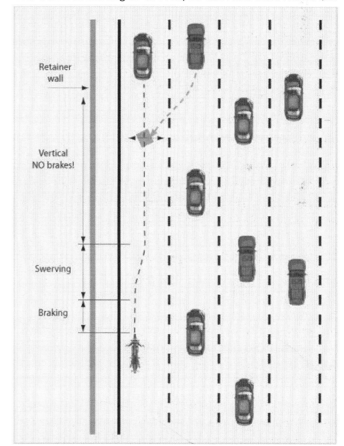

Figure 16: Cardboard box obstacle on freeway

right (staying in the fast lane, as there was traffic in the lane to the right).

Then the wind changed directions, and the box was once again directly in front of the bike.

>**No more swerves**!
>
>Treat this thing like it's a scared animal—there's no way to predict what it's going to do. **Aim for where it is now,** and when we get there, it might not be.

He pointed the bike right at the box and ended the swerving effort.

>The box must be empty, if wind is all it takes to move it around. If we hit it, we're likely to ride **over it** and crush it. If we hit it with the brakes on, we're likely to skid when we roll over it.
>
>**No brakes**!
>
>**Straight up**!

The box did not move again before he got to it. He hit it at about 70 MPH. It crushed as the bike rolled over it. No damage. No crash. No skid.

>Yeah!
>
>Anything wrong with the handling of the bike? No.
>
>All is well.
>
>**Breathe**!

The incident was over.

If you think that adrenalin just affects your muscles, think again. All of those thoughts and reactions took place in **less than one second**.

It's also a distinct advantage to have a passenger who's experienced. The rider was able to react with total confidence that there would be no serious distractions from the pillion, like screaming or leaning.

If a rider always covers his or her front brake lever when moving at counter-steering speeds, that rider becomes predisposed to using the brakes when an unexpected threat presents itself and will **automatically** begin braking without losing any time making that decision. But this incident also demonstrates that in most cases, you actually have a lot of time to decide what else, if anything, you need to do in an emergency.

In all of about one second, brakes were used then released, a mild swerve was begun then aborted and a decision was made to run over that box—with the motorcycle vertical and **without using any brakes**. Only about 5 MPH of speed was scrubbed off in the process.

12. Braking while pulling a trailer

All motorcycle manufactures recommend that riders <u>not</u> tow a trailer with their bikes <u>because of increased safety hazards</u>. All towing is at the operator's own risk.

Despite that, many riders, particularly tour riders, feel that the convenience provided to them by the extra cargo carrying capacity of a trailer offsets the increased risks involved. **We do not agree**.

While the laws in the United States are relatively permissive when it comes to pulling a trailer, not all countries are quite so relaxed in what they will allow.

For example, in the United Kingdom, your trailer, including its contents, cannot weigh more than 330 pounds, or two-thirds of the curb weight of the pulling motorcycle, whichever is less. The end of any pulled trailer cannot be more than about eight feet from the rear axle of the motorcycle.

Trailers are usually constructed of tough plastic or aluminum to keep their weight modest. This tends to also keep down the maximum weight of the cargo placed in these trailers. A typical trailer made of plastic weighs about 160 pounds empty and can carry no more than 500 pounds of cargo.

From a handling point of view, a rider should keep the total weight of any trailer, including cargo, to less than one-third that of the weight of his motorcycle.

As mentioned in Volume One, pulling a trailer automatically reduces your braking efficiency.

This discussion explores the reason for that and explains some lessons learned the hard way by those who have pulled trailers with their motorcycles.

See **APPENDIX E – Pulling a trailer.**

a. Braking Efficiency

If all the motorcycle's weight (including the rider) is being carried by wheels with working brakes, then the "braking efficiency" is 100%. In an automobile that has four wheels, if one of those wheels has a dysfunctional brake, then the braking efficiency possible for that automobile is approximately 75%. If a motorcycle stops by using just its rear brake, then during that braking effort, the motorcycle's providing no more than 40% braking efficiency. (Weight transfer removes weight from the rear wheel, as discussed above.)

Trailers do not have brakes unless they weigh more than 1500 pounds, which is unusual. Thus, if the trailer's weight (including cargo) is 300 pounds and the bike's weight (including the rider) is 800 pounds, the best possible braking efficiency for that vehicle would be slightly more than 70%.

If a rider can stop an 800-pound motorcycle (that isn't pulling a trailer) with a 0.8g rate of deceleration, he's generating 640 pounds of braking force. If he starts braking at 60 MPH, he can stop within 150 feet. On the other hand, if he were pulling a 300-pound trailer and used the same braking pressure on his controls, it would take almost 207 feet to stop it. He would be generating a deceleration rate of only 0.58g's.

To stop the bike and trailer within 150 feet, the rider would have to increase the amount of braking force generated by the tires from 640 pounds to 880 pounds. That's the equivalent of 1.1g's of force without the trailer. The odds are high that if he did that, his front tire would lose traction and skid.

The reason for that isn't obvious at first, but it's explained if you consider weight transfer when a trailer's involved.

b. Weight Transfer

A trailer should be loaded so as to have about 10% of its total weight resting on the trailer hitch at rest. Some riders argue that it's fine to have as much as 20% of the total weight on that hitch, but this isn't true.

First, look at the trailer by itself. Like a motorcycle, it has a Center of Gravity. Any weight placed above its CG results in raising it, and any weight placed below its CG lowers the resulting CG. While simply placing all the heavy cargo above the wheels in a trailer will certainly tend to minimize tongue weight, it also tends to raise the trailer's CG—particularly if the rider decides to place some of the cargo on top of a closed trailer.

The amount of weight transfer, in the case of a motorcycle, is a function of the height of its CG as compared to the length of its wheelbase. In the case of a trailer, because it's unlikely to have its own brakes, the amount of weight transfer is a function of the height of the CG above the height of the ball on the hitch, as compared to the distance between the wheel and that hitch.

Acceleration and deceleration cause weight transfer. Because slowing the bike effectively pushes against the trailer at the ball of the hitch, and weight transfer is through the CG, a CG that's higher than the hitch will create a torque that will try to make the hitch dive, just like the bike's front-end.

The higher the CG, the greater the weight transfer will be. Since the hitch is part of the motorcycle's "overhang", aft of the rear-wheel axle, that weight transfer is leveraged into greater weight on the rear tire and less weight on the front one. That leverage can be **profound**.

At rest, if the bike's weight distribution ratio is normally around 45% to the front and 55% toward the rear, then an 800-pound motorcycle will have only 360 pounds on its front tire. Without weight transfer, because a street-legal tire can support no more than about 1.2g's of lateral force before skidding, a rider could generate a braking force of no more than 432 pounds without losing control.

Without a trailer, weight transfer during aggressive braking can increase the weight on your front tire for most touring bikes to as much as 700 pounds. In other words, without a trailer, the front tire can handle upwards of 840 pounds of braking force.

But if the rider is pulling a trailer while braking aggressively and the trailer's weight on the hitch becomes more than 100 pounds, for example, then it causes about 120 pounds of weight to be added to the rear tire, while it reduces the weight on the front tire by about 20 pounds. Clearly this has adversely affected the ability of the front tire to support high braking forces without skidding.

Handling is similarly affected, even without acceleration or braking. Consider what happens when the bike rides over a dip in the road. As the front-end of the bike rises, the trailer hitch is pulled **down**.

Assume that you have measured the horizontal distance between the ball on the hitch and the axle of your trailer wheels; and that the ball is at the same height as the trailer axle. If you either raise or lower the ball, that horizontal distance must decrease. In other words, this is the same as saying that your "wheelbase" has shortened.

At the same time, unless the CG of your trailer and cargo is at exactly the same height as the ball / axle, it will shift along that "wheelbase" a greater distance than you would expect.

Here's an exaggerated example, to make this point clear. In order for 10% of the total trailer weight to be on the ball of the hitch, the CG of the trailer **must** be 10% of the distance between the trailer axle and that ball (closer, of course, to the axle than the ball).

Now imagine that the CG is one mile above the trailer when the trailer's level and at rest. If you were to lower the ball only a few degrees, the CG would move far forward (indeed, in this extreme case, the CG would move far forward of the hitch itself).

From this imagined scenario, it's easy to see that the higher the CG is, the more significant the weight transfer to the rear of the motorcycle will be, taking it off the trailer wheels.

A motorcycle trailer's CG isn't one mile above the trailer. But it is higher than the ball of the hitch. So, instead of a 30-pound weight on that hitch, there could well be 100 pounds on it if the rider stops fast or rides over a severe dip. That could easily make the front-end feel light and will certainly reduce the front tire's traction.

If, while riding level or at rest, 20% of the total weight of the trailer is on that ball, then upwards of 200 pounds could be added to it as a result of stopping or riding over a deep dip in the road.

Surely this refutes the argument that loading 20% of the total trailer weight on the hitch is O.K. It's not.

B. Aggressive swerve or aggressive stop?

The MSF often leaves students believing that they have a choice—**either** brake or swerve, but don't do both at the same time. Though RiderCoaches do not actually say that, this message is "heard" by many beginning riders. And while it's correct for **aggressive** swerving or **aggressive** braking, normally riders can certainly do both at the same time.

Consider the realities of motorcycle control. If a rider is braking, weight is shifting from the rear to the front of the bike.

A bike's rake and trail cause a "restoring force" that attempts to point the bike's front-end in the direction of travel (to go straight and ride vertical), which resists the rider's efforts to change directions. That's **good**. The amount of "restoring force" is directly proportional to the amount of weight on the front-end. Thus, a weight transfer from braking **increases** that force. Indeed, during an aggressive stop, it's virtually impossible to counter-steer.

Thus, if a rider's performing an aggressive stop, it's foolish to believe that he can, at the same time, swerve in a different direction. And that's also good, for during an aggressive stop, the rider is attempting to maximize his deceleration rate, which means he's close to skidding the front tire. In other words, he has no traction left to consume with the acceleration forces caused by changing direction.

"Delta-V" means change of velocity, and a change of velocity is a change of speed **or** direction. To make this clear, assume you are moving in a straight line at 60 MPH. How fast are you moving to the left? Zero MPH, of course.

But if you change your direction to move slightly left of a straight line, your "speed to the left" during that change was certainly greater than zero, even if your speedometer continues to show that you are maintaining a speed of 60 MPH. You accelerated to the left from zero to something greater than zero. This required energy, and it was felt as "centrifugal force". It was a "Delta-V"... a change of velocity.

But an experienced rider has used his brakes and changed direction at the same time many, many times, so he knows he can do it—he does it virtually every time he pulls into a parking space. A rider **can** do that because he's consuming only a modest amount of traction with modest braking and modest steering input. There's lots of traction left over. So the MSF should advise, as we do, that you cannot **safely** brake aggressively and change directions at the same time.

When you stop aggressively, you must be absolutely committed to it. That is, you must put your mind, body, and soul into **stopping** without losing control. An aggressive stop ends when you are safely stopped, or when you crash. Period.

So why do so many riders seem to believe that they have a choice after they begin an aggressive stop? Could you, for example, decide after you have started an aggressive stop that, despite how quickly you are slowing down, you're still going to hit that 18-wheeler so it must be time to "change your mind", let go of the binders (so that you are not both stopping and swerving at the same time), and begin an aggressive swerve?

Well, of course you can decide to do that, but not without insuring a crash. **You cannot change your mind and have a better result** if you have begun an aggressive stop! (Commitment is good.)

Let's be perfectly clear about this. If a threat presents itself, you have a very brief moment (less than one second of PDR) to recognize it and to decide what to do about it.

Then, in even less time, you must react (move your fingers and begin squeezing the brake lever or apply counter-steering input). If you are leaned over in a turn when that threat appears and you decide to brake aggressively, then you <u>must first</u> use counter-steering input to stand your bike vertical and get it moving in a straight line.

In other words, if you have elected to do an aggressive stop, you have already consumed time. There's no more of that precious reality to squander. What time is left must be used to reduce your speed!

When a rider's in the middle of an aggressive stop, his bike is already vertical, and he's trying to maximize his deceleration rate without exceeding the available traction. He can't be "noticing" things like alternate escape routes, or the color of that 18-wheeler he's heading toward, or whether there's a car behind him and if it will stop as quickly as he can. His attention **must** be focused on maximizing his deceleration rate and remaining in control of the bike. **All the rest of reality is no longer relevant**!

That means that if, during aggressive braking, his mind has wandered into considering alternate choice evaluations (such as whether to abandon the aggressive braking in favor of an aggressive swerve), he's not focused properly or paying enough attention to controlling his motorcycle. Still, some riders will do just that: consider changing their mind. Figure 17 shows this scenario.

Assume that when you begin your aggressive braking, you're moving at 40 MPH. Also assume that you perform an absolutely perfect braking maneuver, but the distance between you and the 18-wheeler is so short that you are going to hit it anyway, at about 20 MPH. Along the way you change your mind. You release the brakes and apply counter-steering input. What's going to happen?

Look closely at the diagram. You can see that if, instead of the aggressive stop you first decided to do, you make an aggressive swerve, the best swerve possible will send you crashing into that 18-wheeler at about 40 MPH.

What on earth makes anyone think that it's possible to muscle a bike into following the dashed line to the left? It's **impossible** to change directions that radically.

You know that, because if you had started the swerve at the beginning of the line instead of braking, the best you could have done was to travel along the dashed line on the left side of the diagram. Believing that if you start a swerve after the distance between you and the threat has evaporated is simply a faulty thought process, or not thinking at all.

No matter what you do, including losing control and low-siding, you are going to hit that 18-wheeler somewhere in the shaded area of the chart. <u>Worse, you will be traveling faster than 20 MPH when you do!</u> Now you see why "changing your mind" after starting an aggressive stop is deadly.

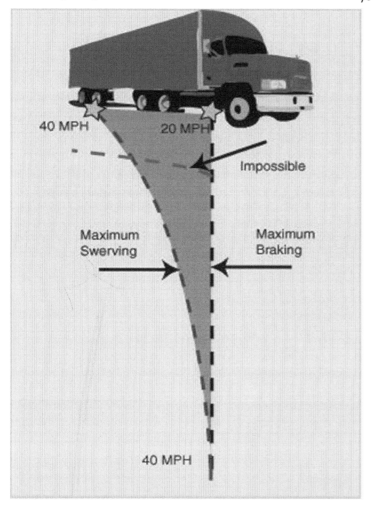

Figure 17: Brake and swerve choices and consequences

But let's play a little with the possibility. (Of course, there are times when you can swerve around an obstacle without hitting it, but this scenario isn't one of those times.) Assume you are able, by magic, to avoid hitting the 18-wheeler as a result of using an aggressive swerve instead of an aggressive stop. We already know that this could only be true if you elected to do an aggressive swerve before starting that aggressive stop. Either, not both at the same time, remember?

Then what?

The unpleasant reality is that you'll be traveling at 40 MPH **in a direction guaranteed to put you into a crash** <u>unless you change it again</u>!

That is, an aggressive swerve isn't just a hard left or hard right change of direction. **It must be an "<u>S</u>" curve.** If you are tooling down the road when a threat presents itself and you opt to do an aggressive swerve instead of an aggressive stop, then after you avoid the threat, you're no longer going in the same direction the road is going. Unless you change your direction **two more times**, you will end up off the road, in a ditch, or on the grill of an oncoming car!

Further, the adrenaline rushing through your body that helped you in your "fight or flight" avoidance decision is now getting in your way, instead of helping.

While you may have managed the bike's **huge** 20-degree lean as you swerved aggressively to avoid hitting the 18-wheeler, you then have to do an **enormous 40-degree** change of lean from one side to the other, and then a **reversing 20-degree** lean to get the bike vertical.

You must make <u>**three**</u> major direction changes of the bike to get back on course. These are almost unthinkable maneuvers while that adrenaline's racing through your blood stream.

The lesson here is this: the advice given by the MSF that "you can either do a stop or a swerve, but not both at the same time", applies **only** to aggressive stops and aggressive swerves. Insofar as that also makes it sound as if those are roughly equal choices in terms of outcome, **it's not so!**

A competent rider knows that an aggressive stop is almost always the safer of the two choices.

Braking **always** leaves you moving slower at impact (if there is an impact). And it's **far easier to control** than an aggressive swerve.

So, in summary, you should almost always elect to do the aggressive stop instead of as aggressive swerve as it's **easier** and **safer**, and the results are far more predictable.

It's wishful thinking to believe that when you elect to do an aggressive swerve, you have "plotted a course" beyond the initial hard right or hard left avoidance trajectory. No rational person elects to make a hard turn right or left into the unknown while driving at 40 MPH, and it's even less likely at 65 MPH.

An aggressive swerve is so unthinkably stupid more often than not that you should put that "choice" in your luggage and concentrate almost exclusively on developing your aggressive braking skills. A rider should be so predisposed to make an aggressive stop that he **wastes no time** making that decision. Get on the binders and control-stop the bike as soon as possible.

Don't argue with yourself about what to do. In a real emergency, you have **no time** to contemplate magic. Hope is not a plan.

C. Safety margin

It's one thing to practice skills in a controlled environment at close to a rider's personal limits. It's quite another to ride on public roads anywhere near those limits. In order to get better, riders need to push their limits. But once a rider has attained a level of proficiency with his skills that he's satisfied with, the vast majority of his parking lot practice sessions should be used merely to maintain those skills, not to improve them.

Beyond skill development and maintenance, however, is the development of behaviors that tend to minimize risk. These behaviors construct and maintain a safety margin that allow a rider to absorb small mistakes and to provide the time and space needed to utilize skills.

Exercising good judgment is fundamental to being a competent rider.

Good judgment, for example, is what causes a rider always to insure that adequate safety margins exist when riding. Counter-intuitively, human nature being what it is, a safety margin can sometimes invite behaviors that are far more dangerous than what a rider would consider if the margins did not exist. Good judgment requires accurate information to work with, something that's often hard to obtain.

1. Risk compensation

A competent rider provides himself or herself one reasonable safety margin by wearing a helmet, but he's aware that this behavior doesn't eliminate risk.

The National Highway Traffic Safety Administration estimates that an unhelmeted rider is 40 per cent more likely to suffer a fatal head injury and 15 percent more likely to incur a non-fatal head injury than a helmeted motorcyclist. NHTSA also claims that motorcycle helmets reduce the likelihood of a crash fatality by 37 per cent.[4] Those facts alone are sufficient to convince most safety-conscious riders to wear a helmet.

The problem with those facts is that they are incomplete and not well known. Riders who wear helmets have an exaggerated belief in helmet efficacy at protecting a rider from injury and death. Any time a rider who's moving at highway speeds crashes, that helmet will be essentially worthless in saving his or her life or preventing serious injury. While it's true that most motorcycle fatalities derive from head injuries, losing a leg or an arm or sustaining serious chest trauma are serious injuries, by definition. Death from crashing is merely an injury taken to the extreme. Helmets play no role in protecting from these kinds of injuries or death.

Beyond a helmet, safety-conscious riders wear other substantial safety gear, including gloves, heavy jackets, some form of leg protection against abrasion and small-scale impacts like stones or flying insects, over-the-ankle footwear, and eye protection. When riders wear all that non-helmet gear, the odds are very high that they will also wear a motorcycle helmet; but it's not infrequent that a rider who wears a helmet lacks almost any other form of safety gear.

But let's stick with the idea that motorcyclists have an exaggerated opinion of how safe they will be if they are wearing a helmet. For many of these riders, that sense of safety leads them to take risks that they would avoid were they not wearing the helmet.

This is called 'risk compensation': increasing the risks taken based on the belief that they are 'safer', or lowering risks taken based on the belief that they are less safe. In effect, wearing a helmet provides a meaningful safety margin, while risk compensation erodes that margin.

Another example of risk compensation is the result of formal training. There's a widespread belief that taking and passing an MSF beginner riding class results in safer riders—riders who are less likely to be hurt or killed while riding their motorcycles.

In fact, many studies have been conducted trying to prove this to be true, but the results do not show that it is. In fact, some of the results actually show that a trained rider is more likely to become involved in an accident that causes his or her injury or death. (See the discussion of this at the beginning of Phase 3.)

An exaggerated regard for how "safe" a rider feels isn't necessary in order to find a rider increasing his or her risks and eroding safety margins. A more formal concept called "risk homeostasis" tries to explain this phenomenon.

2. Risk homeostasis

Gerald J.S. Wilde, a professor emeritus of psychology at Queen's University, Kingston, Ontario, Canada, developed a hypothesis about risk known as "risk homeostasis".[5] This hypothesis argues that people have a personal level of risk tolerance—that they tend to maintain. Thus, when they believe, for whatever reason, that they have become "safer"—have become "bullet-proof"—they naturally seek additional risk to bring their sense of risk to a level approximately equal to what it was before they felt safer.

Training, experience, and wearing a helmet while riding tend to make riders feel "safer." Those riders then tend to behave in ways that are more risky than those who have not been trained, who have limited experience, and who do not wear helmets. This is essentially "risk compensation" with a new name. A rider who believes he's "safer", for any reason, tends to increase risks and erode safety margins.

As an example, when a rider's on a motorcycle that's ABS-equipped, he's likely to be somewhat more aggressive on the road. Though a two-second following distance seemed appropriate when riding without ABS, he may tend to follow just a little bit more closely because his bike has ABS.

"Risk compensation" means that riders increase or decrease the amount of risk they are willing to accept based on the

---

[4] NHTSA, *Traffic Safety Facts 2004*, available at: http://www.nhtsa.gov/people/injury/new-fact-sheet03/motorcyclehelmet.pdf. DOT HS 809 905.

[5] Wilde, Gerald J.S., **TARGET RISK 2: A NEW PSYCHOLOGY OF SAFETY AND HEALTH**, PDE Publications (2001). ISBN 09699124-3-9.

level of risk that they believe exists, while "risk homeostasis" means that riders attempt to maintain a given level of risk which is personally specific.

The problem with both concepts is that humans are incapable of determining the actual level of risk with specificity; and experience tends to reduce our sense of risk level irrationally. For example, a rider may well feel that the risk level is close to his or her tolerance level when riding at 60 MPH if he's relatively inexperienced; but after hundreds or thousands of miles of riding experience at speeds that high, his tolerance level increases to speeds greater than 70 MPH, or 80 MPH, or higher.

Obviously the risks have actually increased, but the perception of risk has diminished. Both risk compensation and risk homeostasis find the rider willing to ride at faster speeds, which isn't at all the same thing as maintaining a given level of risk.

Neither risk compensation nor risk homeostasis compels increasingly risky behaviors. Though an experienced rider might feel that it's just as "safe" to ride at 70 MPH as it is at 60 MPH, he's not required to ride at 70 MPH. He or she can believe and **feel** that a 1.5-second following distance is just as "safe" as a full two-second following distance, but that rider will still observe at least the two-second following distance rule, so that his safety margin is maintained.

A competent, intelligent, and informed rider elects to maintain his or her safety margins at all times.

3. Always have an "escape path'

A fundamental concept for newbies as well as experienced riders is that you should **always** have an escape path while riding a motorcycle. No one seriously argues with that bit of wisdom. Yet there are far too many injuries and deaths that result from failing to understand that very concept.

Perhaps the concept's a little bit too obvious to be taken seriously. Advice like "Look where you want to go" or "If you look at that pothole you are approaching, you will hit it" involves **understanding** the essence of target fixation before this gets the attention of, and meaning to, the listener.

Similarly, advice like "Ride your own ride" requires that you **understand** that some riders have better skills than you do at a particular task; so if you follow the herd, there **will** be times (tasks) that you will confront that are beyond your abilities. Unless you have the background and temperament that allow you to see a "bigger picture", this kind of advice is trivial and easily ignored—meaning, it has no value for you.

So let's get back to "escape paths". Assume you have practiced and developed a certain skill level at all the common tasks required while riding. You can, for example, confidently and smoothly handle a curve in the road posted for 35 MPH at, say, 55 MPH without dragging a peg or losing traction. But you should <u>**not**</u> ride that curve at 55 MPH. It's simple advice, but you may be unwilling to accept it.

You need to have experience (background) and temperament going for you before you can **understand** it and allow yourself to be persuaded to accept the advice as meaningful.

When you ride your motorcycle you are **often** confronted with the unexpected. Riding would be boring if it were not for those moments. Phase 2 riders have come to believe that they can handle virtually anything in the way of "unexpected" because they have, so far, successfully managed to do so. Their reflexes are quick, their judgment is sound, they tend not to panic, and both the rider and his motorcycle are "healthy". But sooner or later an "unexpected" will occur that's slightly (or grossly) beyond their abilities. Then what?

Go back to that skill that you demonstrably have: the ability to handle a particular curve at 55 MPH. At 60 MPH, you'll drag a peg or lose traction. <u>**Your**</u> skill level at that particular task is 55 MPH. What do you do if it turns out that, for one reason or another, you find yourself moving at 60 MPH in that curve? Or suppose what looked like a 55 MPH curve turns out to be ever so slightly tighter than you thought?

What happens, of course, is that you find yourself forced outside of your skill range.

Now you find yourself dragging a peg. Catastrophe? Not at all, so long as you can change the lean angle of your **bike**. You could, for example, simply lean your body (not the bike) deeper into that curve. Your bike's lean angle will diminish, and your peg will no longer be dragging. It becomes a "pucker moment" that safely passed because **you had something in reserve**–an **escape path** (or a **recovery technique**).

An "escape path" need not involve changing your direction of travel. It may be no more than a little more traction, or slightly more braking pressure, or a little more throttle, or as just demonstrated, a recovery technique. Or, it might actually involve a change of travel direction—tightening a turn until the bike assumes an extra five degrees of lean angle or aiming for a space between cars.

So far we have discussed skill levels as if they were limits beyond which you **cannot** safely continue. Now consider that if you ride **at** your skill levels, <u>**you are always at the threshold of loss of control.**</u>

Such behavior is simply not the way to maximize your odds of escaping the riding experience throughout your career without injury or death. Your survival depends on thinking smarter—because there **will be** an "unexpected" event in your future that pushes you beyond your limits.

Go back to that 35 MPH curve. If a rider drags a peg at 55 MPH, he can almost always recover by simply leaning his body into the turn. So, from a skill level point of view, why not make it a practice of always leaning his body into his turns? That way he's increased his skill level (say, for example, to 60 MPH on that particular curve). But simultaneously, he's **removed his escape path**—the recovery technique—from his tool bag. And now when that "unexpected" event occurs, he has nowhere to go but **down**!

It makes far more sense to **not** ride **at** your skill level and always to keep a bit of reserve. Call that "defensive riding", "having an escape path", "having a recovery technique in your tool bag", or "maintaining a reserve", whatever you like. But if you ride **at** your limits all the time, eventually you can expect to call it "eating the pavement".

It should be clear that stunters and racers often ride at the limits of their skills; and when they exceed them, they get hurt. These materials weren't written for them. Instead, they were written for people who **never** want to experience an injury or to die because of riding their motorcycles. This Phase 2 information was written for competent riders who wish to become mature riders by experiencing many years and tens of thousands, or even hundreds of thousands, of safe miles on two wheels during their riding careers.

4. Following distance

Safety margins change based on the situation. A rider should be perfectly happy to maintain a two-second following distance if he knows the people he's riding with, and if he's well rested and mentally alert. However, as he progresses through a 200-mile day trip with a group, he's gotten tired and isn't as mentally alert as when he started that ride. The situation has changed; and the rider should increase his following distance. Toward the end of the ride, he should maintain about a three-second following distance to insure his safety margin is adequate.

A competent rider adapts the "rules" to the situation.

5. Tires

Before your ride, you inspect your tires. Suppose you notice that the tread on one of them is nearly showing its wear indicators. You believe you have another 500 miles of life on that tire—but your life depends on your tires' performance.

A competent rider will abort his ride before it starts and, instead, head for the shop to replace a worn tire.

That last 500 miles might be only 300 before the tire self-destructs, if the rider has misjudged. A rider conscious of his safety margin would rather not have to deal with a self-destructing tire, even if it means replacing a perfectly good tire prematurely. The cost will be substantially less than a hospital visit.

6. Medication

Competent riders tend to be older than newbies. Two things about older riders should be understood:

1. Older riders break more easily than do younger riders; and

2. Older riders tend to have more medical issues than younger riders do.

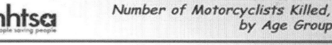

Figure 18: NHTSA chart of fatalities by age

The first item goes a long way toward explaining why, as the motorcycle riding population gets older, there's a disproportionately larger increase in deaths and serious injuries among older riders. The annual accident statistics produced by the National Highway Traffic Safety Administration (NHTSA) bear this out, as shown in Figure 18. An accident that's easily survivable by a younger rider whose bones are stronger and more resilient may become a disabling and or even a fatal accident for older riders. Older riders are not unaware of their increased vulnerability. They would be more inclined to maintain safety margins while riding in order to avoid these serious consequences, one would think; and yet those statistics suggest otherwise.

Older riders probably **do** tend to avoid more threatening situations than do younger riders, but they simultaneously encounter situations that are more threatening to them because of their diminished capacities to deal with them—often as a result of medications (item two in the list above).

Consider how this affects an older rider's safety margins.

Assume you're out on the road and a headache begins. At the next stop, you take some over-the-counter medicine to get rid of it. No problem with that, you think, especially because you're not taking any other medication nor have you been doing any drinking. An hour later, you fail to negotiate a turn and end up hurt...or dead.

Or you have an abscessed tooth, and your dentist prescribed a 10-day supply of penicillin. You're not allergic to it and not taking any other medication. The swelling has gone, and so has the pain. But the curve that you took a little fast turned out to be your worst nightmare, and you couldn't negotiate it at all. Penicillin, it turns out, does not cure road rash, nor the loss of that leg.

These are not examples that just can't happen. They have! Over-the-counter medication does not have to cause drowsiness to be a problem. Even after reading the warning labels and finding that there are no side effects to be worried about, older riders should still be careful. An experienced, certified MSF instructor recently described an accident that simply should not have happened. He was not riding too fast. The road and weather were perfect. The curve was relatively tame. But the anti-histamine he took to help him get over a pollen-induced headache caused him to become confused and less than competent in that curve. He ran off the road and was very lucky to survive the experience.

In the case of penicillin, one MFS instructor-candidate was in the middle of a training class and out on the range working with "students" on one of the more complex exercises. The abscess he had was no longer a problem, and he had only two days left of the medication to go. Suddenly he got terribly confused. When asked to end the exercise by the other instructor, he was to signal the students to "restage" and direct them to the staging area. Instead, he merely slowed them all down as they passed, then **walked off the range** as if the exercise was done. The students kept riding around the range, without supervision. It could have been worse. He could have directed them into trouble. As it was, they were all lucky.

Why did these things happen even without the complication of mixing other drugs or alcohol? Because some medications act very strangely in combination with a hot environment! It was well over 90 degrees, and he had been out on the range all day long. Heat was also a contributing factor in the incident where the other instructor ran off the road. Both were older riders.

If you find you're fighting a headache or some other pain and decide to take care of it and continue your ride, think again! At the very least, slow down and remind yourself that while you may think you're 100%, the headache or other pain has already told you that **something** isn't right with you. You took some medication that you hope is strong enough to get rid of those **symptoms**. If it's strong enough to do that, it's strong enough to make you less than a 100% rider.

In the real world, you may have to ride some distance before you can get off the bike and park it until all is well with you. Build a safety margin for yourself. **Slow down** and drive with the knowledge that you are **not** 100%. No shame in that. But dying to prove how tough you were isn't the smartest thing you ever did when you were alive.

7. "Just in time" is too late

A competent rider is never late.

This means he's not late in recognizing or reacting to a threat, not late in joining a riding group, not late in going through traffic lights, not late in performing preventative maintenance on his motorcycle, and not late in terms of reaching his destination (unless it would have been dangerous to be on time). If you engage in chronically late behavior, you're dangerous to be around.

A rider who tends to be late all the time will probably take extraordinary risks to "try to get there on time" (meaning that he started out late and tried to make up the time). He will tend to tailgate on the road and speed just a bit more than the next guy, speed up when a light turns yellow instead of reaching for his brake lever, and "forget" (because he didn't have time) to do a walk-around inspection before his started his ride. This type of rider is well advised to take the car instead of his motorcycle.

Another type of rider whom others won't appreciate is one who's always "just in time". He arrives just as the rest of the group is getting ready to start their ride, for example. This type of rider is almost as dangerous as one who's chronically late. He plans to get his motorcycle inspected just days before his inspection sticker lapses; or, as mentioned earlier, he won't replace a worn tire until the wear bar shows.

This type of rider is usually more dangerous to himself than to others.

Consider, for example, the case of the rider who scheduled major motorcycle maintenance to be performed a day or so before the start of a long day tour. She picked up her bike from the dealership after the shop had done the work on it for her. As part of the repairs, she had the cams and lifters replaced on the right side of the block. She rode the bike home and commented that the bike had never felt so good and smooth. She was thrilled with the work.

The next day, along with a buddy riding drag, she took her bike out for a 200-mile ride in order to lay out and pre-ride a poker run. After a total of 12 miles, the engine blew.

She was going 70 MPH and was in the fast lane of a four-lane freeway. She heard a metallic grind. Then the left side of her engine housing **disappeared**. The bolt holding the flywheel backed out and ripped the metal casing apart in the process. Oil sprayed out to the left and saturated her chaps and boot. About two quarts were lost in a matter of seconds.

She signaled that she was going to pull off the freeway by going left into the center median. The drag bike saw from behind her what had happened and insisted that she move **right** instead. He secured each lane, and they did just that—moved right across four lanes and off to the side of the road.

She did not freeze. She did not panic. She did not "hit her brakes". Instead, she smoothly eased her bike to the right and coasted off the freeway without losing control.

Lest any reader doubt the wisdom of moving four lanes to the right instead of one lane to the left, remember that oil was gushing out on the left side. If she had gone left to exit the freeway, she would have risked riding over that oil with her back tire. When the riders stopped and got off the bikes, major amounts of oil were still dripping under her bike.

The mechanic who did the work on her bike was **world-class**! After seeing what had happened, and turning white as a sheet, he insisted that the shop technicians hadn't been anywhere near that part of the engine while replacing the cams and lifters. Nevertheless, he promised to fix the bike at his cost because "it looks bad for us." It was later determined that he had used a wrench on the flywheel bolt to crank the engine in order to set the timing of the cam he installed. He told us that he, not some other wrench, might in fact have loosened the bolt without realizing it.

The message should be crystal clear: **Have your maintenance done long before you leave on your tour. Ride your newly-maintained bike for at least 100 miles first.** Even the best "wrench" makes mistakes. Those who aren't the best make more of them. "Just in time" is simply too late if you believe in maintaining a safety margin.

D. Endurance is part of a "safety margin"

In the year 2004, there were 5,780,870 registered motorcycles in the United States, and they traveled 10 billion, 48 million miles.[6] Though that sounds like a lot of miles, it means that the average motorcyclist traveled only 1,738 miles in a year. That's about 144 miles per month. That means that there are a lot of motorcyclists who don't ride motorcycles. They make a typical day trip of only 50 miles perhaps twice a month, and often they travel on the same favorite route every time. They are newbies, in other words, every time they get on their bikes, no matter how many years of riding "experience" they might have.

A competent rider tends to maintain his competence with frequent rides which are often long, and he rarely sticks to the same route.

It's not unusual for a competent rider to average 150 miles on a typical day's ride. Many will take extended riding trips over multiple days and sometimes over more than a thousand or two thousand miles if they are on a tour.

---

[6]NHTSA, *Traffic Safety Facts 2005: Motorcycles.* DOT HS 810 620.

This raises the issue of endurance. A rider who can only just manage a 50-mile day trip is simply not equipped to attempt an extended riding trip without first engaging in some conditioning rides.

1. Conditioning rides

Preparing for an extended ride or tour can take several months of effort. When a rider's able to handle a day trip of about 150 miles, with a single rest or meal stop along the way and without becoming particularly tired, he's ready to begin conditioning for longer rides by extending those day trips to about 200 miles and even sometimes 250 miles.

While participating in these conditioning rides, if the rider finds himself unusually stressed or tired, he should immediately abort the outward bound part of the ride and head toward home.

If you are **tired** at the destination, you will likely be **very tired** when you get home, **but <u>not exhausted</u>**. So, when the rider feels tired, he accepts that as his half-way point. He shouldn't subject himself to the situation of being **very tired** when he gets to the half-way point, because that would insure that he would be exhausted on the way home.

By taking one conditioning step at a time, intelligently, he ends up ready for a few 300- to 400-mile touring segments on his extended ride.

2. Conditioning helps to build muscle

A rider's left hand is critical for maintaining control of the bike at slow speeds. His left hand is also what he usually relies on to "weld" him to his bike on long-distance rides. The left hand on the grip is what assures him that all is well—by feel and position. "Feathering" the clutch also depends on fine control of the muscles of the left hand.

In an emergency, the right hand fingers do most of the work, so they should be loose and flexible at all times. Conditioning rides help both hands' muscles improve their endurance.

3. The secret of endurance is comfort

Being able to handle long-distance rides, which requires a rider to have the endurance to remain alert and in control, is not entirely a matter of conditioning of your body. Indeed, though physical conditioning is important, your comfort while riding is even more so.

A hard seat, a helmet that fits poorly, a posture that is other than upright, severe vibration, insufficient clothing to handle cold or wet weather, infrequent pit stops to stretch your legs and visit the restroom, insufficient water and food—these all shorten your endurance, because they're uncomfortable.

In addition, loud noise damages your ability to hear over time. Loud noise dramatically lowers your comfort level and, thus, your endurance. Wear ear plugs when riding to save your hearing, help maintain your concentration, and prevent rider fatigue. They won't interfere with your awareness of threats around you if they fit properly.

E. The value of planning

You know by now that "just in time" is not the kind of planning that improves a rider's odds of surviving on public roads. Real planning is essential.

A famous pilot's maxim says: "A superior pilot uses his superior judgment to avoid having to exercise his superior skill."

A competent motorcyclist will adopt exactly the same concept for his sport by substituting one word: "**A superior <u>rider</u> uses his superior judgment to avoid having to exercise his superior skill.**"

As a Phase 2 rider, you've survived long enough to develop your skills. Now it's time to improve the exercise of your judgment in those fractions of seconds you have to make a decision. This starts long before you turn the key.

In order to achieve "superior judgment", a rider must necessarily have a great deal of experience; and that experience often derives from having exercised rather poor judgment—or, in the case of the newbie rider, to move from having insufficient experience for making a judgment call at all.

But if you have managed to survive your tenure as a newbie, one can assume you've developed both excellent skills and sound judgment along the way. During Phase 1, the passage through your newbie phase, the emphasis was necessarily on skill development. At this point of your riding career, however, the emphasis shifts toward mental processes. Many older riders say, "Riding is 90% mental," and by that time in their riding careers, it probably is, for the physical skills they needed were mastered long ago.

<u>Anticipatory reflection</u> is the heart of the safety mindset.

Being minimally prepared is essential to survival on the roads. To enjoy longer rides, however, far more detailed planning will add to your comfort and reduce your stress. Planning reduces the number of events that depend on that preparedness; and if they occur, they aren't a disaster.

Newer riders take shorter rides, and they are almost constantly confronted with "learning experiences" during those rides—that is, "unexpected events". These events happen so frequently, in fact, that they cease to be unexpected at all. With experience, a rider learns to expect the unexpected.

More seasoned riders, especially those who have become competent, enjoy longer rides—sometimes crossing state lines over a long weekend. Touring by motorcycle may entail riding many hundreds, even thousands, of miles. The longer the trip, the more substantial planning efforts are needed. It may seem obvious, but the idea that a very experienced rider would simply decide to aim for the bluest sky when touring the country on his motorcycle, having no destination or schedule—or plan—is a fantasy. Taking off without a plan is destined to produce an unsatisfactory experience.

1. Pre-ride checklist and "flight plan"

Three hundred miles away from home isn't the best place to discover that you left your medication in your medicine cabinet, your cell phone plugged into your kitchen outlet next to your toaster, or your extra underwear in the dryer. There are simply too many things you'll need when you're out on the road to rely on perfect memory during a scramble to beat the morning rush-hour traffic and get on the road.

Airplane pilots wouldn't think of taking off without having first gone through a written pre-flight checklist. That's just one reason why airline travel is extremely safe. Is it possible that we can learn something from those pilots?

Part of your pre-ride activity—something most riders find fun, too—should be to look at your maps, determine a likely route and destination, and create a "flight plan" to leave with someone who will be expecting you back from your ride.

Again, pilots file these plans for the same reason you should: to help someone locate them if they don't come back on time. Here's how one rider remembers to do it now:

> This rider recently took an impromptu 130-mile solo ride on his Gold Wing. The trip was uneventful. Still, it was not the smartest thing he's ever done.

It had been his practice always to let someone know where he was going, his probable route, and the time he expected to return if he took off by himself.

Filing that "flight plan" makes more sense if traveling on back roads than it does if traveling on freeways (which is what he did), but the fact remains that if he had had an accident 60 miles away from home, it might have been a long time before anybody realized he was in trouble.

He always wears an emergency tag which includes, among other things, the name and telephone number of the person to contact in case of trouble. That served as a backup plan instead of the "flight plan". Because he wasn't traveling on the back roads, he was relying on the emergency tag.

Figure 19: Emergency Medical Tag

The fact remains that letting someone know where you intend to be, the route you plan to take, and when you expect to return time is a very savvy thing to do, tag or no tag.

His partner chewed his leg off about eight hours later when he mentioned that he had taken that little trip without letting her know!

You should file a "flight plan" with someone who expects to hear from you when you return. One person did know where he was going and when but did not expect a call when he returned. This isn't a good example of the "flight plan" described above.

What's a reasonable use of this practice? Is filing a flight plan a "safety issue" when you are traveling freeways from one location to another near home? If you're involved in an accident on a freeway or another well-traveled surface street, you're not likely to end up undiscovered for hours or days. In that case, a flight plan is merely a courtesy. It could be as short as: "I'm going to take the bike to the dealership on the north side, and I expect to be back shortly after noon."

But if you're on a camp-out and you decide to do some trail riding, or you plan to ride back-country roads, or it's a multi-day trip, you should file a much more detailed plan. Then it becomes a safety issue.

Another tip that works for many riders is to keep maintenance logs that record what was done, when, and at what mileage, just as airplane logs are kept. If you plan a ride of any serious distance, it's a good idea to have your bike checked out shortly before you go, so that any mechanical problem can be diagnosed and dealt with from home. (These logs can be invaluable in case of an accident or when you decide to sell your bike, too.)

Your future motorcycling experiences will not, hopefully, end after the next ride. It makes sense, then, for you not to have to rely on your memory to be sure you are properly prepared before each ride.

Instead, make a thorough checklist and rely on it. Break it into meaningful subsections such as "day trip" and "overnight" or "extended trip". Update the list with experience.

See **APPENDIX H – An equipment and camping checklist**.

A competent rider does a pre-ride "walk around" in which he checks the fundamental heath and adequacy of his motorcycle for that day's ride.

Many riders use T-CLOCK or some similar mnemonic to remember what to look for, but a written list will make sure you do it the same way until you have a routine established.

Because you also do a quick pre-ride parking lot practice session (five minutes) to confirm that both you and your bike are functional and ready, your checklist should include those two activities so that you don't forget them and just ride off.

2. Route

Once you're beyond the fundamentals and looking for a "real" day trip as opposed to a commute, you'll probably have a destination in mind in your area.

If you ride with a club, the Road Captain or the club's officials will probably pick a destination and a route, or you may find some friends who want to join you for a pick-up ride on short notice and who are prepared to go.

A day trip means getting out of your neighborhood and your town or city. It may be shorter, but it's usually between 100 and 200 miles in length. For experienced tour riders, a day trip could mean going much farther.

A day trip for lunch could cover over 400 miles with people who are enthusiastic about a particular region or town.

If you select the route, keep in mind these factors:

1. Light and visibility
2. Traffic density
3. Availability of gas, food, and assistance
4. Variety of roads and terrain

Here are some quick notes about each of them: Remember that you must see and be seen, so plan your route to avoid riding into the sun when it's on the horizon, and to give yourself options if visibility diminishes.

While rush hour is fairly easy to predict in big cities, riders may be surprised to find it in small towns, too. Market days are common in farming areas, and festivals of all kinds dot the calendar. Think about the environment where you plan to ride in terms of who the other drivers will be, and what will be on their minds other than your safety.

The tools that make planning a trip so much easier today include detailed satellite photos and online maps that show hotels, restaurants, fuel stations, and much more. What they may not show is whether the place you intend to stop is still open for business, or what its hours are.

So long as you're in an urban zone, you'll usually find what you need without a problem. If you're in a heavily-traveled tourist area, however, you may experience long waits or price gouging that you could have avoided by changing your route. And if your day trip takes you into open country and off the beaten path, you need to be sure you can get fuel and help, in particular.

Finally, you probably want to try riding all kinds of roads once you're out of the city and away from the familiar ones you travel all the time. Chances are good that skills for riding in the twisties are not ones you'll gain during your morning commute. If you have a choice, plan to ride on novel roads and under new conditions in the morning, when you're fresh (or soon after you start your ride, whatever time that is).

By the time you've finished the outward-bound part of a day trip, which might be three to four hours of riding, you don't need to take on an adventure on the way back.

Even competent riders will experience mental as well as physical fatigue toward the end of a long ride.

Day trips may involve rural areas where riders can poke along on slower roads, to enjoy the scenery and the variety of terrain. On the way back, it's common for riders to travel by freeway to make the best time. This also lowers their risks from cross-traffic or other sight-seeing drivers late in the day.

These factors are even more important on longer rides, so it's good to start thinking about them for day trips.

If you make a mistake in your planning, it's easier to correct it when you're in an area where you know the local roads and can make different choices if need arises; and if you find yourself stressed, you'll be at home when the ride ends, without having to look for a hard-to-find vacancy at a motel in a strange place.

3. Packing

For a day trip, you must carry a number of required items, depending on the laws of your state. Your driver's license with your motorcycle endorsement on it and your liability insurance documentation are required by law.

Your cell phone, money and / or credit cards, and medical insurance card are enough for some riders (probably male). But an overnighter or a trip of longer duration is much more demanding. Not only should you make and look at your pre-ride checklist, you must decide where to pack those items.

For example, depending on the style of motorcycle you ride, you may have some form of luggage compartment on your motorcycle in the form of saddlebags (hard or strap-on) as well as a top-box and possibly carry-on luggage that you will strap onto your pillion.

If you have no luggage, you may need a backpack in order to expand your carrying capacity. Wherever you put it, it takes only a little foresight to know that a map of your travel route shouldn't be stored at the bottom. It also makes no sense to pack any extra heavy tools you might wish to take with you in your top-box or carry-on luggage.

The heavier an item is, the lower it should be packed. The more quickly you may need to access an item, the nearer it should be to the top. Fortunately, except for ladies' purses, heavy items are not usually needed as often as light-weight cargo such as shop rags, cleaner for your windscreen, or a bottle of drinking water.

If you plan to carry a co-rider, you'll want to discuss how limited your cargo space will be before he or she arrives with three changes of clothes and a bowling ball. Also, any time the trip will involve going shopping, extra space must be left on the outbound leg of the trip to allow the rider to pack and strap down any purchased items, unless the vendor or store will ship them home for you. This means souvenirs, as well as safety chrome that hasn't been installed yet. As the rider who's in control of the bike, you have to make the decisions about what you can carry and where it has to ride.

If you're going to stay away from home overnight, toiletries and a laptop computer belong in the carry-on luggage, as you will no doubt take that luggage into any motel (or tent) where you billet at the end of a day's ride. Expensive items shouldn't be left unattended on your bike, and you'll want to bring along your bike cover if possible to protect anything a thief might take, like a GPS. This means leaving room in a saddlebag for carrying that bike cover, even though this item is often bulky and takes up a lot of space.

You'll have a certain amount of cargo on your bike for regular riding, such as your rain gear; but you may have to shift it around to add what you want for a longer day's ride; or you may make a calculated guess about having good weather and decide to leave your rain gear and rubber overshoes at home, in order to have a change from boots to regular shoes.

Don't wait until ten minutes before your departure time to decide what to take and how to pack. Once you find a place for it, you also must insure that your cargo's strapped down with bungee cords, cargo nets, Velcro strips or whatever method you want to use; and it must be strapped tight, without dangling cords or hooks, so that nothing vibrates loose and falls out without your knowing it.

This process can be a series of trial-and-error maneuvers, depending on how much you have to pack. It's a good idea to put the items you plan to carry on a sheet on the floor near the bike the day before your trip, to gauge their weight and mass. You may even want to do a trial-run of your checklist and your packing.

Once you've established the way you want your cargo to ride, it probably will change a little during the trip as you become more efficient at packing and unpacking; but you'll have the basics in mind, and you'll know how many straps or cords it's going to take to hold everything on securely. Be aware of how added weight will change your bike's handling.

Wherever you elect to store your cargo on your motorcycle, you can assume that virtually every pound of what you take with you will be added primarily to the load carried by your rear tire. That is, **it will change the location of your Center of Gravity and will affect the way you steer and brake**.

See **APPENDIX B – Path of travel**.

4. Time and time of day

Some riders have clocks built into their fairings or magnetic clocks that attach to their instrument panel. No doubt many riders have to be conscious of the time of day in order to get to work, avoid rush-hour traffic congestion, or reach their destination by day's end.

For longer rides, however, it's probably not useful to maintain an awareness of time of day except in a geographical sense; that is, where's the sun, how much daylight do I have left, how long do I want to ride into twilight and darkness, how well do I know the roads I'm traveling in poor light, and how long will it take to get home or to shelter.

If you're riding solo or with a co-rider who "goes with the flow," the time you spend on a motorcycle can be one of the best parts of your day or your week. If you tend to let your rides get long as you soak up the experience, be aware of your co-rider's needs and different perspective behind you. Take a break at least once an hour.

Day trips often involve other riders. It's possible you may not have ridden with most of them before, when you first decide to go on a longer ride with them. Allow yourself some time at the beginning of the event to introduce yourself, socialize a little bit, and find out more details about the ride so that you can decide if you want to commit to it.

Attend a pre-ride briefing. Most group rides require that the participants meet at a certain time (and it's often earlier than the normal work day begins); that the riders are gassed up, fed, and otherwise ready to leave at the designated departure time; and that they arrive in time to hear the pre-ride briefing from the Road Captain, or at a minimum, that they discuss with fellow riders the rules of the ride.

If the Road Captain has ridden this route before, the organizers may be able to guess with fair accuracy what time the ride will end.

However, remember that your personal ride ends when you decide it does. Even if you're far from home, even if you had planned to travel with a group for several days, you can change your mind. Certainly on a day trip, you should feel no reluctance to turn back, or to stop, if that's what you need or want to do.

For example, if on a group ride, the route takes you into a setting sun that will leave you blinded by glare for more than a second (or into any other situation you consider dangerous—that is, you hear that "inner voice" telling you to stop), you should put your safety first and courteously depart the group. Let the Road Captain know you're leaving, though.

If you feel that to continue a ride with a group means that it will be making demands that you don't enjoy in order to get home by a certain time, or that the group isn't allowing enough time to reach its destination, or that it's making moves that exceed your skill level, leave when your own schedule or your own inner voice suggests it.

A competent rider should be able to find his or her way home alone, if necessary, in the dark and in rainy weather, and should have the equipment (maps, flashlights, cell phone, credit cards, etc.) to handle an unexpected solo trip as easily as if another rider was along. Finally, if your commute or your longer day trip results in a ride home after dark, **slow down**.

In many states, a big hazard for riders is deer (discussed in Volume One in detail), and they're almost impossible to spot at twilight until they're in front of you.

If you're riding at highway speeds on your return trip after dark, don't over-ride your headlights. Use the lights of adjacent drivers, particularly drivers ahead of you, to help you see what's coming up in your path of travel. Don't tailgate and don't ride in another vehicle's blind spot. Drop back and allow yourself to be seen. If it's not unreasonable for another driver to say, "I didn't see him" during daylight hours, it's even easier to be missed at night.

If you foresee that you're going to ride frequently after dark in order to take long day rides, consider adding running lights on the front and extra brake lights on the rear. Especially at night, you must make an effort to be conspicuous, so that other drivers know where you are.

5. Emergency preparedness

Almost everyone who rides a motorcycle today also carries a cell phone. Even wearing ATGATT and carrying a phone doesn't mean the rider's prepared for an emergency, though.

In the section of this book about group riding is a discussion of some guidelines about how to handle a disabled motorcycle or an impaired rider. The rules for responding to an emergency on any given ride should be covered during a pre-ride briefing so that every member of each group knows what to do.

Besides a cell phone, a rider should make room on his motorcycle for a First Aid kit. Remember to take it out and check it occasionally. Items deteriorate or tear open and get dirty, medications expire, and gloves may have been taken out for non-medical uses and never replaced. If there's no other justification for adding saddlebags to a bike, carrying your First Aid kit, flashlights, maps, and rain gear ought to be enough right there.

Riders are strongly recommended to take a Red Cross or similar emergency response class and to stay certified in CPR (cardiopulmonary resuscitation). Road Captains may call upon any rider in an emergency to help handle a patient or control an accident scene, and if you have training in these areas, it's much appreciated by your group leader or Road Captain to let them know.

Once 911 is called, emergency care for downed riders is usually beyond the scope of basic First Aid, but many classes will offer tips to make the rider comfortable until qualified medical caregivers arrive. If the ABC's have been satisfied (air, breathing, circulation) and bleeding is under control, then the uninjured riders should choose who will perform several immediate accident scene management tasks.

Not everyone is going to be prepared to carry out certain jobs, depending on their skills, emotional maturity, and connection to the injured rider. Sometimes a rider can assist simply by keeping an overwrought person away from the scene. Motorcycle injuries can be very gruesome to see.

Having someone stay near the injured rider's head, to keep them talking if possible, will help prevent panic, while others may collect the rider's gear and keys, locate driver's license, medical and insurance information for police, keep other vehicles away from the downed rider and bike, talk to wrecker crews to arrange for the bike to be hauled off, obtain police report numbers, call relatives, and so forth.

Finally, if there's a group, one uninjured rider or more should stay with the injured rider in the emergency room, either by riding along in the ambulance or by meeting the patient there. Just as no group should leave a rider stranded by the side of the road without assistance, similarly no group should leave a rider alone, afraid, and injured in a hospital among strangers, awaiting care.

One person should also be designated to collect cell phone numbers, email addresses, and other relevant information that will allow those who need or want to stay informed to do so, and to pass information along to other members of the group.

When a motorcyclist is involved in an emergency out of town or out of state, it may take hours or days before a relative is notified or before someone can get to the location to monitor events. One or more riders may elect to stay in town, helping to coordinate the details and provide support to the injured rider until family members arrive.

It's not uncommon, however, for a group of tour riders to decide to continue a trip once an injured rider has received medical care, after his or her bike is secured, and relatives have arrived. Similarly, it's not unusual for part of a group to split off and continue their trip while others remain with the injured rider.

This isn't heartless. For many riders who tour, the trip has been planned months, even years in advance, and they've invested a lot to make it happen, including getting vacations arranged and time off work, taking children out of school, or arranging for pet care while they're gone. It's reasonable for some members of the group to want to carry on, while others may cancel and go home. Having good communication in these situations is vital.

a. Communications

General communication equipment and methods have been discussed previously. In an emergency, however, some specific items are worth mentioning.

1. If you're in an area without cell phone service or without a 911 dispatcher, you may be able to flag down a trucker to relay a request for help. Some of them have CB rigs with a signal booster. This is illegal under federal communications law, but it may be useful if you can't get through any other way.

2. If you do have a CB radio or cell phone, don't hang up until the 911 dispatcher tells you to. It may be necessary for the dispatcher to get directions from you or ask you to identify landmarks in order to get help to you.

3. If you're not talking to a 911 dispatcher, stay off your phone and CB until the person who's giving the dispatcher the information has hung up. It's difficult enough to concentrate when trying to give information about a crash or an injured rider without the competition of other conversations.

4. If you have to ride out for help for another rider, leave water for the injured rider, and shelter him or her if you can. Make sure you know exactly how to get back to the scene of the accident. Stop and call 911 at the first possible opportunity to get help on the way.

In the unlikely and hopefully rare event that you have to deliver news of a death to a rider's family member(s) or close friends, make every effort to do so in person.

If officials have already done this, show support to the family and friends of the deceased however you feel you can.

If you are still out of town, try to find mutual friends who can be with the rider's family back home. Don't be surprised to encounter anger and anti-motorcycling comments.

b. Foul-weather gear

Before you select any item of gear, consider how it's supposed to perform under the greatest stress to which you may subject it: that is, if you're in a crash and sliding along the pavement. Don't put any kind of material next to your body that's likely to melt from abrasion. That's nylon, Dacron, plastic, Spandex, and so forth. The layer that's right next to your skin should be made of natural fibers like cotton or wool. Cotton jersey undershirts and bottoms are available now that feel like silk, stretch for comfort without synthetics, and offer both softness and warmth.

The topic of rain gear and rubber overshoes came up earlier, but that's not the only foul-weather gear a rider may need.

In addition to a water-proof jacket and pants, some gloves are better than others for grasping slick, wet grips and wet chrome levers. Soft leather gloves will immediately wilt and grow soggy when they're wet. Most motorcycle-purpose gloves, even leather ones, tend to be water-resistant with gel pads inside. Some riders prefer gloves that have an extra-grippy design, such as ones used for hunting and fishing.

On one occasion, a rider who was caught in extreme cold while touring used her rain gear to prevent frostbite by adding it over other layers, but what should those other layers be? What else would a rider need for a day trip?

Three extremes require extra gear. Riding in rain was already mentioned, but riding in very cold or very hot weather brings its own problems.

If you don't have electric heating accessories (tour bikes offer heated grips and seats), you'll have to find other ways to stay warm and dry while riding. In addition to heavy gloves, glove liners are a useful item for cold-weather riding. They come in silk and in synthetics designed for explorers in extreme cold.

For riding when it's below 40 degrees F., you can use layers starting with sweats or cotton longjohns next to the body; two pairs of socks; leather, denim, or abrasion-resistant synthetic pants and possibly chaps, too; and finally a shirt, a turtleneck sweater, and a sweatshirt under a riding jacket; or the fleece inner lining that comes with your jacket may take the place of the sweatshirt, to reduce bulk.

That may seem like a lot of clothing, but cold air is insidious, especially at highway speeds. And one part of the body still gets cold: the neck! A scarf or a muffler tucked inside the collar of your jacket may solve this adequately; or you may decide to get a balaclava, the kind of headgear that has an opening for your eyes but covers everything else on your head. These are made to fit down on the neck, and they can be a big help to keep that cold air from whistling up into your helmet and around your ears. They are thin so that they will fit under your helmet. You can wear them with the opening below your nose, as shown in Figure 20, or above it for extra warmth. The thin material allows you to breathe through it.

Figure 20: Example of a balaclava

Finally, part of your cold-weather planning should include some way to nourish your skin and lips. Even if they aren't directly exposed, they will chap in the cold air, and it's easier to get windburn than you might think. Moisturize.

If a rider adds that much clothing for riding in the cold, it might seem reasonable to remove as much clothing as possible for riding in hot weather. But this is true only to a certain point. The basics still remain true: you should cover any skin you can't afford to lose. This means long pants of a shred-resistant material; an abrasion-resistant, armor-padded jacket; boots that cover the ankle; gloves; a helmet; and eye protection. If you're determined to wear all the gear, all the time, you won't ride in less than this, no matter what the temperature is.

If it's hot, what can you take off?

You may shed the long-sleeve shirt under your jacket, and in some cases, reduce the weight of the jacket itself. You may be able to take out the jacket's liner and open any zippered vents across the back and down the sleeves.

Some manufacturers sell mesh jackets specifically made for summer riding, but you have to demand quality with this type of item. The material must not be a synthetic that shreds or melts with abrasion. Read the tags, and do your homework before you buy.

You can also shed the long pants and ride in shorts or light fabric pants, so long as they'd covered by leather chaps or a riding suit. (With chaps, though, there's risk to the buttocks.)

Heat will cause other medical issues, discussed earlier; but you can reduce it with two inexpensive pieces of gear. Wetting down a headskin to put it under your helmet cools your head if you open your helmet vents. Wearing ice around your neck in a neckerchief or Kool Kollar cools your body overall. These allow you to ride on days when it hits 100 degrees F.

If you're tempted to ride without all your gear because of the heat, forget it. Besides the safety factors that should be obvious, there are major health dangers from putting your skin—arms, hands, neck—directly in the sun for hours while you ride. In addition to ending the day lobster-red, uncomfortable, and having endangered your skin cells, you will dehydrate fast if you ride with the wind on your exposed arms and face.

F. Extraordinary parking lot practice

From time to time you may need to prepare to perform a motorcycle-related behavior that goes beyond your normal riding skills, such as carrying a passenger or pulling a trailer with your bike. It simply makes no sense to try these kinds of behaviors on public roads without practicing first.

1. Carrying a passenger

Would you really allow your wife or significant other to board your pillion for a 100-mile ride without first having learned how to handle the bike with a passenger on it and without practicing what you learned? It follows, then, that sooner or later, a passenger should join you on a parking lot to do some practicing.

A competent rider is aware that a wife or child absolutely should not be his first passenger!

Until you are a competent rider, you shouldn't even think about carrying a passenger. But when you decide to do so, how do you get the experience to reduce the risks?

Start with another motorcyclist who has experience carrying passengers on his bike. (An inexperienced passenger won't tolerate these practice sessions or understand why you need them.) Have that person take you on his bike as his passenger. It's astonishing how many riders will decide to carry a passenger without ever having been one themselves.

You'll quickly learn the feeling of being absolutely helpless and completely dependent upon the skills of the rider. You'll wish you had asked a number of questions, if you don't already know the answers, such as: Do you have insurance? Is your license current? Have you inspected the bike today? Are you taking any medications?, and more. You'll hope the rider has given you a pre-ride briefing, so that you don't have to worry about what to do. You'll learn how and when to mount and dismount the pillion, and what the rider is doing while you're climbing aboard. You'll learn what's expected of you as a passenger, such as keeping your feet on your pegs and not attempting in any way to affect the lean angle of the motorcycle from the rear seat. You'll learn how to communicate with the rider when you must stop for some reason, or if you want him to slow down. You'll learn not to stand on your pegs and grab him by the helmet if you have a panic attack, obscuring his view!

Finally, you should learn how to deal with an emergency that "takes out" the rider—meaning, how a passenger can actually take control of a moving motorcycle from the pillion and safely drive it to the side of the road to a dead stop before it falls over, saving your own life and that of an incapacitated rider, too. When you begin to carry a passenger, you'll want to teach this skill to the person riding behind you.

See **APPENDIX F – Passengers are <u>not</u> helpless**.

Once you have learned how a passenger feels, impose on that experienced rider again and have him be your first passenger on a parking lot. This is your first **passenger-oriented** parking lot practice improvement session.

Don't assume an experienced rider knows everything you're going to explain in your **pre-ride briefing**, described in more detail on page 75. Though you're going to stay in the parking lot, one point you should discuss is what to do if you drop the bike. You'll have to decide whether you can really put out a foot and catch your bike on the way down with a passenger's weight on the back, or whether that will break an ankle. But what should your passenger do?

In most cases, the passenger should do exactly what the rider does: step far out on the downside of the motorcycle, and **let go with the downside hand**! (Most co-riders will hold on to the bike by a grab bar or the rider's backrest.) If the rider fails to let go of the downside grip or the passenger holds onto the downside grab bar, he will be thrown to the ground, landing on a hand, shoulder, or hip.

One exception: if the bike's a big touring model, the motorcycle will likely have engine guards that catch it before it falls completely on its side. If the rider drops the bike, it will lean and touch the ground; and he must still let go of the downside grip. But the co-rider's legs will be clear of the ground so long as he keeps them on the floorboards or pegs as the bike goes over. On these large bikes, the passenger may sit so high that it will be impractical to step away.

Assuming the bike isn't a touring model, if both rider and co-rider step wide and let go with the downside hand, the motorcycle will come to rest between the rider's legs, and between the passenger's legs, too. This prevents both from being trapped under the motorcycle or burning a leg on a hot exhaust pipe. For your first parking lot practice sessions, an experienced rider will appreciate these instructions, whereas a wife or child will be alarmed. But riders drop their bikes with passengers on them far more often than a non-rider or newbie would believe, simply because they stop the bike on a slope from which they don't know how to start again, or because they short-leg it, or they make a very slow, tight turn in a parking lot and lose control. An experienced rider who's wearing proper gear is unlikely to be hurt if this occurs, and the same is true for the co-rider. Remember: you will have to make precisely this kind of maneuver **the first time** you try to find a place to park in a parking lot, with your passenger behind you worrying, if you're not already proficient at this.

Once you begin, your exercises must include doing normal stops until you are absolutely confident of being able to put both feet on the ground when (and not before) your motorcycle has come to a complete stop with a person on the pillion. Then you'll progress to performing very slow-speed, tight turns. An experienced co-rider will completely understand ragged starts, less than smooth stops, and your insecurity leaning the bike with him on the pillion. He or she will **not** add problems by distracting you or by engaging in other unsafe behavior behind you.

Then you move on to practice performing quick-stops with your passenger aboard. Having a passenger's added weight doesn't mean that you will automatically take more time or more distance to stop in an emergency. This is untrue, whatever you have heard, and **you must get it into your head that <u>you will be able to make that stop just as fast with or without a passenger</u>**. But be satisfied with a 0.6g deceleration rate when practicing with your passenger on board.

In a real emergency stop situation, you will revert to using your personal limit braking skill, or perhaps a little more. Even at 0.6g's, however, both you and your passenger will probably experience a clicking or bumping of helmets when your passenger slides forward during an aggressive stop. This will confirm for your passenger an important reason for wearing that helmet, and it will familiarize you with one of the distractions that you cannot avoid—though you **must ignore it** in an emergency situation.

Only after you have attained confidence in handling your bike with an experienced passenger on board should you attempt to take a "layman" on your pillion. This is when you invite your significant other, your friend, or your teenage child to join you for a little parking lot practice together.

Your objectives should be never to startle or scare your passenger, never to lose control, and never to need extra steps (hops) as you bring the bike to a stop. Your starts and stops should be as smooth as glass, so that your passenger never quite knows exactly when the bike has started to move or when it has come to a stop. This should be a confidence-building session for both of you, not one in which you are testing limits or providing "thrills". Practice before you subject an uninformed person to your learning curve. And once you engage in the "real thing", no surprises!

2. Practice for pulling a trailer

There are three exercises which you need to practice when you first attach a trailer to your motorcycle: braking, path of travel, and backing up.

To practice braking with a trailer, you should load the trailer with either a representative cargo or a sandbag weighing approximately what a normal load would weigh.

The whole purpose of practicing braking with a trailer is to become familiar with the lowered braking efficiency of your motorcycle entailed by pulling a weight instead of carrying an equivalent weight. Your efforts should be to accomplish a 0.6g stop while pulling the trailer.

Tour riders often carry a passenger and pull a trailer at the same time. These riders should practice their braking skills with both a passenger aboard the pillion and a loaded trailer. A 0.8g stop while pulling a trailer is simply too dangerous to practice. In order to achieve that deceleration rate, you'll be compromising the traction limits of your front tire.

Practice for improving your skill as to path of travel is simple. Put a cone or marker on the parking lot surface, and learn how **wide** your front tire's path of travel from that cone must be in order to miss it with your trailer tire as you make your turns.

The problem with backing up a motorcycle with a trailer attached is familiar to anyone who has ever pulled a trailer with their car or truck. That trailer will go in exactly the opposite direction you want it to, unless you steer the front-end of the bike in the opposite direction and then correct your steering to follow the trailer's path.

There's absolutely no way to get good at backing up with a trailer attached to your bike except by practicing.

G. It may be true – they don't see you

An article in the March 2005 issue of the British magazine *Bike* describes a study indicating one reason why, when someone claims not to have seen a motorcycle before a collision, they may be telling the truth.

The study identified a phenomenon known as **Moving Camouflage** and an ancillary concept called the **Looming Effect**.

1. Moving camouflage

When an object approaches you along the same line of sight as a background point of interest, there's little in the way of change that's visible as you look at that approaching object. As a result, you may not notice it.

Figure 21 provides a concrete example of this phenomenon. Though usually associated with stationary points of interest in your background, such as a building, from the diagram you can see that even another moving vehicle can cause this phenomenon.

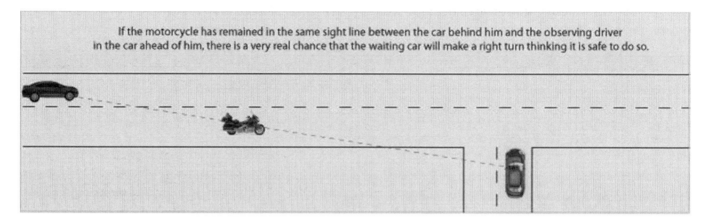

Figure 21: Moving camouflage

2. Looming effect

An approaching object always appears to get larger, the closer it gets. But the difference in size (the amount of size change) is very small when an object moves from 1000 ft. to 900 ft., as compared to when it moves from 200 ft. to 100 ft.

In the latter case, the change is dramatic. The object coming into view is now a **looming threat**. When that happens, the moving camouflage phenomenon ceases to exist.

In Figure 21, the motorcycle is approximately at the place where the looming effect would overwhelm the moving camouflage phenomenon. The bike would suddenly be visible to the driver of the waiting car. Figure 22 shows how an object suddenly seems much larger when it's closer.

The best way to overcome the moving camouflage phenomenon is to vary your lane position as you approach a threatening vehicle—to become visible because of a change in your behavior. Other ways to stand out could be tapping on the top of your helmet or standing on your pegs. Flashing your lights is discouraged, however, as that may be misinterpreted as a signal for the other vehicle to proceed in front of you.

H. Traction and weight management

During a recent safety presentation to a group of BMW riders, a great deal of time was devoted to the subject of traction and weight management.

As the discussion went on, several riders argued with assertions made about the consequences of aerodynamic drag.

One statement was, for example, that at 75 MPH, depending upon how large your frontal surface area is, your bike could have a weight transfer of about 100 pounds from the front tire to the rear due entirely to wind resistance ("downforce", discussed earlier).

Another disputed statement was that a rider could experience a total lift of about 50 pounds caused by pressure differentials. Late in the presentation, another person challenged the idea that riding with your jacket unzipped could cost you about one HP of power; and that it could remove as much as eight pounds of weight from a front tire.

To demonstrate the truth of those assertions, we created an Excel model.

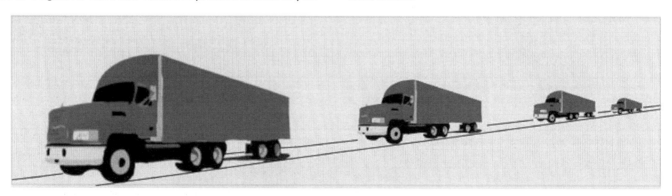

Figure 22: Looming effect

Here's an example of the output from that model:

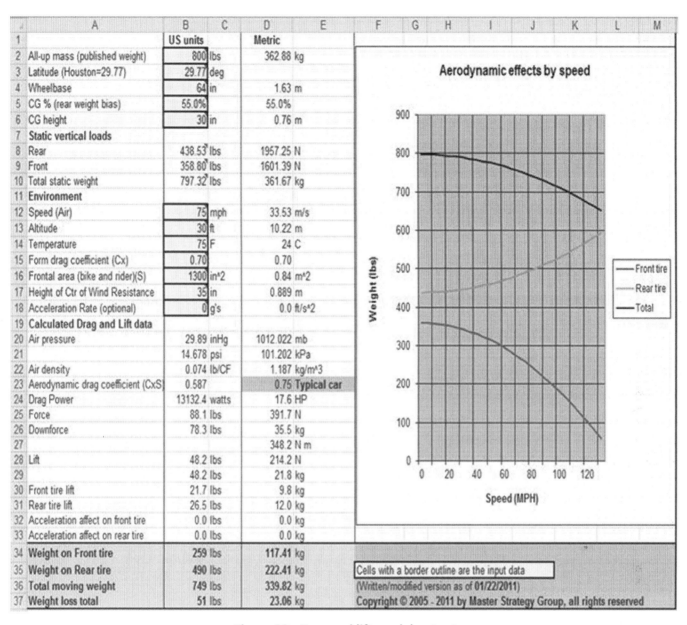

Figure 23: Drag and lift model output

See **APPENDIX G – How the drag and lift model works.**

At rest, this bike has 439 pounds of weight on its rear tire and 359 pounds on its front tire, as shown on lines 8 and 9.

However, when moving at 75 MPH, the weight on the rear tire has increased to 490 pounds, while the weight on the front tire has decreased to only 259 pounds (a loss of approximately 99 pounds) as shown on lines 34 and 35.

The total weight of the motorcycle has decreased by 51 pounds, as shown on line 37.

(In case you're wondering, at rest this bike weighs only 797.32 pounds, instead of 800 pounds, because it's far from the equator where gravity is strongest.)

All of these changes are the result of aerodynamic drag and lift, and they assume a constant speed. Obviously, there's a speed beyond which you can no longer control your motorcycle, because there's no weight left on the front tire and, thus, no traction.

Notice that, for this particular bike configuration, that speed would be about 150 MPH.

But there are other forces that affect weight on your tires. Most notably, if you apply a driving or braking force, you will cause an acceleration or deceleration which, as you know, causes a weight transfer to occur.

Accelerating at a rate of 0.5g's is not beyond the capability of most motorcycles. If we input that acceleration rate into the model (line 18), we will see the resulting weight on our tires as shown in this graphic:

The total weight doesn't change in any way, but there has been a significant **weight shift,** away from the front tire toward the rear. Now the weight on the front tire is only 71 pounds, as shown on line 34.

The rider is perilously close to losing control of his motorcycle. Even though he's only moving at 75 MPH, he's accelerating. Thus, he has only the weight (and, thus, traction) on his front tire that he would have had at about 130 MPH!

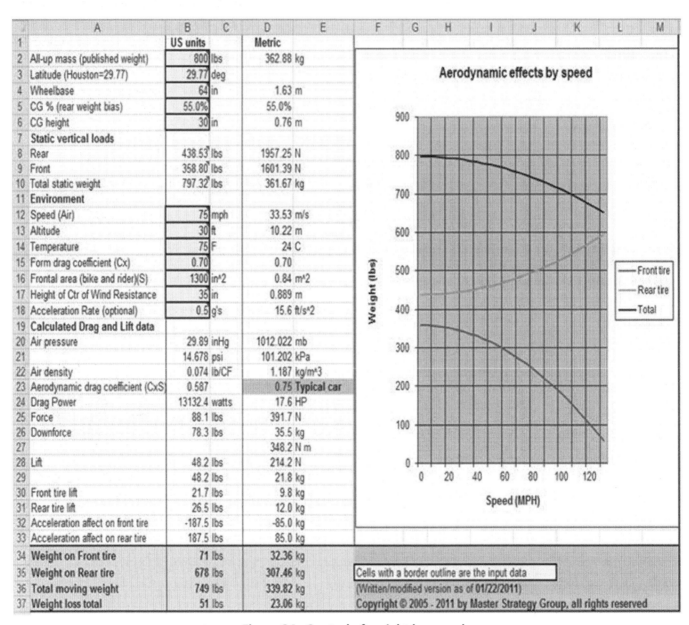

Figure 24: Control of weight by speed

What this means is that you can use more rear brake without skidding the rear tire, the faster you're moving. And, the faster you are moving, the easier you'll skid your front tire by using your front brake.

A competent rider understands this dynamic and controls his tire traction with respect to his speed.

I. Maintenance and how the bike works

Most motorcycle riders are not capable of doing major mechanical work on their bikes. To them, "preventative maintenance" means checking their tires for wear and proper air pressure, for a proper amount of oil in their crankcase, and for a good charge on the battery. A few riders may even be able to change the oil in their bikes, but not many.

In order for you to be able to ride safely, your bike must be healthy. It must function properly and dependably. But vibration and mileage take their toll on the health of a bike. Even the small flying insects you run into as you ride take a toll, and not just on your paint job.

The more you understand about how your bike works, the more likely you are to detect problems before they compromise your safety. If you know that your front-end shocks are leaking oil, for example, the more likely you will take the bike to a dealership for required maintenance before they fail, instead of ending up on the ground wondering what happened after they do.

1. Shock absorbers

Most motorcycles today have a pair of fork tubes for their front suspension and one or two shock absorbers in the rear, connected to the frame via the swing arm. Shock absorbers do not absorb shocks. Springs do that.

When your bike hits a bump in the road, your wheels can do nothing but follow the curve of that bump. Your tires compress fractionally, but not enough to make a meaningful difference in the effects that bump will have on the rest of the bike, and you.

If the wheels of your bike were connected directly to the frame, without springs and shocks, the bike would rise at least as high as the bump, almost instantly. And, if it were severe enough, you would be left in the air when the bike came back down. Your hands would probably not be jerked off the grips; instead, they would be pulled forward with the rest of the bike, while the rest of your body was still in the air—and then, worse, you would come down. Hard.

The fix is to keep as much of the bike, other than the wheels, from rising in reaction to that bump. In other words, to make as much of the bike as possible "sprung weight". A tremendous amount of kinetic energy is imparted to the wheels when they hit that bump. That energy must be captured before it's transferred to the bike's frame. That's exactly what the springs do. By compressing, the springs absorb the energy from the wheels.

If all you had between the wheels and the frame of your bike were springs, then the only difference the springs would make would be to provide a short delay before the bike was tossed into the air after hitting the bump. Once compressed, springs can only decompress. The energy that the springs will exert during decompression is almost equal to the energy that went into compressing them. Almost, because a token amount of the kinetic energy will be converted to heat to make up the difference.

What the shocks actually do is to slow the decompression of your springs **dramatically** (and in the process to convert much more than a token of the total kinetic energy stored in those springs into heat).

A shock absorber consists of a tube filled with oil, which acts as a hydraulic fluid, and a piston that's not physically connected to any part of the tube. It slides up and down within the tube, pushing its way through the oil. The piston is connected to one end of the shock absorber via a metal rod, while the tube is connected to the other. One end of the shock absorber itself is connected to the frame of the bike, while the other end is connected to the wheel hub (or to the swing arm that's connected to the hub).

When the wheel moves up towards the rest of the bike, the piston is pushed through the oil. The oil provides resistance to the piston's movement, slowing it down. As it does so, kinetic energy is converted to heat. (This is why you change your shock absorber oil regularly—heat breaks it down.)

The oil in these tubes would totally stop the movement of the piston, were it not for the existence of a valve in the piston that allowed the fluid to pass through it. This is because, like water, the oil cannot itself be compressed. That valve can be made to allow fluids to flow faster in one direction than the other. For example, you would probably want your springs to compress faster than they are allowed to decompress. Without that valve, your springs would not compress at all, leaving you in the same situation, with as harsh a result as if the wheels were directly connected to the frame. Similarly, if the springs are too strong for the load they're carrying, too much of the kinetic energy will be conveyed directly to the frame of the bike, because they will compress too slowly, if at all.

But just as slowing the compression rate of the springs too much results in ineffective control of bumps, allowing their decompression to happen too quickly is just as bad. Were that to happen, you would have a "pogo stick" reaction to bumps. It's essential that the design of the springs and shocks on your bike take into account how heavy the bike is and what kind of riding you do.

All such designs are compromises, however; and you can do things to totally frustrate the designer's intentions—and end up hurt or worse as a result.

For example, when you put a passenger or heavy luggage on your bike, you should increase the tension of the springs surrounding your shocks. Failing to do that can overload the system and get you close to an extreme level of response from them. Likewise, taking a street machine off-road and pretending it's a motocross machine can do the same.

But even assuming you don't do anything that extreme, you'll find that the design of your shocks isn't perfect. (If it were, you'd never feel a bump in the road.) The fact is, sometimes the road surface changes from perfectly level to bumpy. Some of those bumps (and potholes) can be awesome. This is where a few dollars can make a difference.

You can replace the springs that come stock on your bike with a set that are called "progressives". These provide a normal, soft ride until they are confronted with an unusually severe bump, at which point they get harder and harder to compress. While the oil in the shocks cannot be compressed, air can be. Thus some shocks are "air-assisted": in addition to the oil, a small amount of air is in the tubes. These "air-assisted" shock systems are sometimes attached to an onboard compressor that can be used to increase or decrease the pressure of the air, thus making the shocks either harder or softer, without having to change the compression of the springs when your load weight or the road surface changes substantially. (Also, of course, you can increase the weight of the oil in the shocks to slow them down.)

The shock absorber "system" on your rear wheel tends to have larger springs and to have them mounted on the outside of the hydraulic tubes. Though there are some exceptions for unusual designs with a front-end swing arm, the ones in the front are generally contained within the fork tubes. If you take a close look at your shocks on each wheel, you'll find that the ones in the rear are typically angled forward from the wheel to the frame of the bike; while the ones in the front are angled backwards. These angles tend to be directly in-line with the weight shifts that result from acceleration and braking.

It's essential to maintain the angle of the front shocks (inside the telescoping fork tubes). This angle is usually called the bike's "rake". Along with the front-end "offset", this establishes the bike's "trail" and determines the bike's handling and steering control. It affects the righting force, too.

The more extreme the rake on your bike, the "slower" your steering will be…except at extremely slow speeds—when extreme rakes often result in the wheel quickly "flopping" over and dumping the bike if you do not have your hands firmly in control of the grips.

If you lower your bike by shortening the front and the back shocks, the wheelbase is also shortened (the distance between the front and back tires). Since your front wheel touches the ground more closely to a point directly under your handlebar, your steering "quickens" as a result.

Even shortening the shocks by only one inch could result in steering so fast that your steering damper (another small shock absorber) could not safely handle it. The result would be violent swings of the wheel from side to side, known as a "tank slapper", and with high probability a dumped bike. (Overstated, for if you absorb some of the oscillation into your arms and avoid transferring that into the rest of the bike through your contact with the seat, or if you use some braking-caused weight transfer to the front of the bike, then you can abort the "harmonic" set up in a tank slapper and avoid dumping the motorcycle. A tank slapper may start so suddenly, however, and become so violent that the rider will fail to react. At speed, this can be deadly.)

In short, your shock absorbers are designed to help keep your tires on the ground regardless of surface imperfections, so that they can work for you. They make your bike controllable. To maintain them, make sure they receive factory-recommended oil changes. Do not modify them. Adjust them for major changes in the weight of your vehicle or expected road conditions, and they will do their jobs reliably.

As to preventative maintenance, you should be most concerned about your **front** shocks, for unless the fork tubes are covered by gaiters (protective sleeves), as with most off-road bikes, then they are more exposed to the elements when you ride. During your pre-ride check, inspect the fork seals for signs of wear, and examine the forks for signs of an oily sheen on them.

Most importantly, **after each ride** take a cloth to them and remove the grime. The flying insects you run into while riding end up crushed on your forks and leave an acidic mess that eats fork seal rubber. If you let them dry out, the bug carcasses are abrasive; they will wear your fork seals as the seals slide over the decaying bodies. A simple rubdown of the forks with a clean cloth after each ride can save you hundreds of dollars over the life of your motorcycle.

2. Keeping the rear tire on the ground

Most motorcyclists prefer that their riding be uneventful. They might consider the ride itself an event; or they are riding to or from an event; but along the way, they want that ride to be **controlled** and without any other events that are potentially dangerous.

In order for a motorcycle ride to be "uneventful", both tires must remain on the ground and not be skidding or sliding. That seems pretty obvious, because when one or both of their tires leaves the ground, that tire is no longer a means to control the machine. Then it merely goes along for the ride until the tire hooks up again. When traction has diminished to the point that steering input becomes imprecise (or non-existent), or braking becomes ineffective (or non-existent), an event has occurred.

The previous section established for you that it's your shock absorbers that try to keep your tires on the ground. What good, after all, can your brakes or throttle or steering input do, if the tires themselves have no traction because they are off the ground?

Your shock absorbers work for you for the same reason that you are not crippled or killed every time you pull the trigger on a pistol or rifle: the bullet has far less mass than either you or the gun. A compressed spring in your shock absorber can do only one thing—decompress. Like ignited gunpowder, that decompressing spring pushes **equally** on the wheel (bullet) and the bike's frame (the gun and you).

Because your wheels are substantially less massive than the frame of the bike, they move farther and faster away from the spring than does the frame. In other words, after you hit a bump that compresses the springs in your shock absorber, the decompressing springs push your wheel away from the frame of the bike so that they regain contact with the ground much sooner than they would have, had they been rigidly connected to the frame of the bike.

Thus it would seem that shock absorbers are ideally designed to keep your tires on the ground, and for the most part, this is correct. But there's one situation in which their design works in exactly the wrong way: they cause your tires to be lifted off the ground instead of pushing them toward that surface. This is the case **when you use your rear brake**.

It's your rear shock absorber that starts most rear wheel skids, not excessive weight transfer.

Most riders probably think that if the rear tire comes off the ground during braking, you're doing a stoppie. But this is rarely true. A stoppie is **not** an event defined by your rear tire coming off the ground. Rather, it's an event defined by your bike's frame moving upward and lifting that wheel off the ground in the process.

A stoppie can only be caused by excessive use of the front brake, resulting in enough weight transfer from the rear of the bike to the front so that the rear-end of the bike has a negative amount of weight left on it. The use of your rear brake, alone, cannot cause a stoppie. But your rear brake, alone, can **easily** cause your rear tire to lift off the ground entirely.

How is that possible? Well, consider the function of yet another motorcycle component—the swing arm. That part connects the rear wheel with the frame of your motorcycle via a pivot point located near the middle of bike's frame.

When you accelerate, that pivot arm pushes the frame of the bike forward **and upward**. (Yes, your bike's rear-end gets **higher** as a result of acceleration, not lower.)

When you use your rear brake, the swing arm is pulled level; and in the process, it pulls the frame of the bike **down** as the wheelbase lengthens.

Said differently, when you accelerate, your rear shock absorber extends; and when you use your rear brake, your rear shock absorber contracts.

Now recall that your rear wheel is substantially less massive than the rest of the bike. So when the rear shock absorber contracts during braking, the rear wheel will move **up** farther and faster than the rear-end of the bike can move **down**.

The result will be a dramatic loss of traction on the rear tire. If your use of your rear brake is aggressive enough, the rear tire will be lifted off the ground.

Thus, long before a simple weight transfer caused by braking can unload all the weight from your bike's rear end, the shock absorber will suck that wheel off the ground for you. And that's exactly what you don't want it to do. You want your tires to stay on the ground.

Shortly after your rear tire lifts off the ground, the lumbering mass of your bike's rear-end falls enough to push that tire back into the ground. This is why your rear tire "chirps" when you are too aggressive with the rear brake: it's losing traction and "bouncing" on the roadway surface.

This is just one more reason that **it's never appropriate, never—not once in your life—to use your rear brake aggressively.**

From a safety point of view, you should seriously consider setting the pre-load adjustment on your rear shock as if you are always carrying a passenger. This will result in a slightly harsher ride without a passenger aboard, but it will reduce the odds that you will skid your rear tire.

3. Tires

Excessive tire wear (and / or cupping) is a problem that most motorcyclists experience over time. Too often this is simply the result of failing to maintain proper tire pressure. However, this is far from a complete answer.

Cupping is a phenomenon that's absolutely normal! **Excessive** cupping or **excessive** wear on one side of the tire as compared to the other is not.

There are at least seven causes of cupping and / or uneven wear in the front tire, other than inadequate air pressure. Here they are:

- Most roads are banked away from the center. Thus, if you ride with your motorcycle vertical, as most riders do most of the time, the side of your tire closest to the center of the road wears more.

- Your tires "scuff" when you force a speed change with them. The rear tire scuffs when you accelerate and when you brake (and every time you ride in a direction other than straight ahead). Thus, it tends to have even "cupping" as compared to the front tire (which scuffs when you brake but not when you accelerate).

- Wheel alignment isn't usually a problem with motorcycles, but it can be.

- Carrying an unevenly divided load (all your tools, jumper cable, etc.) in one saddlebag can result in your riding the bike in an orientation that's subtly other than vertical most of the time.

- Setting your TRAC (torque reactive anti-dive control) unequally can easily cause uneven tire wear. TRAC systems were designed in the 1980s and fitted to some brands of motorcycle to reduce front-end dive during braking.

- If one of your front shocks is defective, you will experience uneven tire wear.

- Excessive use of the front brake will result in excessive cupping.

Then there's the issue of punctures.

Sometimes you can't win. A rider recently had to replace a virtually new Elite II rear tire on his motorcycle because it had picked up a couple of small nails. You might think this was an excess of caution, for all he really had to do was plug the tire, right? Wrong!

Here are a few things you should know about tire plugs:

- Almost any single puncture (through the tread) can be repaired by the use of a tire plug.

- You cannot put more than one plug within the same quadrant of a tire—safely.

- You cannot put more than two plugs into any tire—period.

The manufacturers of tire plugs specifically disavow the safety of both of the last two items. They also will void their speed warranties as a result of **any** tire plugging. Your tire is probably marked with an "H" speed designation, meaning it's rated for safety up to 130 MPH. If you have even one tire plug in it, you should not drive faster than about 80 MPH using that tire.

The rider who had to replace his tire had picked up three small nails in it. All three leaked air when he removed them.

Unfortunately, it cost $150 for another new Elite II. But life is too important to be left in the hands of three plugs when the manufacturers refuse to stand up for their safety.

Note, every reference made here about "tire plugs" refers to tire repair plugs professionally installed from the inside—**not** the emergency roadside repair kits which install from the outside of your tire.

And then there's dry rot.

Keeping your tires in good shape includes constant attention to them, maintaining proper inflation at all times, and a little luck in avoiding road hazards. But dry rot is a problem some tires seem to experience regardless of these precautions, particularly if a motorcycle isn't ridden year-round.

There are a few simple things that you can do to minimize dry rot:

- Don't store your motorcycle near electrical appliances. Ozone is generated around electrical appliances and is primarily responsible for the cracks in your tire rubber.
- Don't use products designed to make the rubber look nice and clean and bright black. These products also rob the rubber of some of the chemicals with which they were manufactured, which are designed to minimize the effect of ozone.

Also, don't park your bike in a spot where the tires sit on oil spots. The oil will deteriorate the tire rubber over time.

Finally, there are tire additives.

Long ago, tires were made of rubber—solid rubber. They worked, but they produced a dreadfully hard ride. Then someone came up with the idea of making them pneumatic (filled with air). Tires became far better as a result, and far more comfortable to ride on.

Over the years, tires have steadily gotten better in other ways, too. They are produced using better rubber compounds. Today's tires also benefit from the addition of steel belts, better biasing techniques, radial designs, and better tread designs. Tire manufacturing has become a well understood science, not an art.

As motorcyclists, our lives depend on our tires. We tend to buy the best tires made, and tire manufactures have never stopped trying to make them even better.

One has to wonder, then, why some motorcyclists completely abandon the idea that the tire manufacturers **really** know what they're doing when they create our tires.

For example, some riders have decided that for a few dollars they can squirt some magic compound into their tires and never have to worry about a flat tire again. They believe that this same goop even magically balances their tires for them, so that they no longer have to rely on a trained mechanic to do that for them mechanically. They believe that if their tires are punctured after squirting this wonder product into their expensive tires, they can disregard the problem altogether, because air won't leak out through the puncture; instead, it will seal itself automatically. And they believe that once the magic stuff is squirted into their tires, they don't have to tell anybody about it.

These are the same kinds of motorcyclists who are easy targets for sales pitches for such things as gasoline treatment additives and instant weight loss pills.

Note, this isn't to suggest that all additives are useless or hype. But we do argue that it should take a lot more than a clever sales ad to convince you to deviate **in any way** from the advice of professional mechanics regarding care and maintenance of your motorcycle and its tires.

Virtually all motorcycle tires are now tubeless by design and are built to resist the loss of air from a puncture. You don't have to add anything to them other than air. If the puncture's large, the built-in puncture sealant won't be totally effective. But that's not a bad thing. A large puncture means that you have had significant damage to the belting of the tire. It should be replaced, not covered up!

There's no excuse not to have your tires mechanically balanced when mounted. No amount of internal "balancing goop" substitutes for a properly mounted and balanced tire when you first start riding on it.

Thus, products that are designed to be squirted into a tubeless tire make very little sense. Do you think that a tire manufacturer would fail to make the very best and safest tire they are capable of making for use on motorcycles? Do you think they never heard of puncture sealants? Do you think that they should have to stand to a warranty if the inside of a tire has been coated with a chemical compound that it was not designed to have to deal with?

If you have a tire repair kit that includes a pressurized can of gas to inflate it after the repair, **you must tell your mechanic that you have used it before you ask him to remove your tire**! Some of those compressed gasses are flammable and can **explode** if the tire is exposed to a spark while the bead is being removed from the tire rim. <u>You</u> would be responsible if that mechanic were to be injured by a hazard you knew existed but failed to warn him about.

4. Electrical system

Sooner or later, you'll need to find and repair a failing electrical component, a broken wire, or a short. Or, you will attempt to add a new device to your motorcycle and have to do some wiring. Following are a set of basics that may not be taught anywhere these days except by experience:

- Just because the motorcycle uses a 12 Volt battery doesn't mean that **lethal** voltages don't exist on your bike. Spark plug leads carry many thousands of Volts! Stay away from them. (Actually, lethal <u>currents</u> kill.)

- The vast majority of "failures" can be fixed with the simple replacement of a fuse—particularly on older bikes that use old-style fuses. If the failing fuse is not visibly burnt, it's often just fractured as a result of age. Fuses are generally cheap insurance.

- Crimp connectors are a **no-no** on motorcycles. Vibration and weathering will eventually make them fail. Solder all wire joints you make, and use a piece of shrink-wrap tubing to finish the job.

- Solid wires are a **no-no** on motorcycles. Vibration tends to fracture them, too. Always use stranded wire. (You should carry a length of stranded wire as part of your "tools".)

- Many circuits in modern motorcycles contain solid state devices (transistors). These can be damaged if you use a test light on them. Instead, use a high impedance digital multi-meter (10-Meg or greater) to test voltage levels in these circuits.

- Any electrical connector that you can pull apart should be packed with dielectric grease when you put it back together. Dielectric grease is **non-conductive**. It's used to keep contacts within the connectors clean and to protect them from corrosion. Connectors in a motorcycle's charging system will melt and fail easily if those contacts are not perfectly maintained, because the slightest increase in resistance will cause a huge amount of heat, based on their large current loads.

- Even with the master fuse pulled, one great danger continues to exist in a motorcycle's electrical system: the starter solenoid. Since the current load necessary to turn the starter motor is so great, that circuit is **not** fused. Thus, if you happen to short the solenoid, your bike's starter motor will engage!

- Whenever adding a component, use a separate fuse and circuit for it. Do not simply piggy-back on an existing circuit.

- Whenever removing your battery, always disconnect the **negative** terminal first. This insures that there won't be a disaster should your screwdriver happen to slip while disconnecting the positive terminal if it hits any bare metal.

J. Attention

A competent rider is familiar with his motorcycle.

Once you have your own bike, your experience with it soon allows you to know without looking where your various controls are, what the bike engine sounds like when it's running properly, and when to shift gears according to how the engine sounds. You even know approximately how fast you are going without looking at your speedometer. Familiarity borne of experience has freed your mind from having to focus on these elements of riding it. They are trivial distractions—unless there's something wrong or unexpected about how they feel or sound. Your mind is capable, when things feel and sound familiar, of being alert for threats that are consequential.

A competent rider recognizes when to pay attention to distractions and when to ignore them.

When the rider needs to pay attention to what that oncoming automobile driver is doing after stopping with a turn signal flashing, he disregards almost everything else, unless that something else is substantially out of the ordinary, threatening, or so unexpected that he simply must pay attention to it.

Wanting to pay attention to the left-turning automobile is learned behavior, but changing your focus of attention to a potentially greater threat is instinctive. It's learned behavior to disregard unimportant distractions, while it's instinctive to zero in and pay a great deal of attention to threats. Once you have passed the beginner phase as a rider, you must learn to manage your attention, because you have a limited amount of it to work with.

1. Limits

When everything's going right, riding a motorcycle is effortless and completely enjoyable. "Right" means that the weather is perfect, traffic is light, the bike is familiar and well maintained, and the rider is rested and healthy. Given these conditions, you have the potential to focus entirely on those things that demand your attention—or to be lulled into believing that you can afford to be distracted for a few minutes. Then you can die in a heartbeat.

On the other hand, there's never a better time to see the fields you are driving past, or smell the aroma of freshly cut grass, or to enjoy the sight of a couple of hot air balloons in the distance, than when everything is going right. Isn't this a safety conflict?

Consider this: "paying attention" isn't the same as "being alert". In fact, it's almost the opposite. They're mutually exclusive concepts, except with respect to whatever you happen to be focused on.

On the other hand, letting your attention "wander" is very much the same as being "alert." There's a lesson to be learned by understanding this distinction.

Assume that you have a limit to how much your mind can pay attention to at any single moment. You can be aware, for example, of traffic conditions all around you, of how fast you are going, of the sounds your engine is making, of the approximate time of day it is, of the words to the music you hear in your headset from your radio or tape or CD, of the surrounding countryside unfolding as you drive by, of the temperature, of how long it's been since you last ate or made a potty stop, and of the general location and status of the motorcycles both in front of you and behind you. It would seem to most people that there's no limit to how many different things you can be aware of at any one time.

This is because you scan for these things quickly and **pay** very little attention to them, so long as each appears to conform to what you expect.

The ability to notice that something is wrong is called being "alert." When, during your scanning effort—i.e., while your attention is wandering—something happens out of the ordinary or is unexpected, then your mind **focuses** on the discrepancy. You **pay** substantially more of your attention to it. And now you find that your ability to be attentive to many things at once has reached a limit!

For example, if you are driving down a freeway at 70 MPH and happen to notice that a truck some distance ahead of you has just blown a tire, then you will be so completely focused on that truck and what is around it, as well as how to react to that event, that you will almost certainly no longer be able to notice the scenery to the side of the road. Those hot air balloons a half-mile away won't be able to get your attention any longer, even if one of them were to fall out of the sky.

Not only is there a limit to our ability to pay attention, but when our attention is focused, our ability to be alert to other things is diminished. **That is dangerous**.

When you have to focus on some aspect of your riding, you're forced to diminish the wandering of your attention. For example, if it's raining and after dark, you tend to narrow your visual focus and concentrate on what you see ahead. By doing so, you don't have the ability to let your attention wander very far, for you have very little attention left. Indeed, if you then discover that you're lost, the very first thing to do is to slow down, so that speed is no longer consuming any of your attention. You have already exceeded your limits. This is no time to have a radio on or to be thinking about where to stop for a meal.

Here's the lesson: **Whenever you must focus your attention on the situation that confronts you, you must at the same time reduce as many distractions as possible.**

- If you're riding an unfamiliar bike, make sure the radio / tape player / CD is off. Don't test any other limits (such as high speed or steep lean angles).

- If traffic suddenly increases or becomes "weird", hit your mute button or turn off your good-time radio, and reduce speed if possible.

- If the weather suddenly turns bad, hit your mute button or turn off your good-time radio, and reduce speed if possible.

Clearly your radio can become one distraction too many.

2. Not the same as being alert / aware

Two motorcycle incidents occurred recently that, thankfully, involved no accidents—but could have. One was funny, while the other was an invitation to disaster.

In the first instance, a motorcycle pulled up to a red light and stopped. There was a police car immediately behind the bike. The motorcyclist decided after about ten seconds that the light was stuck, casually ran the light, and crossed the street. In the police car, both occupants looked at each other and shook their heads.

The officers took off after the motorcycle, lights flashing. The rider was not trying to get away—he saw the flashing lights and pulled over to get his ticket. He obviously had not noticed the police car behind him. We suspect most people would argue that he was not paying attention.

In the second instance, a man was walking his dog. As they got near the end of the block, they approached a stop sign that controls traffic for a busy side-street crossing there. A motorcyclist rode up to the stop sign and stopped. He looked both ways and apparently saw that the only traffic was a dog walker and a city bus approaching from the left. That bus had its blinker on and was slowing for a bus stop. Seeing that the bus was actually stopping, the motorcyclist decided it was clear to enter the intersection and took off.

One-half second later he grabbed a handful of brake and panic-stopped. The car that had been to the left of the bus (and had, thus, been invisible to him) screeched its tires and also did a panic-stop to avoid hitting the motorcycle. They were both successful, but the motorcyclist could reach out with his left hand and touch the car's hood at that time. Close! Some would argue that the motorcyclist was not paying attention.

In both cases, the real issue was that the motorcyclist **was** paying attention--too much of it—and was not alert or aware of his surroundings. It's simply not true that paying attention means being alert or aware. It means, because riders have a limited amount of attention to "spend", that you are focused on something, not scanning with open eyes, and not being particularly sensitive to other potential problems.

The first rider paid attention to the red light. He completely missed the fact that a police car was behind him. He also failed the patience test, as the ten seconds when the red light failed to change color apparently seemed like a long time to him. That lapse of awareness cost him a ticket, but it could just as easily have cost him his life. Entering an intersection on a red light is a bet-your-life decision.

The second rider was paying attention—to the bus. He obviously failed to have anything like a "What if there's a car hidden by that bus?" self-preservation inner dialogue. Instead, with all his attention on the bus, believing that it was not a threat to him, he concluded that there were no other vehicles that might constitute a threat, and he took off from the stop sign—right into the path of the hidden car.

Paying attention is usually the wrong thing to do when you're riding. Being alert and aware of your surroundings ("situational awareness" is what pilots call it) is a life-saving, accident avoidance mental activity.

Pay attention **after** you recognize a threat, in order to assess what you should do about it. Do **not** pay attention before that, so that you can detect all relevant threats.

A competent rider learns to discipline his mind.

K. Conspicuity

We have all heard and lament that car drivers often argue that they didn't see the motorcycle before the collision occurred. Because the real problem often is that they were otherwise busy talking on their cell phones or simply being distracted, we don't credit that excuse other than with a "Yeah, sure." But what if it's true?

Most motorcyclists have heard the word "conspicuity". It means conspicuousness or obviousness. It certainly helps you to be seen if you are conspicuous or obvious, though that person on the cell phone still might not notice you; and even if they do, they may not be able to recognize what they are seeing.

When hearing the word "conspicuity," many riders think "light-colored clothes". That can certainly help—when the sun's shining. But at night you're far better off having reflective strips on your jacket / helmet / motorcycle than wearing a light-colored jacket, as opposed to a black one. Those reflective strips or patches should be across your upper back and on your shoulders (facing to either side) for best effect.

And why do riders tend to think the person who's ahead of him needs to see him more than the person behind him or approaching from the side? The truth is, it doesn't matter where "they" are, they **must** be able to see you and recognize you for what you are.

Curiously, despite the natural desire to be seen by drivers coming toward us, when motorcyclists think about adding extra lights to their bikes, they think about rear-facing lights first. They add bigger, brighter brake lights and even modulated brake lights to aid those who are behind them in realizing they are slowing or stopping. This is curious, because most threats to a motorcyclist are in front of them, not behind them.

Many years ago the railroad industry determined that the most conspicuous lighting arrangement for their engines, and the safest, was a triangle of forward-facing lights with the largest, brightest light at the top and two slightly smaller / dimmer lights mounted horizontally below it. This configuration had benefits that might not be immediately obvious.

Most notably, when a train is moving toward you, the two bottom lights appear to get farther apart. Thus, you not only recognize the lights as coming from a train, but you can tell what direction it's moving. You can even estimate its speed.

A motorcycle can have exactly the same lighting advantage. If you mount running lights below your headlight, you have created that magic triangle. When seen from the front, you no longer look like a far distant car. Since no one expects to see a train approaching on a public road, you are recognized for being "something else"—almost certainly a motorcycle.

Unlike modulating brake lights, modulating headlights are absolutely to be avoided, though some riders insist they are a valuable safety addition. They're distracting and easily confused as indicating an emergency vehicle of some kind. They may be illegal in many states if set up incorrectly. They also, like magnets, strongly attract an oncoming driver's eyes, which increases the chance that he will target-fixate on them. Clearly, that's not the rider's intention.

As to drivers behind you...remember, engine-braking does **not** turn on your brake lights. If you roll off your throttle while someone is following you, you should either lightly use your brakes as well, or simply double-tap your front brake lever to give them notice of your change of speed. Don't give them the excuse.

A competent rider insures that other drivers see him.

II. Group riding

Whenever two or more bikes ride together, this is group riding. Discipline is essential to riding safely with others. Many people compare it to formation flying.

What follows is a brief discussion of lessons learned and disciplines developed during several decades of group riding experience. Understand that these guidelines are not gospel. Motorcycle groups make their own rules of conduct and may impose other disciplines; and those may vary substantially from what you read here.

A. Group riding: why?

There are several advantages for motorcyclists who ride street bikes in a group:

- A group is usually more visible to other drivers than a solo rider;

- Other vehicles can predict what a rider in a group will do, because all members generally maintain fixed positions and fixed intervals between riders;

- In case of a mechanical problem or an accident, help is available immediately to the rider. A member of the group may carry a cell-phone. Usually some riders in a group are trained in First Aid and CPR. They are often aware of safety information and accident management procedures that non-riders may not know -- for example, not to remove the helmet of a downed rider unless breathing is inhibited; where to find particular medical information for a downed rider; how to manage an accident scene to prevent complications, etc.; and

- Many riders find it more fun.

In addition, motorcyclists tend to learn a great deal from each other about their sport. Planned stops along the way offer a fine opportunity to socialize and to share valuable tips and techniques.

B. Group riding: why not?

Group riding isn't for everyone. It requires a certain level of skill and self-discipline. It restricts an individual rider's options as to speed, changes in route, and lane positioning. To attempt to ride in a group without having good basic riding skills and a good sense of what others in the group are likely to do—and what they expect you to do—is an invitation to an accident, one that may involve damage and injuries to more than one bike and one rider.

Those who don't wish to ride in a group but who wish to arrive at the same destination as their friends may serve as a scout if they have a CB radio, or they may just prefer to travel solo and meet up with their friends at the day's end.

In most riding groups and clubs, those who carry out the club's "business" in one position or another are unpaid volunteers. Group riding isn't for everyone, but those who accept these conditions are well cared for, and they know it.

C. Rules: who needs them?

At most responsible group rides, a riders' meeting will be held prior to departure, in order to clarify what's expected of all the riders who are to participate. If you find yourself uncomfortable with the riding style of a group at any time, **drop out**. Your safe arrival at your destination is far more important than conforming to rules you don't like or don't understand.

People who ride in a group usually appreciate knowing what they are expected to do, and what to expect from others who are taking part in a hazardous sport in close proximity to them. Road Captains and those who frequently ride lead or drag can explain to other riders who may show up for a scheduled ride without having any group riding experience what the rules are for that particular group or club.

Every group of individuals has its own dynamic that's established over time. That dynamic should be what determines whether you participate in their activities or not.

When you see many motorcyclists in proximity, whether they are riding or stopped, you may not be welcome just because you're also on two wheels.

Some clubs have strict rules about who can ride with them, what brand of motorcycle others must ride in order to join them, and which rides are open to visitors, if any.

If you find yourself surrounded by strange riders on the road (they may pass indiscriminately on your right and left sides), maintain control, let them ride off into the distance without you, and don't provoke animosity even if you feel that their riding is unsafe. You may not appreciate spontaneous lane-sharing with them, but keep all fingers on your grips and away from your horn, and control your worst instincts. Your first consideration should be self-preservation.

Though most riders have very few negative experiences involving other riders, if things are going to go bad, quite often you can see it coming.

Soon after the first instance of an unsafe practice which seems to be tolerated by the others in the group, indicating that the ride will be a free-for-all in terms of style and discipline, it's time to announce politely that you must leave, and then make your way home. If you observe riders who exhibit a "bad attitude" in general—rude or crude comments, demonstrations of selfishness, or outbursts of temper—consider whether you really want the "companionship" of riders like that, when you may have to depend on their help if there's an emergency. Some groups are simply too dangerous to associate with.

There are plenty of people who would find the style of group riding recommended here to be "too confining" or "not exciting enough" for them. The reality is that riding a motorcycle provides plenty of excitement on its own. Riding in close quarters with others is no place to increase the danger, take extra risks, and up the odds that you won't survive the ride.

Most riders who organize group rides believe that their "job" is to do everything possible to make the experience on the roads as safe and as pleasant as possible for everyone in the group. This is entirely a voluntary responsibility, however. So long as they aren't reckless about their own or others' riding experience, no one in the group will blame the ride leaders, or sue them, for the choices they make or how they direct others. Here's where "ride your own ride" is imperative, for you can't depend on anyone else to control your motorcycle or to determine where to ride or what risks you should take.

D. Common group riding terms

Pack: a number of motorcyclists who ride together, generally without maintaining fixed positions or distances between bikes. Packs are occasionally seen with 20-50 motorcyclists in a single formation.

Group: a small number of motorcyclists who ride together maintaining a generally fixed distance between bikes and maintaining fixed positions within the formation.

On rides in which participation by a large number of motorcyclists occurs, it's common to have riders divided into several groups and to name them Group 1, Group 2, etc. This facilitates radio communication when several groups are listening to the same broadcasts and traffic coordination on the same CB channel. Groups should have no more than about six riders in each one to allow traffic to pass safely.

Road Captain: a person who devises group riding rules or guidelines for a club or chapter of a motorcycling organization, who communicates these guidelines to the club, and who generally plans and lays out group rides. The Road Captain may or may not ride lead for a particular ride and in fact may not even attend it, but he's usually the final authority within the organization about what's going to happen on its rides. Some Road Captains also vet new riders to determine whether they have the skills to ride in a group. He's often the "policy maker" and role assigner, and he's commonly the arbiter for disputes within groups.

When a number of motorcyclists are invited for a group ride, the riders and their co-riders gather at the appointed time and place, often without knowing their specific destination or route from that point on. The Road Captain for that ride will have a route in mind and will usually have pre-ridden the route within the past week in order to look for construction and road surface problems and other situations which might affect the safety of those who are to participate.

The Road Captain usually will hand out maps to the riders or to their group leaders and will have a rough idea of times and distances to be traveled, suggestions for rest stops, food and gas, etc. He will hand out emergency medical information forms and release of liability forms for sponsored rides, to be filled in and signed.

If there are several groups of riders, the Road Captain expects all group leaders to follow the route which has been laid out and not to initiate changes in the route except in an emergency. In case of problems that require emergency personnel or re-tracing a route to find a disabled rider or part of a group which has gotten lost, it's much easier to locate the person(s) sought if all groups follow the same path to their common destination. It's not unusual for groups of riders to be separated by several miles and to find themselves out of CB range from other groups during a long trip or in heavy traffic. It's also not unusual for groups to break up briefly in traffic, requiring a station-keeping rider to serve as lead or drag for a fragment of a group, for a short time.

If there are so many riders that more than one group should be formed, the Road Captain works with the group leaders who have been selected by their rider for each one. Then that group leader will choose a drag bike with whom they wish to work, since these two riders will be the basic team for the group ride.

Group Leader or Lead Bike: a person who rides in the most forward position in a group. He sets the pace for those riders who have consented to follow him and determines the group's direction, speed, choice of lane, and formation. He conducts the pre-ride briefing for that group, paying special attention to newbies or to riders who haven't ever ridden in a group before, or who are not familiar with this organization's group riding guidelines. As a result, there's no doubt who the group leader is and what his expectations are. Authority is established by virtue of the participants getting into staggered formation in the parking lot behind this rider before the group pulls out.

The group leader often must make quick navigation decisions in the face of road hazards, changes in road surface conditions, poor signage, construction, and other obstacles while maintaining control of his or her bike and communicating to all other riders in the group via hand signals and / or CB communications.

The group leader should have communications equipment in order to speak to his drag bike at any time during the ride; the ability to make quick decisions; good judgment; excellent eyesight; and acceptable riding skills. He need not be the best rider in the group, but he will always be one of the safest and most responsible.

It's up to the group leader to select a drag bike with whom communications will be coordinated during a ride. If there are three groups on a ride, there will be three group leaders and three drag bikes working in pairs.

A responsible group leader rides to the level of the least experienced or least skilled rider in the group. At each stop, he confers with the drag bike, who has the best perspective to notice problems with such riders. At that time, any safety-related issues are discussed. Then tips are offered to individual riders privately. Group discipline is thus reinforced.

During the ride, the group leader attempts to give timely warnings of road debris or hazards. He signals lane changes, upcoming turns, and unusual situations such as construction or school zones; chooses places for in-between stops; helps the drag bike manage an accident scene, in case of trouble; and so forth. At the eventual destination, all the groups will join up. These tasks are undertaken by the group leader as a courtesy, to make the ride fun for those following.

However, the group leader's first responsibility is to control his motorcycle and protect himself. If this means the group leader cannot give the riders behind him a warning in time for them to avoid a hazard because he's dealing with it himself, no one in the group has the right to expect him to have protected them, too. If he saw the hazard in time to respond without anyone warning him, then the other riders had the same opportunity to do so without a warning. This is exactly what "ride your own ride" is about.

When the group splits apart at the end of a ride, the self-imposed responsibilities of the Road Captain and the group leaders end, but even then it is not unusual for them to place a phone call or two when they get home to insure that everyone else made it home safely, particularly in bad weather or if a rider had mechanical problems along the way. In that case, a group leader or drag bike might even escort that bike all the way to the rider's home.

Drag Bike, Tail Gunner or Sweep: a person who rides in the last position in a group and who relays information to the group leader regarding the other riders in the group, traffic patterns, equipment problems, etc. he or she observes. While a group is highly dependent upon the skills and judgment of the lead bike, in many ways they are more dependent on the drag bike for successfully arriving at their destination. The drag bike should have a comprehensive First Aid kit, a fire extinguisher, blinking warning lights, and reliable communications capability. He should be trained in current First Aid and CPR techniques.

The drag bike's first, and most obvious, role arises during group lane-changing maneuvers. When the group leader requests a lane change, the drag bike determines whether it's safe to make that change: the riders don't just go charging over into the adjacent lane. He then secures a lane for the rest of the group during lane changes into faster traffic (move first to block oncoming traffic) and close the door (move to block passing traffic) when a lane is lost in a merging lane situation.

If it isn't safe for the group to change lanes, the drag bike must tell the lead why the lane change should not occur at that time. Again, **it's the drag bike who determines if and when a lane change requested by the group leader is to happen**. Note that if the group moves into a slower moving lane from front to back, as is quite common, this is much like a normal car-passing maneuver. This is discussed below with diagrams to explain these patterns in detail. In this case, the group leader does not request a lane change at all. He announces it. The drag bike's only responsibility is to announce when the maneuver is completed.

If the drag bike denies the request for a lane change, he's already told the group leader (and all listeners on their CB's) to "stand by". Then he updates that advisory with the reason that the request is denied, such as, "Hot dog coming up in the left lane." This means that an aggressive driver is about to be in the space where the group wants to move. The proper response for the drag bike is to increase the distance between himself and the next bike in front of him, and to radio ahead to the group leader, recommending an immediate lane change to the right, and saying why he's asking for this maneuver. The riders should wait for that vehicle to go ahead of them, so that everyone can move into the new lane at about the same time.

Additional responsibilities of the drag bike: checking that all bikes have raised their side stands when the group begins its ride and after every stop; assisting any member who's forced to leave the group for mechanical, medical, or personal reasons (a loss of confidence, for example); observing the riding performance of all of the other bikes to determine if there's a particular rider who's mismatched in terms of riding skills compared to the group; watching for any unsafe riding habits of individual riders or the group at large; "closing the door" when a lane is about to be lost to prevent other vehicles from entering the group when the lane squeezes down; and reporting any lighting, tire, or luggage problems in the group.

If a rider decides to leave the group, it's the drag bike who determines whether that's because assistance is required; and he provides it, if necessary.

If a member of the group must stop for any reason, the drag bike stops with him, radioing the situation to the lead bike (so that a new drag bike can be designated, and so that the group can find a safe place to leave the road to wait for them). Except in an emergency, a rider who's leaving the group should have the courtesy to tell the group leader or the drag bike so, to avoid a situation where the group waits for him or spends time looking for a "lost" rider. No one else rides "last" for any reason whatever. Among other things, this insures that the group never loses anyone or leaves a straggler unintentionally at a rest stop. In the case of an inexperienced rider who needs to go home or get help, the drag bike rides escort for that motorcyclist.

If the drag bike observes that a rider does not appear to have adequate control of his bike, he advises the lead bike of this and requests that the group make an **immediate** stop to resolve the problem. If either the lead or the drag bike insists that an individual not be allowed to ride with the group, the group must not allow that individual to continue to ride with them, following the advice of these riders. If the individual in question refuses to leave, then the group should simply stop and not proceed until the rider creating the hazard leaves.

The drag bike may ride in the left or right track depending on the number of bikes in the group. It's preferable for him to ride in the left track, so as to have the same visibility line as the group leader.

Cage: any vehicle that is not a motorcycle, but particularly an automobile.

Four-wheeler: any vehicle that is not a motorcycle except an 18-wheeler, a hack or a trike.

Group Parking: a formation in which all bikes in a group follow the lead bike in single file into a parking lot, making a U-turn such that they can all line up next to each other in the space available with the rear of their bikes against the curb or edge of the lot, the front tires pointing outward.

Parade formation: a formation in which all the motorcyclists in a group ride two abreast.

Single file: a formation in which all the motorcyclists in a group ride in one track of a lane.

Slot: any position within a group of riders in the right track of a lane, farthest from oncoming traffic.

Staggered formation: a formation of motorcyclists in a group in which the group leader rides in the left track of a lane, the next bike in the right track or slot, and the next bike in the left track, and so on. Bikes in a group generally maintain a minimum interval of two seconds travel time between bikes in the same track, and one second travel time between each bike in the group. In a staggered formation, a rider still commands and may ride in the entire width of his lane as needed. Group riders may also ride single file or two abreast.

Station keeping: maintaining a fixed position and interval within a group of riders, but not riding as lead or drag bike. Riders without a CB radio usually ride as station keepers in the middle of a group. Positions within a group are initially assigned by the group leader based on the experience level of the rider, particularly his or her group riding experience, though after a period of time, riders may take any position they like except to ride lead or drag.

Track: the zone of a lane in which a rider maintains his position in a group. A lane of traffic is divided into five zones: the left track is the second zone from the left, the middle of the lane (generally not used) is the third zone, and the right track is the fourth zone from the left. The two zones on the sides of a lane serve as margins. A rider may vary his path of travel from his normal track as is required by a road hazard or by an incursion into the group's lane by other vehicles.

Two abreast: a formation in which the members of a group ride adjacent to each other in pairs, used when riding in parade formation. Used after stopping at signs and traffic signals so that riders can get through an intersection quickly and together if possible.

When departing from a stop, the rider in the left track normally pulls out before the rider on the right, returning to a staggered formation.

E. Preparing for a group ride

Riders are expected to arrive on time at the departure point with a full tank of gas, in proper attire for the conditions, and physically ready to ride (potty stop made, medications packed if needed, sober and alert).

Motorcycle endorsements and insurance should be up to date, and the bike should be in street-legal condition. The Road Captain may ask a rider not to join a group ride if these basic conditions are not met (for example, if a rider is drunk or a bike is mechanically unfit to ride).

If a rider brings a co-rider (a passenger) along for a group ride, he's expected to manage and attend to that passenger's needs personally before the riders' meeting.

The following guidelines are suggested for preparing a co-rider for a group ride:

- Do not permit a co-rider to mount the motorcycle until all riding gear is on and fastened securely (beware of outside pockets!). The co-rider should not mount until the rider is seated and holding the motorcycle vertically, and then not until the rider nods that he's ready for the co-rider to get on. The co-rider should avoid contact with hot exhaust pipes, wiggling out of position once seated, and shouting or making sudden movements of the upper body during the ride. The passenger's feet should remain on the pegs or floorboards designed for them at all times, until disembarking.

- A co-rider needs to know generally what he or she should and should not expect in terms of comfort and safety considerations. If the co-rider wishes to communicate with the rider, the rider should explain how to do this: by thumping on the rider's head? Intercom? Shouting in the rider's ear? Will the co-rider be responsible for copying hand signals given by the rider to others in the group?

- Suggested jobs for the co-rider during the ride: Watch out in traffic for anything that may detract from a safe ride: two pairs of eyes are better than one. Do not assist the rider by leaning in turns, but look over the rider's inside shoulder on curves. Wave at all other bikers, children, anyone who shows interest in the riders, and law enforcement officers on their feet. And -- smile!

- In group riding, if the rider (with or without a co-rider) wishes to slow down or stop during the ride, for any reason whatsoever, he or she may drop out of the ride. If at any time a co-rider becomes uncomfortable during the ride and wants the rider to slow down or stop, for any reason whatsoever, the rider should be prepared to do so as quickly and as safely as possible, if possible advising the drag bike of the reason for terminating the ride.

F. Pre-ride briefing

The purposes of the pre-ride briefing, which is conducted by either the Road Captain or the group leader, are these:

- To review where the group is going, what route it will be taking, and usually to hand out maps;
- To describe how the group will handle lane changing and what to do if it splits apart;
- To specify which channel on the CB the group will be using and to review hand signals as well;
- To demonstrate each hand-signal used;
- To determine the riding experience of everyone new to the group;
- To remind the group that the riding formation will be "staggered", with a one-second following distance between the bike ahead, in order, and a two-second following distance between the bike directly ahead in the same track in the staggered formation;
- To assign new group riders to "slot" positions to ride in until the drag bike is satisfied with their abilities to handle their bikes; and
- To invite all the riders to do a "walk-around" of their bikes to insure that all is in order, and then to take a quick look at the bikes on either side of them for the same reason.

One of the most important rules to be discussed during the pre-ride briefing is known as the "Prime Directive."

G. The "Prime Directive"

Group riding has lots of benefits for its participants, but it also carries a few unique responsibilities. One that's probably obvious is this: **Never hit the bike in front of you.**

Why would this even be an issue? Well, consider the group ride that turned into an accident scenario when the lead bike failed to recognize where he was supposed to make a left turn and drove past that road. The second bike in the group did recognize the turn, however, and decided to make it. He turned left, and the third rider promptly ran into him.

What went wrong? Some would say that if no one had been following too closely, then Bike 2's actions would have saved everyone (other than the lead bike) from having to make a U-turn, and no accident would have occurred. Probably true, but almost any rider with experience understands that the group leader **alone** decides when and where the group will change directions unless there's a contrary safety imperative.

Perhaps the leader had a reason for failing to make that turn. For example, he could have realized that the group was going too fast to make that turn safely. (If anybody in the group understands the danger of making sudden moves, it's an experienced lead bike.) Or suppose Bike 2 had not willingly made that left turn but had had a sudden mechanical problem, such as a flat tire. No one should have followed him!

Since all members of a group are expected to follow the direction set by the lead bike, **except into danger**, everyone (other than possibly the drag bike) should have attempted to avoid Bike 2 and continued straight behind the leader, which is what Bike 3 properly did. Only the drag bike should stop to assist a rider—not the whole group. Remember, the general rule in group riding is that all riders in that group follow the group leader, and no one else.

Bike 2 was way out of line to decide to take over lead position unilaterally; to mutiny, if you will. However, the fact that Bike 3 ran into him suggests that she was either following too closely, or was inattentive, or was so confused by the unorthodox behavior of Bike 2 that she could not react fast enough to prevent the accident. Whatever the reason, Bike 3 failed to observe the Prime Directive.

When you are riding in a group as other than lead or drag bike, your principal activity is "station keeping". This means that you maintain a proper distance between yourself and the bike ahead of you, and you stay alert to the leader's directions or signals. You also pass all hand signals back.

Since the vast majority of accident threats present themselves from the front, each rider should be encouraged to focus his attention primarily ahead. In other words, it's dangerous to spend too much time watching your rear-view mirrors when only other group members are riding behind you. If you accept the Prime Directive and assume that all the other riders have done the same, then you are also tacitly acknowledging that **you trust the rider behind you not to run into you**.

Of course, you may never have ridden in a group with that person before. You may never have even met him before. Further, it's common practice to put the weakest or least experienced riders towards the back of a group. Isn't that more likely to result in an accident, then?

Not at all! The weakest or least experienced riders are in the back precisely because they are most likely to have an accident. If one occurs, this puts the fewest other riders in the group at risk. It also allows the drag bike to observe how these inexperienced riders handle themselves and to work with them at stops about little things that they may be doing wrong that jeopardize themselves or the rest of the group.

As to their potential danger to the riders in front of them, that can be managed. An experienced rider demonstrates savvy group riding behavior, if he's concerned that the new group rider behind him is following too close, by using a hand signal to tell that rider to slow down or back off.

Even though many group riders have CBs, hand signals are used as well, to keep those without them informed. All hand signals from the group leader or from other riders must be passed back; but most riders tend not to originate them, thinking that this is a job only for the lead bike.

But if an individual rider in the group notices a hazard in the roadway, he should point to it so that all riders behind him will be alerted. And an individual group rider can always initiate a hand signal telling the rider behind him to slow down.

On the other hand, no one but the group leader should originate a hand signal telling a rider behind him or her to speed up. This is another way of saying that spacing in a group is usually specified in terms of minimums ("no closer than one second" between bikes while in staggered formation). Any rider may decide to use a larger cushion of space, of course. A new rider especially tends to want a bigger gap between him and the bike ahead until he adjusts to the group's style. The Prime Directive errs on the side of conservative riding. It mandates that you be alert primarily to the front. It mandates that you not follow too closely. It makes you think about what the bike ahead of you (closest ahead of you, not literally "straight ahead") is doing or might do next, rather than what the lead bike is up to, although all riders should maintain situational awareness about what's happening throughout the group.

It also gives you a modest suggestion about what to do if **you** are about to have an accident. For example, if you're riding in the right track and there's a hazard in the road ahead of you, the Prime Directive forces you to tend to turn towards the right to avoid that hazard—thus taking you farther away from the closest bike ahead of you, so that if you crash, you don't bring that rider down, too.

H. Normal group riding maneuvers

1. Entering Traffic

When the lead bike for each group sees that all riders are helmeted, sitting on their bikes, motors running, and ready to depart, he or she will check for traffic and enter the roadway. Usually the group leader won't attempt to exit a parking lot unless there's room for all or most of the group to follow immediately. If the group is split, he will normally take the slow lane and keep the speed relatively low until the group can form up in the positions the riders will keep for the duration of the ride. This may mean traveling slower than surrounding traffic, to encourage other vehicles to pass and to allow the group to form up. Occasionally this cannot be accomplished until the group has made a lane change or entered a freeway, depending on where the entrance ramp may be.

Regardless of the lead bike's signals, a rider is responsible for his or her own safety at all times. Ride your own ride.

Once all members of the group are together, they will take up a staggered formation and will stay in it most of the time during the ride, unless given a signal for a change or the need for a change is obvious. Reasons for changing out of a staggered formation could be a passing situation or poor road surface (single file), a dog or other animal charging the group (split the group), or a traffic signal.

2. Changing Lanes

When a group of motorcycles is changing lanes, many safety considerations come into play. Should every rider move into the adjacent lane at the same time? If not, should the lead bike go first, or should the drag bike move first to "secure the lane"? When the drag bike radios to the group that the lane is secured, is it really? What if another vehicle sees a gap in traffic and tries to cut into the group? If part of the group gets separated from the other riders, should everyone change relative positions (tracks) so that the new lead bike is now riding in the left track? The recommended procedure for a group lane change maneuver depends on how the surrounding traffic is moving at the time.

The goal for the bike which moves first is to create a gap into which the other bikes can fit.

Regardless of what other riders are doing, each rider must personally check to see that the new lane is clear of traffic before entering it.

There's virtually no time, absent an emergency, when a group of riders should all move at the same time into a different lane (though in a well-disciplined group, it may appear to other drivers that they do). The wide gap required for a whole group to move is difficult to find in heavy traffic, and if it exists, it will be an invitation for other drivers to jump into it, perhaps while the group might be moving there, too. Additionally, such a maneuver could be interpreted as "parading", which may arguably not be covered under some insurance policies.

In most jurisdictions in the U.S., traffic laws prescribe that, on a road with two lanes moving in the same direction, the right lane is the slower lane. If a group of riders is going to move into the slower lane from the faster one, the first rider in a group which moves is responsible for creating a gap into which all the following bikes can fit.

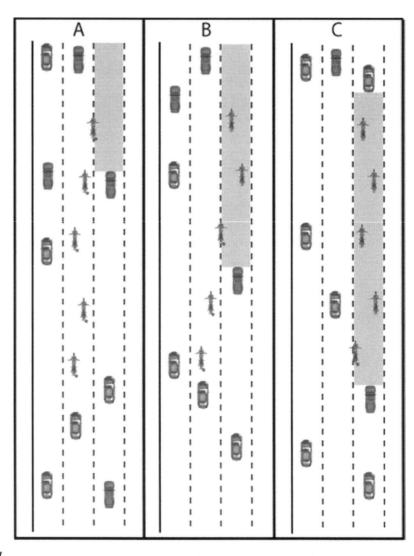

Figure 25: Group lane change into slower lane

This is accomplished by maintaining a constant speed in order to enlarge the gap after the first bike moves. Each bike moving in succession should also be aware of this dynamic. Thus, the group moves from first to last. (An exception is the drag bike, who may move on his own, well after the group has moved, for reasons explained later.)

The first bike to move under these conditions will be the group leader. The maneuver's accomplished this way: the group leader signals for the lane change and announces to the group via CB radio and / or hand signals that the group is moving to the right, front to back. Then, after checking by actually turning his head to see that the new lane is clear of traffic sufficient for one bike to safely enter it, the lead bike moves across the tracks of the current lane, taking up a position in the left track of the new lane, as usual.

By maintaining the maximum speed which the traffic in that lane will allow, the group leader creates a gap into which the next bike in the group can insert, moving into the right track there.

Each succeeding bike follows this pattern: signal right, move right in your own lane, head-check, enter new lane, maintain speed to create gap, and take up regular position (left or right track) in the new lane.

The drag bike in this pattern is normally the last to enter the new lane, unless "closing the door" was possible. As the bikes move quickly and re-form their group, it's rare that a four-wheeler will move up into the gap in the new lane. If a cage moves into the gap, the next bike to move must tuck in behind it and wait for the group ahead to slow up, encouraging the cage to pass. When the cage passes the slower forward group, the whole group can re-form into a normal riding configuration.

The same basic lane-changing principle for entering slow-moving lanes also applies when a group is entering faster-moving traffic where at least two lanes of traffic are moving in the same direction; that is, moving from the right lane to the left. The first bike to move creates a gap for the remaining bikes. Since traffic is pulling away from the group as each member enters the lane, this maneuver is done back to front, as shown in Figure 26.

The maneuver is accomplished in this manner: The group leader signals for a lane change and announces to the group via CB radio and turn signals that the group will be moving to the left, back to front. Then he asks the drag bike to "secure the lane" to the left, to which the drag bike should normally respond with "Stand by."

All station-keeping bikes maintain their position while this occurs, putting their own turn signals on to indicate to the bikes behind them, and to other vehicles, that there's a move to be made. Now **the drag bike moves first** when a space in the lane to the left opens up and radios to the group leader and the group, "The lane is secured."

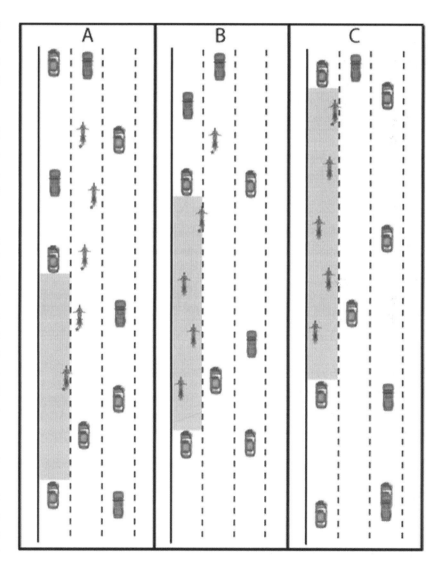

Figure 26: Group lane change into faster lane

No one is to change lanes at this point, however! First, each rider must make certain the lane is clear by actually turning his head to insure that there's no other vehicle still approaching the group in the left lane. If a vehicle is still moving up beside the group, the drag bike will usually say, "After the red truck," or "After the station wagon," etc.

Whether a warning is given by the drag bike (who may have other concerns with the traffic to his rear), **each rider must do a head-check before entering a faster-moving lane**.

The second bike to move will be the one in **front** of the drag bike. That rider moves across the tracks of the current lane, does a head-check, changes lane and then takes up a position in the same track of the new lane as the one in which he was originally riding.

By dropping to a speed slightly slower than the rate at which traffic in that lane has been traveling, each bike creates a gap into which the next bike forward can insert. Each rider follows this pattern: signal left, move left in your own lane, head-check, enter the new lane, maintain (slower) speed to create a gap, and take up your regular position (left or right track) in the new lane. If a cage moves into the gap, the next bike to move must wait for the cage to pass, so that a gap appears again. Then the maneuver can be completed and the group can re-form into a normal configuration.

The group leader in this pattern is normally the last to enter the new lane. As the bikes move quickly and re-form their group, it's rare that a four-wheeler will join them, but the riders usually have no idea if that's true without some feedback from the group itself via CB or by checking their rear view mirrors to see if the group is now intact again.

3. Breaking up is hard to do

If a lane change results in the group's changing formation—for example, if the bike which was unable to move into the new lane slows down and becomes for a time the group leader for the left lane, while the rest of group moves ahead in the slower lane--or if the bike which was unable to move right is forced to **pass** the slower group—should the new group leader take the left forward track?

Ordinarily, no. Only if the group breaks into two obvious sub-groups and becomes separated for a substantial period of time should the "new lead bike" move into a new track to the left, if that has not been that rider's normal position. Otherwise, this will be only a temporary break in formation, and the riders will quickly enter the new lane and re-form as usual behind the group leader, in the positions they were riding in originally.

Why doesn't the "new lead bike" change tracks? Because during any period in which the bikes are changing tracks, the spacing between them is cut in half, drastically reducing the reaction time and space available to the rider in case the bike directly ahead of him becomes a problem. In a lane change, this period is fairly short. But if the "new lead bike" shifts position and all the bikes following attempt to adapt to the new configuration by changing to a different track, they will then have to change back when the original group re-forms. There's no real reason to put the riders in additional jeopardy this way in order to have the "correct" formation, just for short periods.

Forcing all the bikes in the rest of the group to change track position is especially hazardous in the case of a new group rider who has become accustomed to riding in the protected "slot" as opposed to facing oncoming traffic in the exposed left track position. In most cases, anyone who's riding in a group will quickly adapt to this change of conditions and track positions, but there may be times when a new rider who's trying to learn this whole concept will be very uncomfortable changing tracks. The drag bike should pay special attention to inexperienced riders under these conditions.

This pattern may occur not only during a lane change, but also during a passing maneuver or when a group gets separated in traffic because of signal lights and traffic flow. Note that the forward group will also have a "new drag bike" temporarily, though ordinarily the time when the group is separated is quite short. This is another good reason for riders to learn to ride in these leadership positions and not to depend on their usual riders to assume them all the time.

The original drag bike will usually notify the group leader via CB after a brief separation that the group has re-formed by saying, "We're family."

4. Passing

On a busy two-lane road, oncoming traffic typically prevents a group of riders from passing a slow-moving vehicle while in formation.

Each member of the group must accomplish two lane changes in order to pass, and this usually is done on an individual basis, so that each rider is sure when to move.

Regardless of what a rider is told by others in the group about oncoming vehicles, <u>each rider must personally check</u> to see that the oncoming lane is clear of traffic before entering it to pass.

If oncoming traffic requires the group to pass individually, the group leader will signal the group to move into a single-file formation and will announce that the group members are to pass the vehicle one at a time. The forward members of the group will gradually position themselves in single file in the left track to prepare to pull into the oncoming lane.

The group leader will usually wait for a gap in oncoming traffic that's big enough for more than one bike to pass, but this isn't always possible. When a safe interval is observed, the group leader will put his left turn signal on and pull into the oncoming lane. After passing the "obstacle," looking in the rear view mirror for clearance, and actually turning his head to be sure the lane is clear, he then signals that he's moving into the right lane and does so, taking his normal position in front of the slower vehicle(s) in the left track. He must then maintain or even slightly increase his speed.

As with a lane change to the right, each rider should be aware of the need to create a gap into which the next bike in succession can fit after overtaking an obstacle. For this reason, each bike should maintain speed after passing, until the drag bike has passed and the group has re-formed.

Special care should be taken when passing not to focus on distant oncoming traffic to the point of establishing "target fixation." The rider should continue to scan the environment for hazards and should plan escape routes in case of the unexpected; for example, the "obstacle" may come to life again when he sees motorcycles passing him and may accelerate while a rider is still in the oncoming lane, exposed to additional risk.

After he's passed the slower moving vehicle, the drag bike will usually notify the group leader that the group is intact again by saying, "We're family."

5. Spacing out

Especially on less-congested rural back roads, the riders in a group may spread out to create larger intervals between motorcycles. This allows a rider to relax a bit to enjoy the scenery and the ride. If no four-wheelers are trying to pass the group, this is fine. However, the riders should remain close enough to each other to be able to see hand signals being passed back from the lead bike.

Also, if a group is at maximum size (eight bikes should be the absolute limit) and the riders spread out too much in hilly terrain, CB radio communication between the lead and the drag bike may be severely tested or lost. They can't work together if they can't communicate.

It's possible that a rider will also "space out" in terms of losing his concentration and will forget to practice safe riding strategies. If the rider has become too fatigued to ride properly, the drag bike will usually notice this first and will advise the group leader that a rest stop is needed.

If a rider's not riding safely enough to avoid endangering others in the group (because of lack of experience, medical problems, fatigue, or some other reason), the group leader will usually discuss the problem privately with that rider at the next stop. If a problem cannot be solved reasonably in this way, the group leader has absolute discretion to request that a rider leave the group and is entitled to expect the group to support this decision.

In the case of a mechanical or minor medical problem, it's not unusual for another rider (usually the drag bike) to accompany the distressed rider to get help. Sometimes, if the group leader just re-assigns the riders to new positions within the group, this is enough to bring a spaced-out motorcyclist back to a state of alert awareness.

6. Checking out the curves

On any stretch of curvy road and in any corner, a group may ride in single-file momentarily, to enable each rider to corner at his own speed and to have as much room as possible for maneuvering. This is especially important to riders with little experience in a group, as they may "wobble" or be nervous about making turns with another bike to their side or riding close behind them.

This is an accepted variance to staggered formation; usually the group leader won't signal for single-file at each turn but will expect the riders to choose their own desired path of travel through the twisties.

I. "Caution / Warning / Danger" Signal

Though it's not yet a universally agreed-to signal, this one should be. That is, whenever a rider observes a potential threat or wants to announce that he may need to change speed quickly, that rider is obliged to tap his front brake lever twice in rapid succession.

Any rider following that bike should do two things when he observes that signal:

- Slowdown in order to widen his following distance; and
- Repeat the signal to insure that bikes following receive the warning

If no emergency exists or a rapid speed change isn't needed, or if it occurs quickly after seeing that signal, then all bikers can assume the potential emergency has passed and can resume normal speeds and spacing.

Nothing was lost, yet everyone took defensive postures, just in case. That, after all, was the purpose of the signal in the first place.

J. Joining a group

How do you join a group of riders you don't know? Can you just catch up with them and get in line or join their formation? Must you have the same kind of motorcycle they are riding? Will they get bent out of shape if you join them without an invitation?

Consider the following before you link your fate to strangers.

The group of motorcyclists that you want to join has more in common than that they happen to be riding together at the moment. Their history as a group may be no more than an hour old, but it exists. They could, for example, have just met each other for the first time at a dealership and be participating in a dealer-sponsored event. Or they could all be members of a motorcycle organization who often ride together.

Whatever its history, for however long the group has existed, the riders may have more in common besides riding together. As an "outsider", you might or might not be welcome.

If you happen to have a CB radio on your bike and at least one of the members of the group also has one—a fact you deduce based on his having an antenna on his bike—and if you can find the channel that other rider is using (assuming his CB radio is on), you can simply hail the group on your CB. Make a friendly remark that they look good, and ask where they're going. It will quickly become obvious to you if the group may be willing to let you join them or not.

If you don't have a CB, or if no one in the group of strangers does, or if no one responds to your attempts at a radio exchange, don't draw too many conclusions from a failed attempt. However, these are some other realities to consider:

- The group may have one or more drunk or drugged members in it;
- The group may be out looking for trouble;
- The group may just have experienced trouble with someone else trying to join them, uninvited or otherwise; and
- The riders, despite appearances, may have no idea whatsoever about how to ride safely as a group.

It makes little sense to join an unfamiliar group, even if you do manage to make radio contact. But if that's what you want to do, consider doing it this way:

- If it becomes clear from a CB radio chat that you would be welcome to join the group, find out where they plan to make their next stop. Tell your CB contact that you would like to join them at that stop and will follow them until you all get there. Tag along behind the group, but **not** in their formation. Stay behind their last bike with a distance at least **three times** what the group is using, because most groups give the drag bike unique responsibilities (such as securing lanes). Don't interfere with his duties. In other words, follow the group to their next stop without actually joining them.

- If you're unable to make radio contact with the group, **do not join the group uninvited!** Since the group has not yet made it clear that they are willing to have you join them, you should not tag along quite as closely as described above. In this case, you must not appear to the group or to other drivers as though you are a member of the group who's just lagging a bit. Ride in a different lane if you can. Let a car or two get between you and the group. If you and the group are the only riders on the road, follow with at least **five times** the gap that's being used by the group between its members. Then pull in to check them out when they make their next stop.

- At the first stop, park your motorcycle somewhere in sight of the others, but **not** as if you are already a part of the group. Approach the first rider who appears willing to engage you and introduce yourself. If there's a pecking order in the group and someone else decides whether or not an unknown rider can join them (this is almost always true), you will be told about it. The person who will make that decision is probably a group leader or Road Captain, and a responsible one will ask you some questions first. In turn, you should ask for a pre-ride briefing. While you're in conversation, find out about the group, its "rules of the ride", and keep a careful eye out for signs of drugs or alcohol. Just because you meet **their** approval doesn't mean you should automatically assume they're a good group for **you**.

If they are, then have a good time. Don't press your skill level to "keep up", accept the Prime Directive ("**N**ever hit the bike in front of you"), and make some new friends.

K. Size matters – the "rubber band effect"

While most riders know that it takes about one second to recognize and begin to react to a threat ahead of them (PDR), it usually takes from two to three seconds for riders to recognize and to begin reacting to a **gradual** change to a faster speed by the bike in front of them in a group.

A couple of seconds doesn't sound like much. With two seconds for PDR, small group of bikes can usually handle that gradual acceleration; but at three seconds, some serious problems result. This becomes particularly important if there are six bikes in the group or more. Group leaders in particular need to be aware of how this kind of trouble can develop.

At 60 MPH, your bike moves 88 feet per second. Assuming that you maintain a one-second gap between bikes in the group, then each rider is about 88 feet behind the next one. At 70 MPH, the gaps would be about 103 feet.

Assume that the lead bike increases speed from 60 MPH to 70 MPH. It takes about two seconds to do so if that rider's casual about it (using an acceleration rate of 7.5 ft/sec^2), though she could do it in half that time. What happens to all the bikes behind that lead bike?

Most people assume that each rider will simply follow suit by accelerating modestly at the rate of about 7.5 ft/sec^2 (5 MPH/Sec) and, thus, the riders will maintain their group with the same spacing between bikes as before. But that's not what actually happens.

After the first second of modest acceleration by the group leader, the distance between the lead bike and the second one has grown from 88 feet to 92 feet.

One second later, the gap has become 103 feet. By coincidence, this is exactly what the new distance between bikes should be while riding at 70 MPH. However, the second bike has not yet even begun to accelerate. That rider's now moving 10 MPH slower than the bike ahead of it.

The gap between the bikes will continue to grow until the second bike is also moving at 70 MPH, some two or three seconds later. That is, if the second bike realizes that the first one is pulling away from him and begins to accelerate within only two seconds. If he does, then he, too, will be traveling at 70 MPH within another two seconds. If it takes him three seconds to wake up and recognize a widening gap, and then to react to it, then it will take another two seconds for his speed to match the speed of the bike ahead of him.

In the best-case scenario (a two-second react / respond time), the gap between the bikes will now be 117 feet.

If it took three seconds for the second rider to start to speed up, that gap would have grown to 132 feet. Clearly once the speed of both motorcycles is the same, the gaps will remain the same.

But since the group prefers to travel with a "one-second" gap between bikes, the second rider **must go faster** than the first one for a brief time in order to catch up and be back in the same relative position as before the first rider started to accelerate.

If we assume that the riders in this group are conservative, and that individually every rider elects never to travel more than 5 MPH faster than the bike ahead of them when they're closing these gaps, then the second bike will continue to accelerate for one additional second and will attain a speed of **75 MPH** while the first one continues at 70 MPH. In fact, the second bike will have to ride for **two seconds** at 75 MPH, while the first one rides at 70 MPH, in order to close the gap to 106 feet. Then he takes one more second decelerating to 70 MPH, during which the gap between them is reduced to the desired 103 feet.

This example of the dynamics between just two bikes usually causes no grief and is easily understood. Farther back, it's anything but trivial.

Let's look at the third bike in the group. About two seconds after the **second** rider begins to accelerate, the third one follows suit. Three seconds later, the gap between the second and third bike has, as expected, become 117 feet. But, because the second bike is traveling at 75 MPH at that time rather than 70 MPH like the first bike, **the gap continues to widen**; and within one more second, it becomes 128 feet.

Clearly Bike 3 must accelerate more to catch up to the second bike than the second bike needed to, in order to catch up with the lead bike. Indeed, the third bike will have to accelerate to 75 MPH and will have to maintain that speed for **four seconds,** instead of the two required by the second bike, in order to close that gap.

Worse, the next rider, Bike 4, will find that the gap which he has to close has grown to 132 feet before it begins to shorten; and then only if he accelerates to **80 MPH** instead of 75, because the third bike is traveling at 75 MPH rather than 70 MPH when the gap has reached 132 feet. The gap would be larger still if Bike 4 accelerates only to 75 MPH.

In a group of just six motorcycles, Bike 6 will find the gap between himself and Bike 5 has grown to 143 feet before it begins to close. He will have to accelerate to 80 MPH, hold that speed for three seconds, drop to 75 MPH for an additional three seconds, and then finally drop to the group speed of 70 MPH, in order for all members of the group to end up with a one-second gap between them at 70 MPH.

Further, it will be at least 11 seconds after the lead bike has started to accelerate before the sixth bike does. Imagine what will happen during that time **if the lead bike applies his brakes** in anticipation of a curve!

This example demonstrates what all riders in a group experience: the "rubber band" effect. Imagine how **profound** this effect becomes at the end of a string of 20 bikes, rather than only six.

And what happens if the lead bike, upon exiting a 35 MPH curve, gooses his bike to 60 MPH as fast as he can?

The group leader is in the best position to mitigate these problems, and here are several ways to do so:

- The lead bike can change speed more gradually;

- The lead bike can announce speed changes over the CB and, thus, reduce reaction times for all;

- All bikes in a group can stay alert and thus react faster to changes in speed of the bikes farther ahead than the one immediately in front of them;

- The members of a group can avoid cranking their throttles up to excessive speeds just to keep the group spacing "correct"—in other words, they can speed up and re-establish spacing gradually;

- A good group leader can avoid accelerating within 15 seconds of entering a curve (assuming he then must slow before actually entering it);

- The "one-second rule" for spacing between bikes should be abandoned whenever the group is riding "twisties" (because it makes sense only when traveling on an open highway); and

- The lead bike should never permit his group to become larger than six bikes if even one of the riders is inexperienced with group riding. It should never be larger than eight bikes, even if all riders are familiar with each other's riding habits.

For some riders, understanding the rubber band effect brings the disappointing news that huge group rides, like holiday toy runs, charity events, or memorial rides, should be avoided. Correct! Find another way to support these causes.

Once you've ridden in a crowd of several hundred motorcycles, with riders around you whose riding skills are unknown, on bikes in all kinds of condition, and you see that the group is rubber-banding at speeds up to 100 MPH near the front (despite the presence of law enforcement), while somewhere riders behind them are coming to a screeching stop, you'll realize you're really not missing anything good.

And if you think that the "rubber band" effect is a problem when accelerating, think of what happens during braking!

L. Closing the gap after a rider leaves

Because group size matters, the question arises of what to do if one member of the group drops out of the ride. Should the remaining group members maintain their lane positions, or should they rearrange into a new staggered formation?

This isn't hard to answer: they should regroup into a full staggered formation and shorten the remaining group size by about two seconds' worth of space.

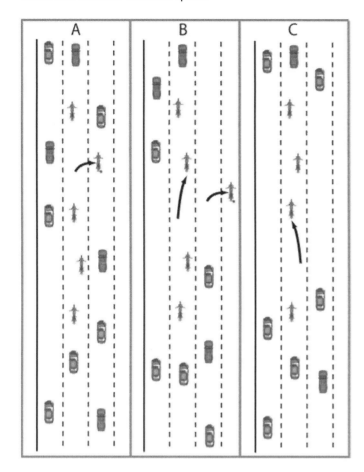

Figure 27: Closing a gap within a group

No matter whether a rider exits to the left or right of the group, the remaining members should regroup as shown in Figure 27.

The concern about bikes "crossing paths" expressed by some group riders is exaggerated. The same thing happens if any member elects to shift lane position in order to avoid a roadway obstacle, and nobody would dream of being critical of that move.

As you can see in the diagram, the remaining bikes advance forward in the group and shift lane position along the way one bike at a time.

In the real world, all the riders after the exiting rider will probably adjust their lane positions at about the same time.

M. "Closing the door"

An experienced drag bike rider can add considerably to the safety of a group ride.

For example, assume a group of motorcyclists are riding along and pass a sign indicating that a lane of the road will soon be lost. This could be because of construction or simply because the road narrows by design.

Normally, the lead bike will position the group so that they are in the remaining lane well before the other lane collapses. The danger comes when some vehicle tries to race along that collapsing lane and runs out of road. Then he has no choice but to jam his way into the middle of the group.

An effective lead-bike / drag-bike team cures this problem before it happens. As soon as either of them realizes that one of the lanes is going to disappear, the drag bike is asked to (or merely announces that he's going to) "close the door".

This means that, while the group is positioned in the continuing lane, the drag bike rides, by himself, in the collapsing lane. As soon as the collapsing lane has disappeared, the drag bike returns to the rear of the group. He then says to the group leader, "We're family", indicating he's back in his usual position.

Figure 28: "Closing the door"

In Figure 28, the drag bike is riding in front of the car in the lane which will soon disappear. If the car driver intends to move ahead of the group or into it at the last minute, the drag bike has closed off that opportunity.

N. Groups of two

It will often happen that you and your friend or your spouse are out for a ride on separate motorcycles. One of you is more experienced, one of you is more skilled at navigation or some other aspect of riding (possibly the same person). Which of you takes the lead? Which track of the lane does that person ride in?

First, assume one of the two riders is essentially a newbie.

Contrary to the usual arrangement described previously for group riding, here the group's most experienced rider belongs in the lead, because it's the lead bike's responsibility to establish speed, select a path of travel, initiate lane changes, navigate, and encounter trouble first. This is too much for almost any new rider to handle.

The newbie is gaining experience and may well be "pushed" over his or her ability if required to take on the many responsibilities of group leader. Also, the rider in the lead position should be in the left track of the lane, because that's the position that provides most visibility (for oncoming drivers, as well as the lead bike). This provides some extra protection for the less experienced rider, who is farther away from the center line and from oncoming traffic. If that rider is leading, he's lost this protection.

If the less experienced rider is not a newbie (meaning, this person has ridden in groups several times and is in complete control of his motorcycle on the road), then either of the riders may take the lead position. The less experienced rider may wish to learn how to lead a group; or the more experienced rider may wish to assess the riding skills of the other one, which is best done by watching from behind.

The safety rationale that stipulates that the lead bike takes the left track of the lane is persuasive most of the time. However, in the case of a person who may be an experienced rider but who has **no** or very little experience riding lead, then both riders can agree that the lead will ride in the right track until that person has gained more experience.

In this case, the inexperienced lead bike is trading the somewhat greater safety of better visibility in the left track for the greater safety of being farther away from oncoming traffic in the right track while he's learning to cope with all the other demands of riding lead. This is the **only** scenario where the lead bike can justify being in the right track for any extended period of time.

If both riders are inexperienced at riding lead but are reasonably skilled riders, either can take the lead; but it should be from the left track of the lane, as is normal—and the spacing between bikes should be doubled.

Finally, if both are inexperienced at riding lead and both are also relatively unskilled riders, then **they should <u>not</u> ride as a group**. If they intend to ride "together", then they should do so in single file, with twice the normal group spacing between them. This pair of riders should find an experienced lead bike to tutor them in group riding, or otherwise obtain group riding experience while gaining their essential riding skills, before they ride together as a group of two.

Why suggest that a relatively unskilled rider get any group riding experience? This may actually be the safest way for a new rider to gain riding experience in general, if the other group members are highly skilled. In a group, other riders are available to offer help in case of trouble and make the unskilled rider more visible. Once each of the riders who want to ride together has ridden with others who have more experience, then these new riders will have a much better idea of how to ride together when they are alone and what to expect when traveling in their group of two.

O. Super-Groups

When motorcyclists gather for a group ride, there may be many riders and co-riders who want to participate. If there are more than six, then two or more groups should be formed. The entire set of these small groups is a super-group. Since each group is an autonomous organization with its own group leaders, drag bikes, and station-keeping members, each having their own responsibilities, the Road Captain will function as leader of the super-group.

In addition to the duties described earlier, if the super-group is large enough (for example, at a charity run), the Road Captain is responsible for arranging to have police escorts for traffic control, if needed.

He also acts in a supervisory capacity, in that the group leaders will all report to him.

What that means from a practical point of view is that he can "fire" group leaders who are not performing their responsibilities in a manner satisfactory to him.

But what he does not do is select the group leaders. Should he "fire" a group leader from the super-group, that leader's entire group is not to participate in the super-group on this ride until they choose a different group leader. The Road Captain may designate a set of riders whom he believes would make good group leaders, but the selection of the lead bike is the responsibility of the members of each group. **They must agree to be led by <u>and</u> to back up their leader.**

P. What to do with the impaired rider

During a group ride, the drag bike may see that one of the group's members slows down dramatically when entering curves. This is a sure sign that the rider is being pushed. If the drag bike observes that a rider does not appear to have control of his or her bike adequate to continue the ride as a member of the group at all, then he **must** advise the group leader that there's a problem and request that the group make an immediate stop to resolve the problem.

If the problem is a dangerous level of inexperience, then this is almost always resolved by the group leader's asking the rider to stop riding with the group. Usually this rider will be offered an escort to a safe destination. Typically the drag bike will act as escort, and the group leader will designate someone else, usually the next most experienced rider, to assume the position of drag bike for the rest of the ride.

If either the lead or the drag bike insists that an individual should not be allowed to ride with the group, the group **must not** allow that individual to continue to ride with them.

On rare occasions, the problem turns out not to be an inexperienced rider, but one who is impaired by alcohol or drugs (prescription or otherwise).

The first sign of this may be when someone notices that one of the riders is acting erratically. He's weaving in his lane, unable to maintain proper following distance, riding **on** the line between lanes, or doing something else that indicates he is not quite fully in control of himself and his bike.

Understand that it's far more likely that you'll notice that one of the riders is impaired when your group is at a pit stop. For example, if you all have stopped at a restaurant and enjoyed a meal, during that meal you may notice a rider's slurred speech, or that he suddenly nods off, or that he orders and drinks an alcoholic beverage (or more than one).

As soon as possible, the group leader must be notified of the problem by the drag bike or anyone else who sees it, so that the situation can be taken care of before an accident ensues. The group leader should immediately stop the group at the side of the road or take an off-ramp and lead the bikers to a convenient stopping place. Then what?

For alcohol is not the only impairment threat. It's possible that one of the riders has taken some drug or medication that's active in his system and was even before the ride began. The effects of that drug could begin to "hit" during the meal or while out on the road. If a rider is seen taking pills at a stop, it's a good idea to ask him or her if she's feeling all right. This will usually elicit an explanation about which medication the rider's on; and if it doesn't, the drag bike should pay special attention to this rider.

Although the first thing to do is to make sure that the group leader or the Road Captain is informed of the situation, that's not the same as saying that from then on, the situation should be handled by that person. When the bikes are not moving, the Road Captain and the group leader have only the authority given them voluntarily by the rest of the group's member. **The most important person in the group is <u>you</u>** (even if the bikes are moving).

In cases involving drugs, alcohol, or medical problems, **an impaired rider must not be allowed to ride his or her bike at all. His participation in this group ride is over.**

If one of the co-riders traveling with someone else in the group is also a capable rider, that person may be asked to ride the impaired person's bike to a safe place for overnight storage. Even if the bike cannot be secured temporarily, the impaired rider should not be allowed to ride it. The motorcycle will probably be O.K. for some time where it is; and even it weren't, the rider's life **will** be in jeopardy if he or she keeps riding.

If the individual in question refuses to cooperate, the group should simply stop and not proceed while he or she remains. Some riders suggest taking an impaired rider's keys, though it may invite an unpleasant confrontation. If the rider refuses to give them up, someone in the group may attempt to disable his motorcycle in a non-damaging way (by letting the air out of his tires, for example). If he insists on getting back on the road alone, this is the time to consider whether law enforcement assistance is needed to keep an impaired rider from getting killed. If the rider becomes belligerent or unruly, it's time to leave the scene. Avoid confrontations with impaired persons; arguments with such people can't be won.

And here's some extremely important advice in such a situation: **the impaired rider should not be allowed to assume co-rider (passenger) status**!

The group leader, drag bike, or group members should arrange for some other form of transportation for that person. Call a cab if necessary.

Sometimes riders will observe a group member consuming a single alcoholic beverage and will be told that he's fully in control of himself and should be allowed to continue with the group. This statement simply can't be trusted: there's no way to know whether this is really the only alcohol the rider's consumed, or whether it will mix with some other substance (such as medication) to make the rider dangerous. One or more members of the group may opt to stay behind with that rider for an hour and let the others continue their ride in the hope he will show no impairment and is really in control of himself; but only if he turns over his keys. After that hour, he can ride again, but not with the group! And no one escorts a previously-impaired rider home. No one should be put in the position of compromising his own safety by doing so. Escorts are reserved for those who have minor mechanical problems, not those whose judgment is faulty.

If a group leader and other group members are unwilling to deal with these highly restrictive rules, even though the situation may be uncomfortable, then it's time for you to disengage and ride on your own.

The group leader and the drag bike are a team designated by the group to conduct them safely to their destination. As you can see, these are not symbolic positions. They require maturity, experience, training, cooperation, good communications, and good judgment. And, occasionally, your thanks.

Q. Responsibilities of other riders

Members of a group other than the group leader and the drag bike are not there just to follow orders and play "follow-the-leader." If you think group riding is generally just following along, you should abandon that impression immediately.

When you join a group ride, you agree to be led by its group leader and shepherded by its drag bike. You agree that you will station-keep (maintain proper spacing and a staggered formation) throughout the ride. And you agree that you will adopt the Prime Directive. You agree to back up the decisions of the Road Captain, the group leader and the drag bike. But there's more.

For example, you agree to follow the lead bike **except into danger**. You agree to rely solely on yourself to determine that a lane change is safe for you to perform. You agree, in other words, to be responsible for your own safety. Riding in a group is much more than being a passive component. It involves being an **active** participant.

Lest you think that you are nevertheless still just following the leader, here are some real-life situations that may change your mind.

A group of seven people on five bikes went out for a short ride together of about 150 miles. One of them was a newbie to the group and to group riding. That rider received a pre-ride briefing in which the group leader explained the concept of group riding. He had also received written group riding guidelines the week before. Because there was a new rider in the group, the ride started out very conservatively.

The group leader decided to place the new person in the slot immediately in front of the drag bike. When the group got to a freeway, the lead bike kept the group in the right-most lane. This was done to give the drag bike an opportunity to gauge the skills of the new rider before the group increased its speed and moved left into the fast lane. The drag bike observed that this rider had fine control of his bike, but he was clearly anxious about being in the right lane. And indeed, there was a lot of merging traffic before the group got through traffic and out of town.

Someone in the group who was equally anxious about riding in the right lane said on the CB: "Hey, I have it on good authority that there are two more lanes on this freeway." The group leader responded by asking the drag bike to secure a lane to the left. He did so, and the group moved to the left. In other words, one of the "followers" changed the behavior of the group. He took an active role and asked, in his own fashion, for the group to move out of the slow lane. Had the newbie been having any trouble with highway speed or with control of his bike in any other way, the drag bike would have vetoed the lane change and advised the group leader to take the next exit instead.

Taking an active role is expected of group riders! And not just to change some group behavior to accommodate a personal desire. Each rider in the group is expected to look out for the interests of the other riders as well.

Another example: As a ride came to an end, the group leader and the drag bike rode home together through some unfamiliar back country roads that had essentially no traffic on them. They traveled at speeds of from 60 to 70 MPH most of the time, so long as conditions were favorable.

This group leader has led groups for in excess of 50,000 miles over the past decade and is very good at it. When she approaches unfamiliar curves, she doesn't push the envelope. But when riding with a familiar riding partner whose skills she knows, it's not unusual for her to take a marked curve at from 10 to 20 MPH above posted advisory speed limits. (For example, if a sign says that the speed of a curve is 45 MPH, these riders will usually take it about 55 MPH and be well within their skill limits.)

On this ride, they were traveling at about 70 MPH when the drag bike noticed that they were approaching a curve that was posted at 20 MPH! The lead bike had looked down at her instrument panel and hadn't noticed the sign at all. She would never have tried to take that curve so fast, as the drag bike knew perfectly well.

The drag bike announced on the CB radio, "This one's a 20!" The lead bike hit her binders and brought her bike down to about 30 MPH before she entered the curve. Note, the curve had not been visible at all before the drag bike made his announcement, at least not to him. The lead bike had seen the first set of left-pointing arrows indicating that they were approaching a curve but clearly had no idea that it was such a tight and dangerous one. Because the drag bike was pro-active, they both made it through the curve without incident.

In other words, all riders in a group are expected to look out for everybody else. The lead bike at the time was known to be a competent rider, but if the drag bike had simply been a passive rider, "following the leader", both of them would have ended up on the side of the road waiting for a Life Flight helicopter, or worse.

Being in a group provides everyone with many extra pairs of eyes, extra minds to deal with situations that others are not prepared to deal with, extra help in the event of problems, and a community of informed decision-makers. To think that anyone in the group would fail to be active when the need arose is out of the question. To think that anyone in a group of riding friends would have failed to warn the lead bike about the speed of that curve is simply nuts.

No one should follow a group leader into danger. And no one should allow a group leader to enter danger without trying to prevent it. This requires an **active** role for everyone.

R. "Odd Duck" in the group

Sometimes when riders show up for a group ride, all of the motorcycles are similar except one—it's a trike or a hack. What should the group leader do with it?

There are only a few situations in which most group leaders will not allow a motorcycle, of any kind, to ride with their group. First, if it's not street legal, it doesn't go along. If the rider is impaired in any way, he's not allowed to join the other riders, regardless of the condition of his bike. If the group leader requires that helmets must be worn in his group and a rider refuses to wear one, then he must ride in another group where the group leader is more flexible or else abandon the ride if all group leaders require this.

Assuming the group isn't part of a brand-oriented organization, and sometimes even if it is, most group leaders otherwise don't care if the rider's motorcycle is a Honda, a Harley, a Ninja, a trike, or a hack. They are all part of the family and welcome to join the group (assuming the rider doesn't demonstrate a lack of control or unsafe practices). A trike or a hack presents some unique concerns, however. For example, they are wider than the other bikes and effectively must use the full width of a lane. And neither of them are capable of using counter-steering. They literally must be steered through the curves.

What's relevant here is that a rider who follows another bike obtains several visual cues from the one ahead of them. These cues are used by the following rider to anticipate what he must do in order to stay on the road and out of trouble. Such things as lean angle and brake lights are examples of these cues. But there's no lean angle on a trike (or on most hacks), and braking patterns are quite different for these kinds of vehicles.

In other words, a rider cannot casually assume that he can follow one of these odd ducks the same way he would any other motorcycle. Further, because they are so wide, when a rider is following one of them, he's unable to see as much of the road ahead of him as he's used to.

In this situation, the group leader helps the rest of the group by assigning such an odd duck one of two positions within it: If the rider of a trike or a hack is sufficiently skilled that the group leader has confidence in him or her, that rider is asked to ride drag. This very neatly solves all of the major concerns. However, if the trike or hack rider's experience or skills are unknown, or if he or she isn't qualified to ride as drag (or doesn't wish to do so), then that rider should be assigned the second to last position in the group.

There, that rider directly affects only the drag bike. Since the drag bike is presumed to be the most competent and prepared rider in the group, it's reasonable to assume that he or she can deal with the odd duck.

The drag bike's following distance should be increased to about twice normal to account for the abnormal width of the trike or hack, which affects his escape path within the lane ahead of him.

If there are two "odd ducks" or more wishing to participate, they should each be assigned to a separate group, if possible. If there's only a single group, then the "odd ducks" belong at the rear of the group or in a separate group of their own.

S. "Rules" don't outweigh safety

Some common misunderstandings exist about the "rules" for group riding. For example, virtually everyone who has ridden in a group understands that they should try to keep the group together. That has become almost "gospel," yet it's absolutely wrong if to do so would involve increasing risk.

Said another way, though group riders know that they are to follow the lead bike, there's a caveat to that understanding—again, **except into danger**.

Keeping a group together can never have priority over safety.

Here's a common highway scenario, analyzed from a realistic perspective. Figure 29 is a diagram of a situation where a group finds itself riding in the right lane of a two-lane highway as the riders approach an on-ramp.

Here, the group leader has failed to notice that a car is about to try to merge into the highway traffic. If each rider in the group insists on maintaining the same position in order to keep the group together, then that means at least one rider in that group is going to have an encounter with a car's bumper. What should the riders do?

Well, for sure it's **not** up to the group leader to determine what actions to take. E**ach** rider is responsible for his own safety. Each rider in the group must decide what to do about the threat, though there are several things that the riders can do in order to try to keep some semblance of order within their ranks and maintain part of the formation.

For example, Biker 3 might put on his turn signal and, after doing his head check, begin moving to the left lane. In a disciplined group, all the bikes behind that third bike will also see the threat, understand it, and decide to follow him into the left lane. This isn't the "rule"—which would have all the riders after Biker 3 continuing to follow the group leader.

Maybe that's not the best thing they could have done, but it demonstrates positive action on the part of at least one of the riders.

What it leads to, however, is that after the riders move left, the group now covers two full lanes and totally blocks all following traffic.

Since group riders understand that under any normal conditions they are not supposed to pass the lead bike, the group in the left lane will not do so. They'll also be traveling slower than expected in that lane.

That will leave the car driver who entered the highway boxed in and probably pretty angry!

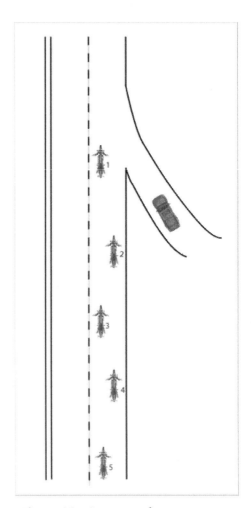

Figure 29: On-ramp threat to group

Traffic in the left lane is also unhappy at having to slow down suddenly to accommodate this partial group.

A second and far more appropriate action for Bike 3 to take is to simply slow down and widen the gap between his bike and the bike ahead of him. That allows the car to gracefully merge with traffic, as in Figure 31. Generally, as soon as that driver sees a way to move left into the next lane, he will do so. (It apparently is "threatening" for many car drivers to find themselves in the middle of a group of motorcyclists.)

When the car has merged onto the freeway and entered the lane, there are then two independent motorcycle groups in that lane. That is, the group is no longer "family." The third biker has temporarily become the group leader of the second group; he is then responsible for navigation for that group.

If the car doesn't move left, the temporary leader can move the second, sub-group into the passing lane and increase its speed until they can safely merge back into the right lane behind the first group, or he can decide to bide his time and simply maintain visual contact with the group ahead until the car moves out of the lane.

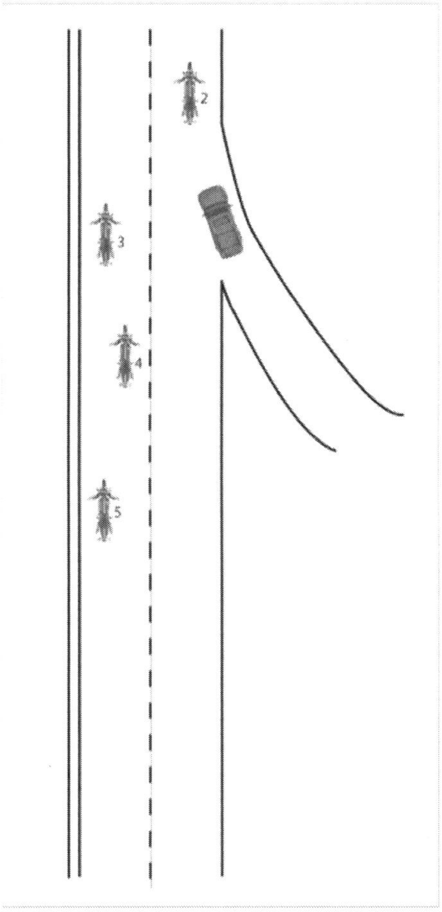

This is a real-world situation in which the "rule" to keep the group together **must** be subordinated to safety. Although many riders believe that only the group leader and the drag bike are to make decisions for the group, each rider is **required** to do so first on his own behalf, then for others. What really should have been done in the example we've just given was for the group leader to move the **entire** group into the faster left lane **before** approaching the on-ramp.

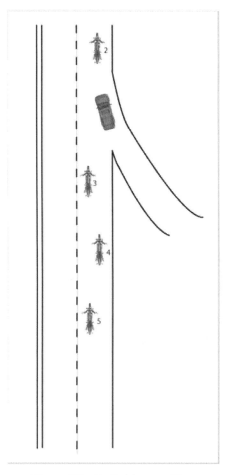

Figure 30: Reaction blocking traffic

That may not always be appropriate, but it usually is; and a group leader who is looking far down the road for potential threats will recognize that a car is on the entrance ramp and about to enter the freeway, in time for the whole group to move left and speed up, or to slow down and wait for the car to merge.

Now consider the situation in which the same group is approaching an off-

Figure 31: Suitable reaction

ramp instead of an on-ramp. If there's a car in the left lane that decides to exit, there's going to be an accident unless someone in the group is courteous enough, **and savvy enough**, to slow down and let that car gracefully (and safely) pass through the group to exit the freeway.

These examples demonstrate why a group leader should not build his groups with more than six to eight bikes.

T. Guidelines for street bikes

Whatever the rules are for your group, it's vitally important that all riders know them. It's your responsibility to know them before you get on the road next to other bikes to ride in close formation; and it wouldn't hurt for you to check with the people you're riding with to see if they're familiar with them, as well. Guidelines for Group Riding may be downloaded for free from our website.

You may distribute these guidelines widely. The print-ready version at http://www.msgroup.org/GroupRidingGuide.aspx can be handed out at the start of a ride. Or it may be easier to send the link to all participants who plan to ride in your group, so that they can read them at home beforehand.

Whatever rules are to be observed, each rider should attend the pre-ride briefing by their group leader and confirm their understanding of anything that isn't clear during that discussion. There must not be the slightest confusion about the group riding rules before the ride starts.

The competent rider understands that multiple fatalities are not uncommon in group riding crashes and knows how to avoid these situations by understanding the group's riding rules and knowing when to ignore them.

Despite these risks, the camaraderie, the shared discipline, and the common support found in group rides can be a rewarding part of motorcycling.

III. Carrying a passenger

Carrying a passenger (or co-rider) can be a wonderful experience for both your passenger and you. But the rider isn't the only person who needs training for this.

For deciding to carry a passenger can be the very worst decision you ever make in your life if you or your passenger end up hurt, or if you lose control of your bike and hurt someone else's person or property. This discussion is intended to help you avoid making a serious mistake.

Before a rider allows a passenger onto his motorcycle, he must insure that it's properly set up. First, the motorcycle should be designed to carry a passenger, which means that it has a pillion for that person to sit on, not merely a padded area intended for strapping a small amount of cargo on the back. If it doesn't have a "sissy bar", that pillion isn't a seat, and the bike isn't intended to carry a passenger safely.

Then the rider should inflate his tires to about the maximum air pressure they are designed to handle (which is imprinted on the sidewall of the tires), and he should adjust the rear shocks to handle the added weight.

A. Six months later, you're still not ready

Putting a new rider and a passenger together is strictly a **no-no**. Most riders probably know that, but here are the issues.

When you move from a smaller bike to a larger bike, the learning curve essentially starts all over again. You must practice starts, stops, and turns almost as if you had never ridden a bike before. However, moving from a larger bike to a smaller one takes about one minute of familiarity, and you have complete control of it (unless you make a radical move from a cruiser to a sportbike, for example).

Managing the effect of added weight in the form of a passenger takes longer practice. After reading pages 39-41, you should understand why.

Remember, it's **not** true that adding weight to a bike increases its stopping distance and time. It merely makes it more difficult to achieve the same stopping distance and time.

Because traction is increased proportionate to the added weight, you can handle more braking. All you have to do is **squeeze the brakes harder** to stop in the same distance and time. If you wish to increase your following distance in an excess of caution, do so, but know how fast you can stop.

On the other hand, adding a passenger changes the dynamics of the bike. A new rider can barely recognize that, even though the dynamics have changed, **the way he controls the motorcycle** has not undergone any meaningful change.

You should have at least **six months** of experience riding your bike solo before you allow a passenger to get onto it. But at that time **you still won't be ready** to handle the added weight! You will need to practice with that added weight before you go out on the street—just like when you graduate to a new or larger bike, and with a specific kind of passenger, before you go out and test other limits.

Never, ever place a passenger (a child or even an animal) on the tank in front of you. You must have clear access to your grips and controls, you have to see the road, and you must be able to maneuver the front wheel without the added complication of a change in handling dynamics or misplaced attention. Passengers belong on the pillion behind you.

In most states, there are laws restricting the age at which a child can become a passenger, or requiring that a small passenger still be able to put his or her feet on the passenger's floorboard or pegs. You must also provide safety equipment for your passenger that fits; and if you care about that person, the passenger's gear should be just as sturdy and as protective as your own.

Your significant other or a child will expect you to be **in control** of the bike if you're taking him for a ride; and if you demonstrate sloppy starts or stops or leans, you will undermine that confidence. Part of establishing that you're a careful rider is to conduct a pre-ride briefing with your passenger.

B. Passenger's pre-ride briefing

Before your passenger mounts your bike, you should explain what you expect from the passenger, and what the passenger can expect from you.

A rider should advise his co-rider that, so long as he or she is on the bike, the passenger's the boss. If the passenger wants to slow down or to stop, for any reason, the rider will do so. In other words, the rider controls the bike, and the passenger controls the rider!

It's important to explain that it's not the rider's intention to scare the passenger, ever, but to help him or her enjoy the experience. The rider's attitude must be to ensure the passenger's safety, above all else. Recall how helpless you felt as a passenger, when you first started practicing this skill?

The only thing you should want to "show off" is that, while riding a motorcycle can never be without risk, you're doing everything you can to make it safe and enjoyable. Your stops and starts will be so gentle that the passenger can't tell when the bike begins to move; and your goal will be a smooth ride.

Before the ride commences, the co-rider must agree to get on and off the bike **only** with the rider's permission.

The passenger must also get on and off only while the rider's on the bike (which is in neutral gear). The rider will have both feet down, with the bike's side-stand **up**. This is because, if the side-stand is down and the passenger plops onto the pillion, that will compress the shocks. The side-stand will prevent leftward movement and will lever the bike to the right—and possibly all the way over onto its side!

The passenger must not get on the bike until the rider is ready for him to mount and **signals** for him to do so, usually by a nod of the head. (This is also true when the rider is ready for his co-rider to leave the bike.)

Finally, when he mounts and dismounts the bike, the passenger must try to keep his weight centered on the bike. That is, he should avoid pulling the bike towards himself. Rather, he should push himself towards the bike.

As to moving around during the ride, the passenger should pretend he or she's a sack of potatoes. (It's OK for a passenger to move about a little, but not suddenly; and he must never lean far off to either side.) The co-rider is **not** to try to help the rider through the turns; he should not lean his body in anticipation of a turn, or when they are in one.

It's helpful to tell a passenger that you've never had an accident (assuming that's true); but that no matter what happens while you're moving, the co-rider is to keep his feet on the passenger floorboards and never, ever, try to touch the ground with his feet to try to hold up the motorcycle.

If the motorcycle is equipped with saddlebags that have guard rails, the rider should point them out and explain that they are heavy steel, like "roll bars", and they will protect the passenger's legs—but only so long as his feet remain on the floorboards or pegs.

C. Restrictions to enforce obsessively

Passengers must have at least the same safety gear as the rider. If you can't provide this, then don't invite or allow another person to ride your motorcycle.

A passenger who shows bare skin is only pleasant to the eye before hitting the ground. A passenger who wears sandals, who has unprotected hands or arms or legs (from not wearing gloves, or wearing short sleeves, halter tops, or shorts), or who wants to ride without a helmet, should not be allowed on a motorcycle—**ever**.

If a person cannot rest his feet on the passenger pegs or floorboards, he's too short to be allowed to sit on the pillion and cannot be a passenger. This is not only common sense; it's also the law in many states.

If the potential passenger must be in any way restrained (tied to the bike or the rider), that person must not be allowed to be a passenger on your motorcycle.

There are devices on the market that allow a child to be strapped to the rider so that they can sleep while riding. Don't use them. **They can be deadly if the child is crushed by the rider as he comes off the bike and hits the ground**.

A person who's under the influence of drugs or alcohol must not be allowed to be a passenger. Note that this includes both adults and children who have an attention deficit disorder and who take (or should take) drugs like Ritalin!

As long as the passenger's helmet has a face shield that isn't raised, any helmet that cover the sides and back of the head (i.e., not a "beanie") is appropriate for passengers, including a three-quarter style. However, the higher the passenger sits relative to the rider, the more valuable a full-face helmet becomes. In a quick-stop, the passenger's face may be planted into the back of the rider's helmet. The passenger can sustain a broken nose, a split lip, or even broken teeth, should any other type of helmet be used. Note that this type of injury is possible even when there's no accident.

D. Communications

Passengers and riders often have occasion to communicate with each other while they are moving. Some riders can only hear the passenger when he leans forward and yells to the rider. However, rider-to-passenger communication then requires the rider to turn his head to respond and yell over his shoulder. This takes the rider's eyes off the road.

Big bikes, especially touring bikes, are often equipped with an intercom system permitting easier and clearer communication between rider and co-rider. If the motorcycle's also equipped with a CB, it will usually permit the passenger to hear and respond to other bikes over the CB, as well as talk to the rider.

To use this equipment, the co-rider must have a helmet with a headset installed, which consists of embedded earphones and a microphone. A cord will usually connect the passenger's helmet to the motorcycle.

The rider should explain the "passenger twist" before the passenger mounts the bike. This is a maneuver whereby the co-rider first connects the helmet cord while facing the bike, then does a full turn clockwise so that the cord wraps behind the passenger before he gets on the bike. Bluetooth-equipped headsets that require no cables are also available for this kind of onboard communication.

The rider should show the passenger how to use the push-to-talk button to talk on the CB / intercom and where it is.

In the absence of an intercom, or when a passenger wears a helmet without a headset built in, the rider and the co-rider should decide on at least a few signals before the co-rider mounts the bike. This should include a signal for an immediate stop, a signal for "slow down", and a signal for a convenient stop, for example at the next town or next gas station.

E. Experienced passengers add value

Passengers, particularly those who are experienced, are not just "along for the ride". They often take an active role to assist the rider. A co-rider is an extra pair of eyes to scan for threats, usually to the side, such as lurking deer. With stepped pillions, or with the remarkably plush passenger accommodations provided on touring bikes, passengers sit higher than the rider and have a relatively unobstructed view that's in some ways better than the one available to the rider. A co-rider can see over taller vehicles ahead of the bike, such as in stop-and-go traffic, to advise the rider of a better lane choice, for example, or why traffic has stopped.

The co-rider can also provide hand signals to supplement the bike's turn signals. Riders should keep their hands on the bike's grips when the bike's moving, so this practice is actually a very helpful visibility aid. For example, a couple who have ridden together for many years developed an effective way for the co-rider to assist the rider when turning, slowing, or making lane changes. The wife put a highly reflective paint on the palms of her gloves which she shows to those following the bike, in an effort to get them to back off if they are following too closely or to give other drivers notice in addition to the bike's turn signals and brake lights. This provides extra visibility and warns others of the rider's intentions.

On longer rides or when touring, passengers may be tasked to provide navigation support if they know how to do so. It's helpful if a co-rider knows or has studied the route, or can read maps without the rider having to pull over for a stop, or can use a hand-held GPS device for that purpose.

A rider can also benefit from a passenger who recognizes that he's getting sleepy or losing concentration and convinces him that it's time to stop. However much fun it is for the rider to control the motorcycle for miles and miles, a passenger may suffer from a lack of stimulation, especially if the scenery isn't exciting; or from wind blast because of the exposure of sitting higher on the pillion. Thus, a rider should plan more frequent stops when carrying a passenger than when riding solo. This can help the rider, too.

Unexpectedly, passengers turn out to be better than brakes in keeping a rider at or below the speed limit. Motorcycles like to go fast. Riders sometimes let their motorcycles get away with it, but when a passenger's aboard, they tend to pay more attention to speed, because it contributes to the passenger's well-being and comfort.

IV. Camping

Motorcycle camping is an experience that many motorcyclists find to be as enjoyable and socially enabling as anything else they have ever done. It's been said, "Adventure is taking inappropriate equipment to out-of-the-way places," so if you're going to do it, you may as well do it with friends.

Though many riders will try camping as a solo experience, sometimes out of necessity (making a long distance trip on a very restricted budget), most find that camping is best appreciated with a significant other or with a riding group.

Depending on climate and your tolerance for exposure, there are three pieces of equipment considered essential for even hardy campers if they want to enjoy the experience:

1. A waterproof tent;
2. A warm sleeping bag; and
3. An air mattress.

In summer, it's not unusual to find campers along the Gulf Coast or in southern states who sleep in a beach towel on the sand under the stars; or in the saddle, in a series of naps; or on a table in a highway's rest area.

You can rough it for one night like this in a really minimal fashion, though you sacrifice comfort and safety, as well as cleanliness in the morning.

But to get the full experience, campers essentially establish a new and sufficiently comfortable "home" for themselves away from the comforts of civilization, where they will stay two nights or more, soaking up the scenery, the social life, and a disengagement with all the demands of their normal existence.

Of course, getting away has its own demands.

One of the first issues is a location where camping is either tolerated or encouraged. In most states, you can't just stop along a highway, pull off the road, and pitch your tent. You need a place for yourself and your bike that's off the road. But where?

Private property owners are generally unwilling to overlook a camper who hasn't asked permission; and if you ask, they'll usually say no. If you stay after you're asked to leave (and that can mean, if you take "too long" to pack up), and if you argue with the property owner or his agent about it, you're looking at an encounter with law enforcement that may escalate.

And what's happening to your camping equipment while you deal with that kind of problem "downtown"?

Decide in advance where you want to stay and why: for example, "This town has great local attractions, good riding roads, family nearby, potential adventures, a campground beside a river, with clean bathrooms and easy hook-ups...." Whatever your reason for picking that location to camp in, scope it out in advance.

You might find that a certain destination doesn't fit into the rest of your tour schedule, once you take a close look at the time it involves for that one visit. A fun idea for a place to see along your route might not really be worth spending a night near it in a campground, just for that visit; or it may hold only enough interest to take you and your fellow traveler(s) an hour or so away from your regular route, so that you can stop briefly and then get back on the road.

Remember, you're going to be paying rent (and probably putting down a deposit) in order to make a little "home" when you unpack and set up camp; and that implies a certain commitment of time or interest to make it worth the hassle of creating it and then taking it down and packing it all away when you're ready to move on.

Allow yourself plenty of time and patience to choose a place where you will make reservations before your camping trip. It can take a serious effort to find a suitable campground in popular tourist areas, especially during holidays, festivals, rallies, and vacation time. You may have to study your maps and be flexible about how close you are to a certain town, like Daytona, or a region with a major attraction zone, such as seeing the maple leaves in New England in fall.

Make decisions and make reservations early. Before you start out on any long trip, know where you're going to sleep every night and for how many nights. You can always cancel your reservation, and usually without charge if you do so early enough on your arrival day.

Note: It's far better to be charged for a room or a campsite you didn't use than to force yourself to get to it that night after you had a problem on the road. Try to know where you're going to end the day, but don't get into a race with the clock if it's not working out. If you have to improvise, you'll have a great story to tell about it later.

Second Note: Making reservations like this allows you to create your "flight plan" with ease before you leave. If you have to change your plans along the trip, remember to call in and revise your "flight plan" with those who are keeping track of you back home.

Why all this harping on making reservations? Well, many franchise campgrounds are booked far in advance, because some campers return to that area at the same time, year after year, and they keep a standing reservation. People have been known to book rooms or sublet apartments at Sturgis more than five years in advance! If an event's coming up that will fill the hotels and motels, chances are it will also fill the campgrounds. State parks and recreation areas also require reservations for certain months, so you should plan your trip carefully and budget for park entrance and camping fees. Though you may find a campground that caters to motorcyclists, even they are rarely free.

Further, it's truly annoying to have a sleeping bag on your bike when you're starting to get tired of riding but to have nowhere to unroll it and rest. This quickly becomes a safety issue, too.

Once you've decided on your travel route, allowed time for lengthy stops, and decided how long you want to spend camping out in a given locale, research campgrounds all around the area. Examine photographs online, use Google Earth to look at the area from a satellite's perspective, read travel reports, and maybe even find other riders who can recommend a campground or advise you where to steer clear.

If you plan to visit an attraction while you're camping out, determine how you're going to secure what you leave behind for half a day, including (perhaps) that "extra" motorcycle. Also check the route between your campground and that attraction, so that you can gauge time and fuel requirements for getting back and forth. It's not unusual to camp more than 50 miles away from your destination.

After you reach that stopping point on the map on your first day of camping, you'll want to know exactly how to get to the campgrounds and into it (i.e., who has the key to the gate?), and that it has the facilities you need that night, whether it's an electrical hook-up or a shower or a reception area with a coffee pot.

It's not unusual for you to have to call someone who controls access to the campground after you arrive. This will often be a person who lives nearby who must bring you a key or unlock the toilet or showers. Get that phone number in advance and put it into your cell phone. (This will be true of many bed-and-breakfast facilities and of some family-run motels, too.)

Though some campgrounds are run by big corporations as interstate franchises, a campground is frequently a small business, privately owned and operated, not a government-run park. Owners often live on or near the site, and their businesses live or die on their reputation. Some places make it clear that motorcyclists will never be allowed to rent a space there, which they see as a marketing plus for the non-riding public who are looking for peace and quiet. Other campgrounds are specifically intended for bikers who tour, or at least they welcome riders.

Be sure your allotted travel time will get you to your destination in time to stop early enough to set up your camp before it's pitch-dark. Even if you had a dozen flashlights with you and six extra people with nothing to do but stand there and point them in the correct places, you still wouldn't have enough light to permit you to pitch a tent, unload your gear, and get it stashed neatly inside once it's really, really dark, and you're tired. Certainly not enough light to do it without resorting to making remarks to your co-rider that you'll regret in the light of day.

Also, reserve a specific spot, not a general "place" in the campground. Your camping site must be level—more level than most—so that you can at least park your motorcycle(s) without worry. If you don't want to fight gravity all night, you'll also want a level place to pitch your tent and roll out your sleeping bag.

Every experienced camper wants that, so in this case, the requirements of your motorcycle may be a definite plus, if the owner is accommodating.

The amount of activity inside a specific campground during the daylight hours may be high or low. In some campgrounds, almost everyone leaves after one night, and there's nothing within the site itself to hold visitors. The site may be virtually empty during daylight hours. In others, people may come and stay without leaving the site for two weeks, socializing with friends who came along with them or meeting new ones. People may cook, eat, and drink with their neighbors, strike up card games, or watch TV, having no interest in tourist places in that vicinity. As with anywhere else, they may also get into arguments and fights when they become uncomfortable and bored. In many campgrounds, alcohol and firearms are prohibited. In others, people can party (and get into a fight) all day. Word of mouth is a valuable tool here.

Before discussing camping equipment, one more reminder is appropriate. When people are outdoors, sounds carry much farther than you may expect or believe, especially when everyone else is quiet and the environment undisturbed. Keep the noise level in your camp low enough that you can be seen as the sane and respectful camper(s) that you are. Don't say things you wouldn't say in a crowded room of third-graders, because voices carry. If you have to pass other tents in the wee hours, remember that people are sleeping inside them with only a thin layer of tarp between you; and even whispers seem loud in the middle of the night after the birds are asleep.

If you have to strike your camp and pack up your bikes in the early morning hours in order to leave according to schedule, keep your voices low and your process orderly. And if someone in another camp has been an inconsiderate slob the night before, carousing and keeping you and your friends awake, avoid the temptation to pay them back by making all the noise you can with your bikes before you leave.

Your decision to go motorcycle camping usually will involve more than one person; and that means taking along at least two sleeping bags even in the best of weather.

If you're camping more than one night, you'll want a tent, a First Aid kit, whatever food and water supplies you want to bring, and utensils, particularly a knife. Though you may be able to shop for food every day, you'll probably need a modicum of refrigeration and storage containers for leftovers, bags for your trash, insect repellant, sun screen, flashlights, soap, cooking equipment, extra clothes and shoes for off-bike activities, and folding chairs. And there may be more items that your particular group enjoys or requires, such as darts, games, and books.

Does loading all this on a bike sound impossible? It's not at all. Two bikes can carry a great deal of cargo without using a trailer; and, by careful planning, you'll manage to avoid having to go back to civilization to buy something you forgot. Lots of motorcycle campers do pull trailers in order to carry everything they want to have with them when they are "roughing it," but motorcycle manufacturers discourage this.

See **Pulling a Trailer**, discussed above.

Without a trailer, everything must fit on your bike, and it's obvious that just the three items listed above, not to mention all the items on the camping checklist, are beyond the limits of what you can carry in a backpack. That means that you must either have big saddlebags (and probably a top box) on your bike; or you'll have to strap these items securely to the bike itself—probably both.

In essence, you're riding a tour bike, no matter what your bike's actual configuration is. And that probably means you can't take a passenger and your camping essentials on the same bike. It also means that you must also carry a supply of bungee cords and cargo nets with you.

If all you carried with you to enable a night of camping was a sleeping bag, a tent, and an air mattress, you would perhaps be satisfied, assuming you can handle being a minimalist; but you would be neither comfortable nor prepared for what you will actually experience.

For example, on almost every multi-day road trip, you'll run into at least one day of dealing with rain or bad weather that requires a diversion, an extra stop, or some other change of plans. If you're camping, you may be glad you brought along something to occupy your time while you sit in your tent and wait for the storm clouds to pass. Thus, besides the items mentioned above, you will need foul-weather gear, changes of clothing, toiletries, a cell phone, perhaps a laptop computer, and much, much more. Unless you have someone in a car or truck in your party who can haul all the equipment you'll need, those items must be carried on your motorcycle.

Figure 32: Cargo capacity of a non-touring bike

See **APPENDIX H – An equipment and camping checklist.**

To give you an idea of just how much cargo-carrying capacity a non-touring bike can support, Figure 32 is a picture of a rider with saddle bags and strap-on luggage. Notice that the luggage on the pillion serves as an excellent back rest. In this case, the bike does have a built-in back rest for the rider as well as a sissy bar, and the luggage is secured around both.

Unlike the very limited cargo-carrying capacity of a top box on a touring bike (from a weight point of view), strapping luggage onto the pillion of a motorcycle enables a rider to carry easily 100 pounds or more of cargo. The bike will handle just as if you are carrying a well-mannered passenger.

If you have no experience carrying a passenger, take some time for parking lot practice with a fully loaded motorcycle to learn how to handle the added and higher weight of your motorcycle, before you head out on your road trip. Without cooking equipment, two riders can easily carry supplies adequate for more than a week on the road.

A competent rider plans ahead for both comfort and safety.

V. Confidence

You entered the competence phase of your motorcycling career as a result of the experience gained from confronting and managing an enormous number of incidents that we've called "expected unexpected threats", learning from each of them, increasing your skill levels with hours of practice, avoiding unreasonably dangerous situations, maintaining a healthy motorcycle, and otherwise demonstrating superior judgment. In a word, you've survived.

Along the way, you've become increasingly confident in your motorcycle's abilities, along with your own. That confidence has allowed you to entertain behaviors that a beginning motorcyclist finds, if not impossible to duplicate, at least well beyond his personal limits. With each new success came increased confidence that you can handle almost anything your part of the motorcycling world throws at you.

You no longer make mistakes because of a lack of knowledge or a belief in myths and misinformation.

With study and now with a learned eye, you've discovered how and why your motorcycle behaves the way it does in a wide range of environments and weather conditions. You've mastered its controls and no longer hesitate to use them as needed, immediately and with precision. These, the fundamentals of motorcycle dynamics, have become your tools. And in order to become competent, you've learned much about rider dynamics as well. That is, you've learned how and why riders behave as they do, in response to whatever the environment throws at them.

It's not surprising that you are now a confident rider. You've earned it in the most honest manner possible—through intelligent effort and experience, and by surviving.

A. Belief rather than fact

Now what confront you are some realities that will probably undermine that sense of confidence you worked so hard to achieve. For example,

- Despite the 50,000 or even 100,000 miles of two-wheel experience you've amassed, you know others who have two or three times as much experience riding motorcycles;

- Despite how fun and thrilling the motorcycling experience has been, the "edge" has worn off; and though you still greatly enjoy the experience, you know there just has to be more to it than you've experienced so far; and

- Despite all the hours and hard work you've put into developing your skills, you simply are not the best—at any of them.

The result: you decide to "test your limits" again, just as you did to grow your skills from those of a newbie to those of a competent rider. This is when your confidence can kill you.

Your confidence is based on a **belief** that you can handle whatever happens to you out there, not on that fact. The experiences you've already had are broad and hugely varied, no doubt. Few of them were so unique that you'll likely never encounter them again. But no matter how many threatening situations you've encountered so far, there are others out there waiting to test you. Some of them could still be beyond you.

It's entirely proper for you to have confidence about your abilities and those of your motorcycle to deal with the vast majority of the threats that you will encounter in the future; but since you haven't been tested with everything that can happen, some of that confidence may be over-confidence. A

belief that you can handle a situation is a far cry from **knowing** that you can. Being able consistently to develop a deceleration rate of 0.8g's during parking lot practice on a pristine surface is good evidence that you can do the same on a highway at speed, and maintaining that ability is ample reason to be confident. But developing a 0.8g deceleration rate on a parking lot does not mean you should believe that you will automatically be able to develop a 0.9g deceleration rate in an emergency situation, if it's required.

It's entirely appropriate to have confidence in your ability to do again what you've done many times in the past, but it's sophistry of the most dangerous kind to have confidence based on belief rather than fact.

B. Survival is a better goal than a gauge

Admit it…you've survived a few situations that could have gone either way. In a number of circumstances, there was an element of luck involved in the outcome.

If you have determined that you are a competent rider based only on the fact that you've survived every threat you've encountered so far, you're using it as a gauge of success, much like the pilots who claim that "any landing you can walk away from is a good landing." Not true!

The appropriate gauge of success is the extent to which **you** managed to **control** the outcome. Survival is the objective, not the gauge.

A competent rider never loses control of his motorcycle or himself. As a result, he's never the cause of an accident.

Some events, however, are entirely beyond the rider's control. Those events must be avoided, if at all possible. If you have avoided an unreasonably dangerous situation, you have controlled the outcome. To believe that you are "lucky" because you have survived threats that could have gone either way is irrational. There's no such thing as "good luck" or "bad luck"; there's only randomness in the outcome.

The fact that you have survived those threat encounters means that you are still able to read this book; and that, in turn, indicates that the coin has always turned up "heads" when you needed it to.

But if you conclude from that happenstance that the next time you flip the coin, it has higher odds of turning up on the survival side, you're just denying reality.

It isn't luck that convinces you to avoid an unreasonably dangerous behavior; it's intelligence. But a history of successful outcomes when you've been confronted with threats that are out of your control strongly encourages the development of what you feel as confidence.

In reality, that feeling is properly called over-confidence. By definition, when the outcome of encountering a threat depends on luck, your odds of surviving it are random.

More to the point, no matter how often you've survived in the past, your odds of surviving the next such threat are no different than your odds were on the first such encounter.

C. Your guard may go down

The consequence of confusing confidence (based on demonstrated and practiced skills) with over-confidence (based on the belief that you can do something, and not demonstrated) is a general lowering of your guard against failure.

Rather than avoiding certain behaviors that at an earlier time you considered to be an obviously unreasonable danger, you willingly entertain those behaviors now, because those risks no longer appear unreasonable to you. Psychological studies show that most people are over-confident about their own relative abilities and unreasonably optimistic about their futures. In fact, most people think they're "above-average."[7] Couple that thought with the desire to reestablish a little more of the thrill and zest you used to experience as a newbie motorcyclist, and you can find yourself pushing limits that have random outcomes you **hope** will be lucky ones. It only takes a single failure of judgment or skill—for the coin to come up "tails" when you flip it—to end your riding career.

This discussion may seem to imply that being confident, as a result of knowing you have handled a situation, is entirely proper, while being over-confident, because you only believe you can handle a situation, is entirely inappropriate and dangerous. But that's not at all the intended message. Being willing to take on an **unfamiliar** situation is largely the result of confidence; but it's often hard to distinguish whether that confidence properly reflects your abilities or not.

Believing that you can handle an unfamiliar situation because it's similar in many ways to situations you've successfully

---

[7] Pallier, Gerry, et al. *"The role of individual differences in the accuracy of confidence judgments."* The Journal of General Psychology 129.3 (2002), p. 257.

handled in the past **is** reasonable. The consequence of your trying to do so will likely be success. You are, after all, not guessing about it, and you have a significant amount of experience and skills working for you.

Where over-confidence can kill you on a motorcycle is when you believe that you can handle **an unfamiliar situation that is not at all similar** to previously encountered situations. In that case, believing you can handle it isn't far from wishful thinking—foolish and irrational.

Even more foolish is purposely to place yourself in the path of unfamiliar threats just to see if you can handle them.

VI. Self-induced new threats

When you were a newbie, you probably rode a small to mid-sized motorcycle. It was adequate to support the kind of riding you did as you learned your skills and gathered the experience you have now. More than likely, you've now come to believe that your first street-legal motorcycle isn't quite powerful enough, or not dressed properly, or lacks the performance reputation that fits your self-image and desires.

Also, while you were a newbie, your typical range on a day ride was probably somewhere between 10 and 30 miles on the road (or a parking lot). Now that you're a competent rider, your typical range for a day trip is more likely somewhere between 50 and 200 miles. A 200-mile ride may not be exhausting, but when you've completed it, you're tired. In fact, it probably takes you most of the next day to recover from it fully. Though your endurance is adequate for this distance, you wonder if it's what it "should be", given that you might want to do some touring in the future—especially if you're aware that some tour riders cover 350 to 400 miles a day or more, often for several days in a row.

Perhaps the time and effort you've spent during your parking lot practice sessions and on your short day trips hasn't prepared you to handle twisties, depending on where you live and the kinds of roads in your area; or you don't take tight turns with the finesse and speed your friends demonstrate on the street. Maybe it's time, you think, to take on some advanced or performance training.

Another thought that might cross your mind is that you're not as skilled as some of your buddies, and some improvements are in order. You achieve a deceleration rate of 0.8g's consistently, which helped qualify you as a competent rider; but if you could only consistently achieve a deceleration rate of 0.9g's, you'd be closer to "world-class". What all of these thoughts suggest is that, beyond being willing to take on unfamiliar but commonly encountered threats during your rides, you're now willing to put some self-induced threats into the mix.

Before you read on, understand that if he decides to accept any of the following self-induced new threats, <u>**a competent rider automatically becomes a newbie again**</u>.

The learning curve may be shorter, of course, but recall that a newbie usually is injured or dies as a result of mistakes made from a lack of knowledge or skills. The changes you're contemplating mean that right now you lack both.

A. More powerful and faster motorcycles

For several decades, the MSF has tried to convey a belief that motorcycle injuries and deaths were in essence the sole result of either rider error or the behavior of others.

The one possible cause that its management steadfastly refuses to acknowledge is the motorcycle itself. Since the MSF is an organization that's owned by and exists, according to its legal status, only to serve the interests of its sponsoring motorcycle manufacturers, that's not surprising.

Those manufacturers, however, have produced machines with vastly more torque and horsepower per weight than ever before. They make machines with shorter wheelbases and higher centers of gravity to facilitate stunting, as well as machines that can easily exceed speeds in excess of twice the legal speed limit on any road in the United States. It's inescapable to conclude that some motorcyclists die each year as a direct result of the motorcycle they were riding, and only secondarily because of rider errors. (Though it would be fair to claim that the precipitating cause of such accidents was rider error in choosing to ride an inappropriate motorcycle in the first place.)

There's no safety rational to justify the legality of "bullet bikes" on U.S. public roads. There's no safety rational to justify the legality of motorcycles that are built for the purpose of performing stunts on U.S. public roads. And there's no safety rational for denying that some motorcycle designs should be blamed for causing certain motorcyclist deaths.

The moment you throw a leg over the saddle of a bike with which you are unfamiliar, even if it's a good fit for you in all reasonable ways, you cease to be a competent rider and become, instead, a newbie.

B. 1,000 miles in 24 hours

Touring the country on two wheels is a pleasure. Seeing the sights, meeting the locals, experiencing the diversity of cultures that exist only a few hundred miles away from where you normally hang your hat—these are part of what "quality of life" means to those of us who regularly hit the roads to tour on our motorcycles.

Note that most of those things require that you actually get off your motorcycle from time to time. But there are people who **really** put mileage on their motorcycles, in as little time as possible—and who honestly feel as if that's what constitutes "quality of life" for them. Some do both kinds of long distance riding.

This discussion may read like a slam at one of those kinds of people. It's merely a reflection of the authors' biases and an attempt to put into perspective some sobering realities about traveling long distances, with the hope that the reader will at least know what he's facing if he decides to participate in one of these races or endurance riding events.

Automobile drivers tend to average about 60 MPH on long trips, while motorcyclists tend to average about 45 MPH, even though both kinds of vehicles are actually moving in excess of 70 MPH much of the time. Note that this average speed includes all the time the drivers or riders are actually trying to make progress going from one place to another, as well as pit stops of all kinds. What it does not include is the time from the last stop of the day until they resume their travels the next day (i.e., while they are resting).

In other words, if a motorcyclist wants to average 600 miles per day on a multi-day trip, it's quite likely that he will be riding more than 13 hours each day. In the case of a 700-mile day, it will be more like 16 hours. If he has any weather problems or unfavorable road conditions to deal with, it's possible to take upwards of 20 hours to do 700 miles in a single day, even riding at highway speed.

It turns out that most experienced riders can do a 13-hour day fairly easily, while very few of them could do 20 hours (or even 16). But after a few 13-hour days, a rider will be exhausted. Indeed, studies have shown that even experienced long distance riders find that after the second day of riding, their endurance begins to fail. They're only able to accomplish about 65% as long a ride on their seventh day as they averaged during their first two days. It's a matter of both physical and mental endurance.

Even the driver of a cage is essentially a passenger, compared to a motorcyclist. It's not unfair to argue that one actually rides in a car and "drives" a motorcycle. And it takes far more skill and alertness to handle a motorcycle. After 16 hours of riding, alertness is history for most riders.

As to physical endurance, for anyone contemplating a **long** tour in a short time, this is a useful tip: if you can allow your elbows to droop while you ride, you'll find that your wrists and forearms won't be nearly as sore or tired as they would be otherwise. If, however, your bike is designed so that you must lean forward over the tank and essentially straight-arm the grips, you'll have fatigue problems early on in your trip.

Still, at least for the first day or two, this pace can be accomplished. Many riders have done it, enjoyed it, and lived to tell others about it.

But this discussion is for those who have not done it and who are considering their first long trip. For the inexperienced, it's better to arrange your itinerary so that you average something closer to 350-400 miles per day rather than 600.

Further, it's wise to make the early days of a road trip the longer ones. Besides being easier and safer for all concerned, this pace assumes that you'll want to spend time in new places farther away from home than those you can reach when you take a day trip. Traveling fewer miles after you've ridden the first two days gives you plenty of time to visit the sights you came to see and to meet the locals if you wish.

There's an award that's well known among touring motorcyclists called the "Iron Butt Award" (some call it the "Lead Butt Award"). This award is given to a rider by the Iron Butt Association® in exchange for proof that a rider has traveled 1,000 miles in any one 24-hour period. The association claims that it's "dedicated to safe, long-distance motorcycle endurance riding", and it sets out rules for its 50,000-plus members. Though it doesn't operate as a formal "club", it does sponsor a number of rallies and other events that provide recognition to those who complete its rides, of which the Iron Butt Award is arguably the most conservative.

The Iron Butt Association® is actually a very safety-oriented group. They preach the good word, and they do all that they can to encourage safe practices during the rides. They strongly advocate proper conditioning of the riders, proper attention to the mechanical condition of their motorcycles, respect for speed laws, etc. They even make available valuable tips for everyone who might want to do some long distance rides.

Unfortunately, because some people can handle riding 1,000 miles in 24 hours doesn't mean that most can. Like racing a motorcycle on the public roads, these events are highly problematic and in some states probably illegal. To a rider concerned about safety and survival, these events should be avoided like road rash.

In a group of riders focused on safety, there's nothing macho about flashing such an award around. Rather, it's like being proud about having done something stupid. Certainly this doesn't mean that everyone who has earned such an award is stupid. Those who have done so aren't necessarily mentally deficient, by any means. Most riders, as well as non-riders, have done more than a few stupid things in their lives, but that doesn't mean they're necessarily dumb. However, for the majority of motorcyclists, doing 1,000 miles or more (1,500 miles for the "Bun Burner Gold") in 24 hours is.

Not long ago, some experienced riders laid out a tour that covered 23 states in 21 days. It averaged about 350 miles per day. Most riders can't imagine wanting to even see a motorcycle for a week after finishing such a tour. So, for many reasons, few riders will ever actually take a tour like that, but it satisfies the curiosity to know it can be done by some.

Certainly, many experienced riders can handle a number of such long days in a row just fine. Though few can finish even one 1,000-mile day safely despite months of preparation and training, most who start one of these runs manage at least to survive trying it.

To ride 1,000 miles in 24 hours, you have to average only about 42 MPH (including pit stops). Some people who want to earn an Iron Butt Award even go to extraordinary efforts to increase their average speeds, including, for example, cutting the number of pit stops they would normally need by about half by carrying additional fuel with them in auxiliary tanks. If somehow you could legally drive at 100 MPH, and if neither you nor your motorcycle were forced to make any stops, then you could earn the award in only 10 hours. But the reality is that you will average closer to 50 MPH if you try it. That means about 20 hours.

Nobody is sufficiently alert after riding their motorcycle for 20 hours to constitute being other than a hazard to themselves and those around them on the public roads.

Anecdotal evidence bears this out: it was reported that the "winner" of the 1999 Iron Butt run was hallucinating towards the end of his ride.

Though no doubt it's a rush to accomplish this feat, that's not the same as saying it is worthwhile—or safe to try. Truckers have laws that proscribe the number of hours and miles they can legally drive on the highways. Wonder why?

Many experienced riders have done their share of long days while touring, sometimes over 600 miles in a single day, usually because of unforeseen difficulties earlier in their route, such as weather delays and hard-to-change deadlines. But despite decades of experience preceding that effort, they often report that they were not sufficiently alert towards the end to constitute being other than a moving hazard. Though they felt a sense of pride in having accomplished that effort (actually, at the time, in having survived it), in retrospect they admit that it wasn't very smart, nor was it safe.

If, for whatever reason, you get yourself involved in an accident while trying to earn an Iron Butt Award, you will have no excuse if somebody (other than you) dies as a result. Pride in the "accomplishment" quickly turns to life-long guilt. The reality is that many motorcyclists can't safely do even 350 miles in a single 24-hour period!

A competent rider knows his endurance limits and doesn't push them excessively to win the approval of others.

If it's imperative for someone to reach 1,000 miles (or more) in 24 hours, then it should be done in a controlled environment. Why not rent a race track?

C. Advanced or performance training

Over the past several years, more and more courses offering advanced or performance-oriented training have become available. Young riders who are willing to take on more risk, in particular, feel an increasing interest in "Track Days"—classes offering to teach riders how to handle a motorcycle near its (and their) limits away from our public roads on a relatively safe race track.

In MOTORCYCLE SAFETY AND DYNAMICS, Volume One, the advice was aimed at relatively new riders. Here, it's assumed that you are no longer new to riding and are, in fact, skillful and experienced enough to have become competent, including competent enough at the basics to take such a class if you wish to. You should understand the caveats, however.

Because we have failed to endorse or to encourage riders to participate in these alternative riding courses, it's been claimed that we deliberately discourage rider skill growth in this direction and oppose riders learning advanced techniques. That has been exactly our intention.

To be perfectly clear, we have very high regard for many of the advanced and performance-oriented courses, for the skills and techniques taught by them, for their instructors, and even for most of their students. What we oppose from a safety perspective is any suggestion that these courses prepare motorcyclists to become better **street** riders. The notion that they will increase their odds of surviving riding motorcycles on our public roads based on what they learn during these classes is simply false.

To the contrary, learning how to handle your motorcycle at speeds of 100 MPH or greater, how to hang off your motorcycle, or how to pick your "best" line through a curve encourages unsafe behavior on our public roads, and illegal behavior at that.

Apparently the DOT's National Highway Transportation Safety Association has a similar opinion:[8]

> Another way driver education can worsen the problem is through courses that unintentionally encourage risky driving. Specifically, courses that teach advanced driving maneuvers can produce adverse outcomes. These courses are currently very popular in the United States as a way to supplement basic driver education. The courses are generally taught by police or in advanced driving schools using test track facilities. **Several studies, however, have shown that young people, particularly males, who take these courses are more likely than comparable drivers without such training to be in crashes** (Jones, 1993; Glad, 1988; Katila et al., 1995). It is not entirely clear why this occurs, but it is clear that superior skills do not necessarily translate to superior driving records and in fact may result in more crashes. Highly trained and experienced racecar drivers, for example, have been found to have worse crash records than run-of-the-mill drivers, adjusting for age, gender, and mileage (Williams & ONeill, 1982). **Advanced skills can translate to overconfidence and risk-taking.** For young drivers, the immaturity factor, involving decision-making and peer influences, may also contribute. Young people may create extra opportunities to try out the advanced maneuvers, showing off for their friends. This is an example of how skills learned through driver education can interact with developmental and lifestyle factors typical of young people and produce unintended results. (emphasis added)

Look at just the three conclusions drawn here more closely. There isn't a road in the United States where it's legal or safe to ride at speeds of 100 MPH or greater. Only a motorcycle in top mechanical condition has even a reasonable chance of surviving the effort, assuming the rider is also in top physical condition, the roadway is free of all defects, the weather is clear, there's no traffic, and the rider **knows** with certainty that there are no blind curves (actually, curves of any kind) ahead. A police officer who happens to observe this effort or who captures the rider's speed with his radar equipment will not be in the least bit sympathetic that the rider learned how to handle his motorcycle at such speeds in a well-regarded class run by people who hoped that he would become a safer rider as a result of their training.

Hanging off a motorcycle is a technique taught by some as a way to "smoothly" and "properly" handle curves and as an advanced skill that will help avoid dragging a peg in a fast curve—plus, it looks so cool. What that really translates into is how to increase your odds of making it through a curve at **illegal speeds**. There isn't a speed-limited road in this country that requires you to lean your bike more than 20 degrees (closer to 15 degrees) when you are riding **at** the posted speed. No body lean is required to negotiate **any** speed-marked curve in the country <u>at legal speeds</u>. You may look cool when your knee is reaching for the ground in a turn, but you won't look quite so cool in a hospital bed; and your body will definitely be cold on a slab in a morgue.

Picking the best line in a curve is a racing performance objective. Usually, the smoothest line through a curve is the one that requires the least steering correction through the turn, because that line is the least destabilizing and requires the least lean angle.

A safer line can often be chosen, such as one known alternatively as one requiring a "late apex" or "late entry", but both of those safer lines require more aggressive steering inputs and steeper lean angles than the smoothest line. Selecting a line through multiple consecutive curves is certainly an ad-

---

[8] From NHTSA, *Feasibility Study on Evaluating Driver Education Curriculum* (2009). DOT HS 811 108.

vanced technique, but selecting it to maximize your speed through those curves is anything but safety-oriented. And in fact, at any legal speeds on speed-marked curves, a rider can choose virtually any path (line) through it without requiring any aggressive steering inputs.

Not encouraging riders to get "advanced" or "performance" training or to participate in "track days" stems from the fact that these courses and events lead some participants, particularly those who are dumb, stupid, naive, immature, foolish, and / or crazy (of whom the population of said participants is greater than zero) to over-confidence and risk-taking on public roads that can, in turn, **kill** and injure riders.

A competent rider learns to control his motorcycle, no matter what, and he learns to control himself.

This is how you improve your odds. The rest is putting your toes over the edge—for fun or thrills, not for survival.

D. Efforts to improve and compete

The only person with whom it makes sense to compete, with respect to your motorcycle usage, is you. You can compare your prior performance in a skill with your best effort from the past, and there's merit in the comparison. You decide, not your buddies, what skill level is appropriate for you to achieve and maintain. No matter how good you are with a particular skill, however, there will always be others who are either already better, or who will soon be.

That's not defeatist in any way; it's a statement of fact. Even if you happen to find yourself being the very best, that status marks you and your accomplishment as a target for others. Unless you are a professional motorcycle rider, working on a course with special protection, a never-ending effort to improve without limit is both unreasonable and dangerous.

1. Road (street) racing

This section could be called "testing limits" instead of focusing on racing. Consider this advice: the MSF properly highlights the need to prepare for your rides. It goes so far as to describe three elements that need to be prepared:

- Your mind,
- Your body, and
- Your motorcycle.

It then advises that a motorcyclist should know and ride within his limits.

And, again, it lists three such limits:

- Your skills,
- Your motorcycle, and
- Your environment.

While that's correct in principle, a rider should to go farther and consider how this advice relates to the real world.

The intention of this advice is spot on, from a safety point of view, but look at it from other perspectives. For example, before you learned to ride, your motorcycle skills were totally limited. Following that advice to the letter would preclude ever taking a motorcycle rider class.

To grow, by definition, one must test (at least stress) limits. That does not mean "stepping over the line". Rather, it means putting your **toes** over that line. To acquire great skill at anything involves a process of pushing the limit line farther and farther ahead of you. Push it too fast, and you might not survive for the next lesson.

Next, the three limits described are not isolated or well defined absolutes. You may be able to scrape your pegs on a certain curve, using a familiar motorcycle, but change the motorcycle or try it on an unfamiliar curve, and your skill limit is probably breached. Said differently, limits are interdependent, not independent.

Because these limits are all functions of each other, a rational person who wants to grow (stretch his limits) must control all those that he's not trying to stretch. One does not, for example, decide to see how far over he can lean in a curve by mounting an unfamiliar motorcycle and aiming it at a blind curve that he has never ridden on before.

Learning to ride motorcycles in the MSF Basic Rider Course is an excellent example of this. The RiderCoaches provide motorcycles of a known quality, on a range of known quality, with instructors of a known quality, using a known and well tested curriculum. The only variable is the individual student's experience. Those students, in turn, are expected to grow their personal skill limits. But motorcycle and environmental limits are not allowed to change. This makes enormous sense.

While motorcyclists must know their own skill limits, the limits of their motorcycles, and the limits of their riding environment, until a rider personally feels that he's "good enough" to satisfy whatever personal needs he has, he should feel free to put his toes over **one** limit at a time, in order to grow.

And to think that there are only three limits to be concerned about is silly. At least one more limit is profoundly important: the **law**.

This section is called road racing, not limits. So what's the message here?

One local rider we know has exceptionally fine motorcycle skills; his motorcycle is of the highest quality and is well maintained; and he tends to ride on the best surfaces possible (meaning, among other things, that he avoids rain when he rides). This man routinely challenges himself, his motorcycle, and his environment **all at the same time**! And, almost by definition, he challenges the law while challenging all the rest of those limits. He considers himself to be a road racer.

And he's not alone. He travels with and **competes against** half a dozen other road racers. This activity always takes place on public roads, often roads he has never ridden before, and always in uncontrolled conditions. He always rides well in excess of posted speed limits. Sometimes he swaps motorcycles with a buddy to see how another bike "feels". And occasionally, he does this after consuming a beer or two.

Because a rider's limits include at least self, motorcycle, environment, and law (and because it makes sense when testing one's limits to test only one limit at a time), then you have to wonder how this guy survives at all. Indeed, maybe you already know why so many such riders don't.

To be completely clear, consider this scenario: a group of two or more road racers takes on unfamiliar roads at speeds far in excess of the speed limit, pushing their skill limits and competing with one another. Here, the entire group is obviously testing too many limits. If someone **dies** as a result of that activity, then **everyone in the group should be charged with manslaughter**.

The only place motorcyclists should compete is on a race course. Road racing isn't "growth". It's reckless endangerment. That's a criminal act.

2. The "world class" rider's personal limits

Of course, some riders are going to become world class in terms of their riding skills. However, it should be clear that these people tend to devote their entire lives to achieving that goal. They are or want to become professional racers, or movie stuntmen, or record holders of some kind. Many of them end up crippled or dead in the effort; but some do succeed. However, striving to become "the best" involves substantial risk—usually far more than anyone other than a professional should consider.

Despite that, this doesn't mean that you shouldn't strive to become as proficient as you can at controlling your motorcycle and yourself. But a rational approach to becoming "the best that you can be" includes a realistic assessment of risk and reward, as well as consideration of the rider's own temperament.

A competent rider knows what his personal skill limits are and knows that maintaining his skills close to those limits is far more important than undertaking a never-ending effort to improve them.

The fact is that, for every human being, no matter how hard you try to get better at certain skills, you simply can't do so. Though it will vary from person to person as to which skill that may be, each and every attempt to get better at that one that pertains to you, or those several, will result in failure. It's better, by far, to maintain excellent skills than to break your confidence, or your body, or your motorcycle, in fruitless attempts to be world class if your limits are lower.

VII. Limited understanding

A new rider gets in trouble as a result of mistakes borne from a lack of knowledge or understanding. Knowing what a clutch lever does, mechanically, is inadequate to protect you from its improper usage.

A competent rider strives to increase his knowledge level far beyond the fundamentals.

Unlike a never-ending effort to advance your skill levels without limit, attaining knowledge is not dangerous and, in fact, can well reduce the danger of motorcycle riding.

There's no way to know precisely which piece of information or knowledge you pick up today will contribute to your survival in the most meaningful way in the future. What you can be sure about, however, is that accumulating knowledge is worth more than the sum of its parts.

Each piece of knowledge that you add to your stockpile fits into the other pieces already there in unexpected ways, leading to insights and a broader understanding than those individual pieces can account for.

What follows are topics that you can assimilate or not, but we believe they have sufficient value to be shared here.

As a competent rider, you probably already know at least 95% of what follows. Consider the other 5% as potentially lifesaving.

A. Weight transfer

When you change speed (accelerate or decelerate) the weight of your motorcycle (including you) shifts in such a way as to put more or less load on your tires.

You don't have to weigh the load on your tires to know this principal with certainty, because you can see and feel it happen when you brake by observing your motorcycle's front-end "dive".

Traction is proportional to the weight carried by your tires. Thus, when braking, your front tire gains traction, while the rear one loses it. Clearly losing too much traction is dangerous, since the result is that your tire will skid.

Weight transfer can be controlled beyond simply adjusting your acceleration and braking rates. That is, how fast you change speeds is not the only thing that determines weight transfer. Surely you're interested in minimizing the odds of losing traction during a panic stop?

1. The result of torque, not a shift of mass

"Weight transfer" is understood to exist and to occur whenever you accelerate or decelerate. However, why it happens and how much weight transfers—and even how fast it occurs—seems to be completely beyond most riders.

Here's an explanation of the fundamentals.

First, "weight" and "mass" are **not** the same thing. Weight is a **force**, mass is not. Weight is mass times the acceleration rate of gravity. Whenever you see the symbol "mg" it means "weight" or "mass times gravity".

Second, gravity acts through the Center of Gravity of a mass.

For those who inquire, most motorcycles are sold with the claim that their Center of Gravity (CG) is "low" by comparison. Naturally, they can't all be lower than every other motorcycle. But the reason "low" is claimed is because the lower the CG is, the more stable a motorcycle feels, and the easier it is to lean without its falling over onto its side.

Figure 33 demonstrates that when a rider's on a motorcycle, the CG shifts both upwards and toward the rear. This is because the rider sits higher than the bike's CG and behind it.

You can investigate weight transfer using realistic numbers to familiarize yourself with magnitudes. For example, assume that the motorcycle weighs 820 pounds without a rider and that the rider weighs 180 pounds. The total weight (mg) of both is 1,000 pounds.

Further, assume that the height of the CG (H) stands at about 24 inches without a rider and grows to about 33 inches with the rider. Without the rider, the CG is closer to midway between the front and rear contact patches than with the rider.

Now assume that a motorcycle has a wheelbase (WB) of 66 inches, and that the length of the front weight bias (F) is about 37 inches, while the length of the back weight bias (B) is about 29 inches. (While this is just an example, the numbers are realistic.)

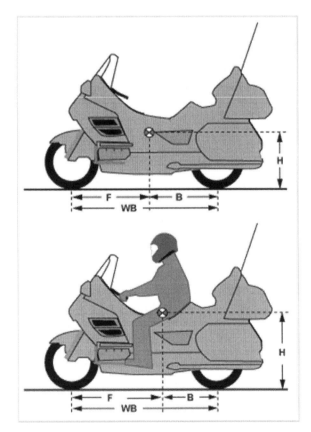

Figure 33: Effect on CG of adding a rider

This is important, because the amount of weight on each tire is determined by dividing the **alternate** weight bias by the wheelbase length and multiplying that ratio by the total weight.

Without a rider, there will be an **average** of 410 pounds on each tire; but the actual weight on each is shown below.

Front tire load =
mg * **B** / WB
820 * 29 / 66
360 pounds

Back tire load =
mg * **F** / WB
820 * 37 / 66
460 pounds

Now we add the rider. Because the CG has shifted toward the rear, the lengths of F and B change. The weight on the rear tire will be about 59% of the total, while the weight on the front tire will be only about 41% of that total.

Notice that the Front weight bias (F) has become about 39 inches instead of 37, while the Back weight bias (B) has become about 27 inches instead of 29.

Now the calculations look like this:

Front tire load =
mg * **B** / WB
1000 * 27 / 66
409 pounds

Back tire load =
mg * **F** / WB
1000 * 39 / 66
591 pounds

Adding lines of force, as shown in Figure 34, we can see that for a motionless motorcycle (one that's at rest) or for one that's moving at a constant speed, gravity pulls the motorcycle and rider down (through their CG), while the ground pushes back with an equal amount upward through the tires.

The amount of Normal force upwards is distributed so that about 40% goes through the front tire and about 60% through the rear.

Gravity is **vertical acceleration**. Here's what happens when the bike is accelerated horizontally by cranking the throttle.

The bike's speed increases in a horizontal direction, as shown in Figure 35. In fact, because its tires have traction sufficient to support it, and because some motorcycles' engines are quite powerful, it can actually accelerate at rates approaching 1.0g (a little more than 32 feet per second per second) or, of course, at a rate smaller than that.

The higher the rate of acceleration, the greater the weight transfer will be, because weight transfer is a function of the rate of acceleration and the height of the CG (H) divided by the length of the wheelbase (WB). That is, the higher the CG is, or the shorter the wheelbase, the greater the weight transfer for any given rate of acceleration.

Adding more force lines, we can explore this more closely.

Figure 35 shows that the engine produces a driving force that's felt at the rear contact patch (only) and is represented by the forward pointing arrow. The length of that arrow is an indication of how much driving force is being sent to the rear wheel. Here, it's about the same length as the length of the arrow representing gravity.

In other words, this shows what happens when you deliver the maximum acceleration force your motorcycle can handle. Resisting this driving force is an equal amount of force (essentially, inertia) that pushes toward the rear through the CG. (Forces must **always** balance).

Because the CG is higher than ground level where the driving force is being exerted, there's a natural **torque** developed

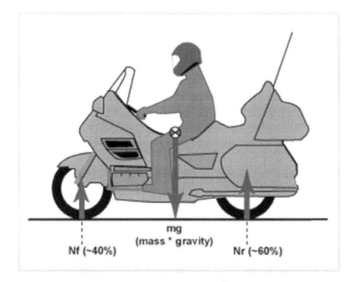

Figure 34: At-rest forces (Weight and Normal)

which tries to twist the motorcycle clockwise (in the diagrams) relative to the Center of Gravity.

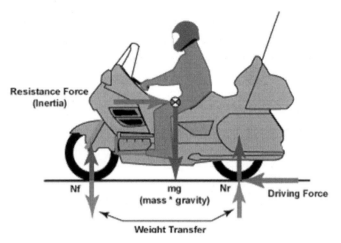

Figure 35: Moving forces (driving and resistance)

That is what causes weight on the front tire to appear to shift to the rear tire. In other words, torque accounts for weight transfer.

The downward pointing arrow at the front tire's contact patch represents, by its length, how much **less** the load is that the front tire now bears, while the lower upward pointing arrow at the rear tire's contact patch represents how much **more** load that tire now bears.

Some readers may notice that both the driving force and the resistance force are **horizontal**. How can they cause changes to the **vertical** forces on the motorcycle?

You don't need to understand "torque" to understand weight transfer. Once again we add some force lines and

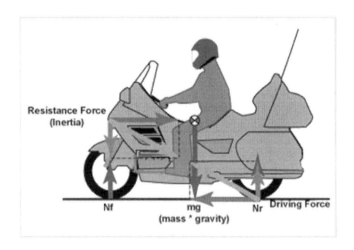

Figure 36: Vectored forces

shift others around to see why. Consider Figure 36.

Since the gravity and resistance force lines are orthogonal (meaning perpendicular to each other), it's simple to demonstrate that these forces combine via vectors into a force that points **down** and to the right.

That's what shifts weight from the front tire to the rear one.

Now, as to how much weight is transferred…

The amount of weight transfer is merely the total weight times the amount of acceleration being applied times the height of the CG, divided by the length of the wheelbase (WB). So, in this example of maximum acceleration, the total weight transfer would be as follows:

Weight transfer = mg * acceleration rate (1g) * H / WB
1000 * 1 * 33 / 66
500 pounds

The load on the front tire, if the bike accelerates at the rate of 1.0g, would be 409 pounds **less** 500 pounds, or a **minus** 91 pounds! In other words, the rider has done a backflip and ended up on the pavement with the bike on top of him!

For those of you who might think this describes a wheelie, pay attention to the fact that the bike and rider flipped over because, as the front tire comes off the ground, the CG gets higher. You've already seen that for any given amount of driving force, the higher the CG, the more weight transfer occurs. Thus, if he were only to do a wheelie, this **requires** that as the front-end comes off the ground, the rider **rolls off** the throttle, so as not to end up on his back.

But if the bike had accelerated at only 0.5g's (a respectable rate), then the total weight transfer would be 250 pounds; and the resultant load on the bike's front tire would be 159 pounds, while the rear tire would be carrying 841 pounds (591 + 250) then. No backflip, no front tire off the ground.

From these simple calculations one can see the following:

- The greater the rate of acceleration, the greater the weight transfer; and
- The higher the CG is relative to the wheelbase, the greater the weight transfer.

And how fast does it occur? **Instantaneously**. But since you can't increase your acceleration rate from zero to 1.0g instantaneously, it's **that** amount of time that determines when all the weight transfer that's going to happen actually occurs.

A final point: **braking is merely negative acceleration**. What is true about weight transfer during acceleration is equally true when braking, though the weight will shift from the rear tire to the front one.

Physics is a balancing act, after all.

2. Braking transfers

Except for wind resistance, essentially all the forces that try to slow you down when you apply your brakes are at ground level; that is, at the contact patches of your tires.

On the other hand, the inertia of your bike works not at ground level, but directly through its Center of Gravity.

Since the CG is higher than ground level, the resulting net force translates into a torque.

In other words, braking does not simply shift weight forward, it tries to shift it down in the front and up in the rear.

The higher the CG is, the greater the torque. (If the CG were at ground level, the torque would be zero.) But this is true, as well: the longer your wheelbase, the less torque is created. This is just another way of saying that the amount of weight transfer resulting from a change in speed is a function of the ratio of the height of the CG to the length of the wheelbase.

Gravity is acceleration. At ground level, gravity tries to make objects fall with an acceleration rate of about 32.2 feet per second per second (shown as ft/sec^2.) This acceleration is called "1.0g".

"Weight" is a force. Weight is how hard a mass is trying to fall to the center of the earth because of gravity. Like inertia, gravity works directly through the CG of an object.

When a rider brakes, he applies force, called a braking force. As stated previously, braking is nothing more than negative acceleration. Thus, when the total braking force is such that the bike's forward speed is being reduced at the rate of approximately 32.1 ft/sec^2, it is decelerating at the rate of 1.0g.

That is, the braking force then equals the weight of the motorcycle (including the rider).

If your motorcycle weighs 1,000 pounds, then braking at 1.0g means you are applying 1,000 pounds of braking force.

You can calculate the amount of weight transfer involved in any stop knowing only the braking force being used and the ratio of CG height to wheelbase length.

For example, assume that the total braking force is 1,000 pounds, that your CG is 20 inches above the ground, and that your wheelbase is 63.4 inches long. Then,

> Weight Transfer = Braking Force times CG ratio
> Weight Transfer = 1000 lbs. * 20/63.4
> Weight Transfer = 1000 lbs. * .3155
> Weight Transfer = 315.5 lbs.

[This discounts entirely the effects caused by tire distortion and suspension compression; not because these aren't important, but because they are of secondary importance in understanding these principles.]

Now, just because the bike weighs 1,000 pounds and is sitting on two wheels, that doesn't mean that at rest, there are 500 pounds on each wheel. How is the weight distributed?

Here again we need to know something about the bike's CG. Only if the CG is exactly in the middle of the bike (between the front and rear contact patches) will the weight be evenly distributed. If the CG is closer to the front wheel than the rear one, for example, then there will be more weight on the front tire than on the rear when the bike's at rest. Further, unless there's an upward or downward movement of the bike, it's obvious that the sum of the weight carried by the front and rear tires must equal the total weight of the motorcycle and rider.

Assume that when the bike's at rest, the weight is evenly distributed. While the 1,000-pound bike is braking at 1.0g, because of weight transfer, there will be 815.5 lbs. (500 + 315.5) on the front tire and only 184.5 lbs. (500 - 315.5) on the rear tire. Since traction is a function of the weight carried by a tire, clearly there's not a lot of traction left on the rear tire at this time.

Look very carefully at what this weight transfer example means. You have probably heard that about 70% of your stopping power is in the front brake. This example shows that we have applied 1,000 pounds of braking power to the tires of the bike. If it were **all** the result of using only the front brake, then we have wasted what traction is still available to us from the rear tire. Worse, we have locked our front tire and started a skid, because virtually all standard tires lose their "sticktion" (stick / friction) when confronted with more than about 1.1g of braking force.

With 815.5 pounds on the front tire, a rider could expect that tire to handle a braking force of 897 pounds (1.1 * 815.5) with reasonable confidence; yet here he applied 1,000 pounds to it.

In this case, the front brakes could deliver nearly 90% of the bike's stopping power, not just 70%. But not 100%, either.

Now let's look at what would happen if the CG happened to be 30 inches high rather than 20:

> Weight Transfer = Braking Force times CG ratio
> Weight Transfer = 1000 lbs. * 30/63.4
> Weight Transfer = 1000 lbs. * .4732
> Weight Transfer = 473.2 lbs.

Now the front tire would have 973.2 pounds of weight on it and the rear would have only 26.8 pounds. This is close to doing a "stoppie"!

What you should notice is that if the CG gets to a height of half the length of the wheelbase, you can expect to do a "stoppie" if you use 1.0g of braking force.

Further, if you use even the slightest amount of rear brake in such a configuration when you're slowing at the rate of 1.0g, you can expect to lock the rear wheel.

One more example: this time the rider will attempt a 1.1g stop with this taller bike:

> Weight Transfer = Braking Force times CG ratio
> Weight Transfer = 1100 lbs. * 30/63.4
> Weight Transfer = 1100 lbs. * .4732
> Weight Transfer = 520.5 lbs.

At this point he's transferred **more** than the entire weight which had been on the rear wheel—he's left the rear wheel with a **negative** 20.5 pounds on it. I.e., the rear wheel has been lifted off the ground!

Notice that the CG does **not** remain at a constant height during aggressive braking. If a rider uses the front brake exclusively, then the front-end will dive and the rear-end will lift. This **could** result in the CG remaining at the same height, but **more likely it will get higher**.

You've already seen that a higher CG means more weight transfer. Further, as the front-end dives, the result of the compression of the front shocks is to shorten the bike's wheelbase. Like raising the CG, this results in a higher CG to wheelbase ratio, and therefore more weight transfer.

[As an aside, if your bike has an anti-dive feature (TRAC, for example), then **more** weight transfer occurs to the front wheel than without it, because that feature keeps the CG higher. In other words, an anti-dive feature **increases** the odds of skidding your rear tire!]

If only the rear brake is used, there will be a weight transfer to the front tire, which will tend to compress the shocks. Additionally, however, use of only the rear brake tends to **lower** the rear-end of your motorcycle and lengthens its wheelbase: the swing arm becomes more level. The net effect is to lower the CG of the bike. This offsets neatly the fact that the compressing front-end shortens the wheelbase at the same time.

Since there's a weight transfer, however, the rear-end gets lighter while braking. This quickly limits how much braking power you can apply before you skid that tire. In other words, you must use the front brake, too, for maximum stopping power.

From this discussion, you can now see that the use of your rear brake along with the front brake can result in less weight transfer than if you use only the front brake. This is why using both brakes at the same time always results in maximum stopping power.

When a rider mounts his motorcycle, he both raises the CG and moves it towards the rear. The heavier the rider, the more significant this change to the CG will be. You've seen that as the CG rises, it causes more weight transfer during speed changes. Raising the CG is far more significant than its shift towards the rear, because the height of the CG is a small distance compared to the length of the wheelbase.

What this means is that the heavier the rider, the easier it is to cause a breakaway of the bike's rear-end while braking.

Is there anything that can be done to mitigate this potentially deadly problem? You bet! In an emergency stop, the driver should bend from the hips, pull his elbows in, and lean forward! This will cause the CG to lower and move forward. Lowering the CG is more significant than its slight movement forward when the rider moves in this way.

In summary, there will be less weight transfer with the rider leaning forward than if he were sitting straight up in the saddle; for there will be less compression of the front shocks and less shortening of the wheelbase. In other words, this means it's less likely that he will lose rear-end traction.

Can you conclude anything else from this discussion? Yes. Always pack your saddlebags with heavy items towards the bottom. Every pound below the CG lowers it, while every pound above it raises it.

3. Accelerating transfers – in a straight line

We've focused so far only on weight transfer associated with braking. It should be obvious that exactly the same phenomenon happens when you accelerate; the amount of weight transfer is determined by your rate of acceleration and the Weight Transfer ratio (height of CG divided by length of wheelbase).

Though you may not believe that you have an "anti-dive" component for your rear wheel like the one in the front, you do. The rear wheel does not push the frame forward directly. It pushes its "swing arm" forward. Since the swing arm pivots on the frame behind your CG, and since that pivot's almost invariably higher than where the swing arm attaches to the rear wheel, an accelerating force applied through the rear wheel tries to lift the frame of the motorcycle.

Rather than calling this an "anti-dive", think of it as an "anti-squat." This keeps the CG higher than it would be otherwise and the result is that there's greater weight transfer to the rear tire (which results in correspondingly higher traction).

4. Accelerating transfers - in a curve

What about weight transfers when you are in a curve?

You've probably heard the terms "over-steer" and "under-steer". Over-steer means that when you're in a curve, your rear wheel's more likely than the front one to lose traction (i.e., your sliding bike will end up pointing towards the inside of the curve). Under-steer is the opposite. Weight transfer to the rear tire from acceleration leads to over-steer (creating a greater slip angle on the rear tire).

Braking in a curve, because of weight transfer to the front, leads to under-steer (creating a greater slip angle on the front tire). Both are deadly concerns if you push tire loads to their limits! If you have a choice, you would almost certainly want a little over-steer rather than under-steer, because a brief slide of the rear tire is easier to correct than a similarly brief slide of the front tire.

It would be a deadly mistake to try to use the kind of weight transfer analysis we have discussed so far in an effort to learn how much acceleration to use while **in a curve** to equalize tire loads!

These weight transfer calculations have dealt with the consequences of longitudinal acceleration—that is, while traveling in a straight line. In a curve, you are also subject to **lateral acceleration**, even if maintaining constant speed. This is felt as centrifugal force.

Unlike longitudinal acceleration, which changes your tire loading in a simple proportion to the Weight Transfer ratio, lateral acceleration increases tire load in proportion to the **square** of your change in speed. The formula to determine this force is:

Force = Mass times Velocity squared divided by Radius
($F = M*V^2/R$)

You can assume that most street tires will lose traction when they are subjected to about 1.1g's of force. So how can you tell whether you are close to 1.1g when in a turn?

Simple. If your effective lean angle is 45 degrees, you are experiencing 1.0g of lateral force. From the formula shown above, you can see that this force is **extremely sensitive** to velocity. A tiny increase in speed could easily push you past the 1.1g limit. This means that using acceleration (speed change) to balance tire loads while in a curve is foolish.

It's true that, in general, you'll want some **minor**—minor!—acceleration in a curve, as this recovers the actual speed lost as a result of cornering; and it makes the bike feel "planted" in the turn. On a closed track, racers may wish to attempt to maximize speed coming out of a turn with aggressive acceleration, but that's inappropriate on public roads.

On public roads, your objective should be to minimize both braking and acceleration while in a turn, in order to maintain your bike's stability. Practically speaking, there's really no difference in the bike's stability whether you maintain a constant speed or you decide to accelerate **modestly** through a turn when riding at legal speeds. This is why you want to be sure the load distribution on your bike is set properly **before** you hit the road.

5. Accelerating transfers - exiting a curve

While modestly increasing your speed or keeping it essentially constant makes sense while you are riding through most of a curve, some people find great pleasure in rolling on their throttle as they exit one.

The previous discussion should convince you that you must be conservative in this practice while you are leaned over hard, and that you need to be widening the curve and standing the bike taller **at the same time** you do this.

You can see the effects of weight transfer instead of doing the calculations. Take a look at the output from this Excel spreadsheet Lean Angle Calculator model.

You can find the model itself at www.msgroup.org to download at no charge. A complete list and description of the spreadsheet models available to you from our website is provided in Section G below.

With the Lean Angle Calculator model, you can modify any of the inputs shown and observe the effect of the changes.

Figure 37 is a sample of the screen displayed while using the model.

This example shows a fully loaded motorcycle weighing 800 pounds which has a Center of Gravity closer to the rear wheel than the front wheel. It's traveling in a curve with a radius of 40 feet at a speed of 23 MPH. The information on the right side of the spreadsheet assumes constant speed.

The graph on the right shows the lateral (sideways) force divided by the vertical force (load) for each wheel as a function of acceleration.

At zero acceleration, the ratio is 0.88 and so is the lateral acceleration (i.e., it's 0.88g). Notice that the effect of acceleration is **radically** different between the front and rear tires.

At the front tire, acceleration merely reduces loading because of weight transfer. Thus, traction is diminishing in proportion to that acceleration; i.e., traction is a function of the types of material that are being pressed together and the force pressing them together.

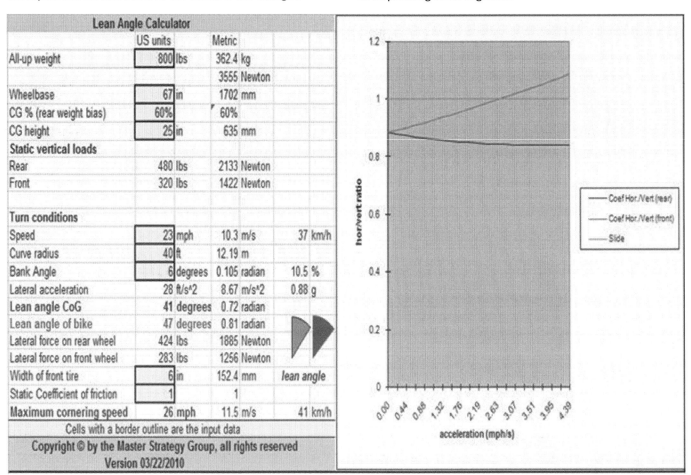

Figure 37: Lean Angle Calculator sample output

Since the load is diminishing because of weight transfer, so is the traction available to that front tire.

The effect of acceleration on the rear tire is quite different. Weight transfer resulting from acceleration increases traction on the rear tire during modest acceleration. But acceleration (increasing the bike's speed) is accomplished using the rear tire only. That is, there is no longitudinal acceleration affecting the traction of the front tire, just the rear one.

Longitudinal acceleration and lateral acceleration are vectored, which means the resulting acceleration force is the square root of the sum of the squares of those forces. (In other words, more than either of them, but not as much as the sum of both.) As the rate of acceleration increases, it quickly overwhelms the effect of increasing load (and thus traction) on the tire and **begins to consume that traction faster than it is being added**.

The lower curved line in the chart shows this effect on the rear tire, while the upper curved line shows the effect on the front tire. The front tire will lose traction first as a result of weight transfer.

So what do these lines ultimately show? If you assume that the Coefficient of Friction for your tires is approximately 1.1, then when either line reaches 1.1 on the chart, that tire will lose traction and skid! The higher the line, the closer to a skid (i.e., the less traction is left).

If you increase speed or decrease the radius of your turn, your lean angle will get larger. When your lean angle gets to 45 degrees, the lines will start at 1.0g; and even a slight acceleration will push the lines over 1.1—which means you will soon be exploring the joys of road rash.

Thus, here are the reasons to care about weight transfer:

- Traction is directly proportional to the amount of weight carried by a tire. Managing weight transfer is managing traction.

- Improperly loading your motorcycle can result in substantial handling problems, particularly in a curve.

- In order to manage weight transfer intelligently, you need to have a good idea of where the Center of Gravity is for your bike and what happens to it when you add a passenger or luggage.

- Traction will probably be lost if acceleration forces exceeds about 1.1g. If you are in a curve and are leaning at 45 degrees, you already have a 1.0g lateral acceleration force.

- Stopping with your elbows locked guarantees more weight transfer and a higher Center of Gravity. Both of these are undesirable in terms of control.

- Rolling **off** your throttle (or braking) when you are traveling a bit too fast in a curve is almost certainly more dangerous than simply leaning farther into the curve, because weight transfer will unload the rear-end, which reduces rear tire traction.

- Under-steer and over-steer both yield slides when load limits are reached. Balancing the weight reduces the risk.

B. Path traveled

When you're riding in a curve, the bike's rear tire travels a path that is inside the path of the front tire.

That means that when you are traveling at slow speeds and trying to get past an obstacle on the roadway, your front tire must provide a meaningful amount of distance between it and that obstacle, or else the rear tire will hit it. Anyone who has ridden a cone weave during PLP will recognize this issue.

When riding at any meaningful speed, a motorcycle's path of travel is far less obvious. The rider's initial impression is that the front tire defines the path and the rear tire simply follows, though it carves a path slightly inside that of the front tire. While this is true, it's not a complete or insightful understanding of the dynamics involved.

If a rider inputs a certain steering angle with his handlebar, he expects that to produce a circular path of travel that's more or less consistent between any two motorcycles he rides. But different motorcycles will travel circular paths that have dramatically different diameters, even using the same steering angle.

Leaving aside the situation where two motorcycles have different wheelbase lengths and different rake angles, which would clearly produce different travel paths, let's consider only the effect of tire slippage. In other words, this discussion will now look closely at the behavior of **the same motorcycle with different tire traction scenarios** in order to see how greatly they affect the motorcycle's path of travel in a curve.

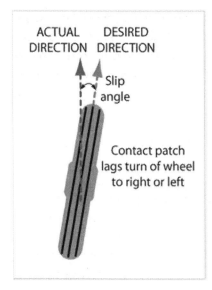

Figure 38: Slip angle

When a tire tries to change its path of travel in response to steering input, its contact patch must slip and lag, adopting the travel direction to which the tire points.

This is partly the result of the tire's sidewalls deforming and partly the result of traction resisting the change of direction. Figure 38 shows how a contact patch lags.

The amount of slippage is a function of the tire's rubber compound, the weight it's carrying, and the pressure of the air contained in the tire. Because of these variables, the amount of tire slippage experienced by the front tire is rarely identical to the amount experienced by the rear tire.

As a result, the motorcycle either over-steers or under-steers as it changes direction.

Since the vast majority of motorcycles carry somewhat more weight on their rear tires than they do on their front tires, most motorcycles exhibit over-steer characteristics.

Automobiles, on the other hand, usually exhibit under-steer characteristics for the same reason: most of the weight is carried by their front tires.

The effect of different slip angles on a motorcycle's path of travel of travel is much greater than a typical rider appreciates. For example, in Figure 39 you can see the actual paths of travel for a motorcycle's CG when in a turn **using exactly the same steering angle** in both circles.

The path with a smaller diameter results from nothing more than a shift of the weight being carried between the bike's tires toward the rear of the bike. If a rider adds cargo toward the rear or puts a passenger on the pillion, this effect increases.

The larger diameter path shows the result of the front tire's having a greater slip angle than the rear tire. This is under-steering. In the larger circle, the rear tire has less weight on it, and there's more weight on the front tire. This might occur when the rider leans forward or when he adds cargo carried in a tank bag or between the front forks. Remember, the air pressure in the tires affects this, too. This is another reason to check your air pressure frequently.

A discussion of how Figure 39 was constructed is presented at the end of this volume, along with a far more detailed explanation of this dynamic. Read it if you want to understand why it is that merely by shifting your weight toward the rear of your motorcycle, you get a much tighter turn than is available without moving that weight.

See **APPENDIX B – Path of travel.**

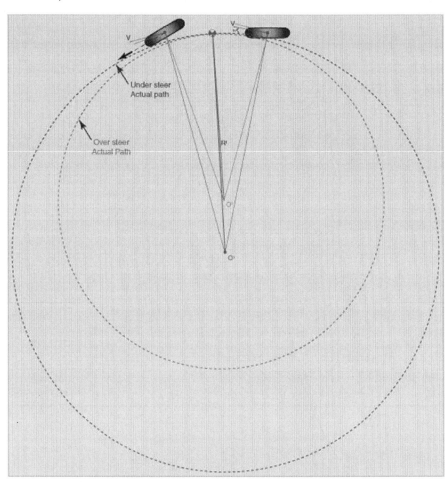

Figure 39: Under- and over-steer paths

C. Neutral steering

Motorcycle dynamics are hugely complex and difficult to quantify, let alone understand. Because they are so complex, it's generally true that even experienced riders resort to over-simplifications, short-cuts, concept-only, and abbreviated realities (snapshots in time) when describing them.

As a result, any discussion that purports to be a critical analysis of the subject is easily sidetracked with honestly held claims and counter-claims by the participants about the specifics. The following section deals with just one such dynamic: the behavior of a motorcycle while in a turn with a specific focus on steering inputs required to **maintain** a curved path. That means the discussion will focus on the part played by "counter-steering" once a bike's leaned over and already riding a given radius curve.

First, some background.

In any discussion of counter-steering, it soon becomes obvious that in order to begin a change of direction (enter a curve, for example), the rider **must** provide a steering input that involves a "negative torque" relative to the direction the rider wishes to move if traveling at speeds greater than about 10 mph. This means that if a rider wishes to cause his motorcycle to move to the **right**, he must input a **leftward** (counter-clockwise) steering torque. As a result of that negative torque, the bike will first lean to the **right** and will **then** begin changing direction to the right.

In virtually all cases, the rider **must** maintain some measure of negative torque throughout the turn in order to maintain it. That is, he must maintain a certain amount of forward pressure on the inside grip throughout the turn, or else the bike will, of its own accord, attempt to straighten itself out and abort the turn—ending up moving in a straight direction. However, there are "tuning points" where a specific speed and turning radius can result in a motorcycle that requires no steering input to maintain its path.

A very experienced (and credible) sportbike rider alleges that his bike provides "neutral steering", so that once he gets into his turns, he's able to provide **zero** steering input in order to maintain them. Indeed, he claims that he could even take his hands off the grips entirely, and the bike would continue the course that it was in before he did so.

Those two positions sound entirely impossible to reconcile, as they appear to be making diametrically opposite claims.

But is that really the case? Could both positions be valid and demonstrably correct? By the time you absorb the following discussion, you'll find that both positions are correct and can be demonstrated. They're both "concept statements" utilizing a host of assumptions and simplifications of reality, and both involve "snapshots in time".

A motorcycle's handling behavior can't be reduced to a magical number or index where the higher or lower that number is, the better the bike is. For example, a touring bike is expected to be stable at virtually any speed; yet it lacks agility. On the other hand, a sportbike must be able to be lean quickly into a turn (it must be "flickable"), particularly at higher speeds; but most sportbikes are not known for being stable while moving in a straight line (some exhibit steering head wobble). Which style of motorcycle "handles better" is a rider's personal choice.

The principal design elements in determining how a motorcycle behaves (its dynamics) include choice of tires (size, rubber compounds, profile), type of suspension, front-end (rake, trail), wheelbase length, location of its Center of Gravity, steering damper resistance, frame flexibility, shock absorber size and flexibility, and much more. Tires are **always** the first design consideration. Almost all other design decisions utilize that consideration.

People who decide to replace a motorcycle's rear tire with an automobile tire have not the slightest idea how that change effects nearly all handling characteristics of their bikes; but that's another story.

As an over-steering vehicle, generally, a bike's rear tire will have a greater slip angle than its front tire while it's in a turn. If you pass its critical speed then, the rear tire will be the one most likely to slide out from under you, leaving your bike pointed **into** the turn.

As we saw earlier, an over-steering vehicle tends to carve a tighter turn, while an under-steering vehicle tends to carve a wider turn for any given steering input.

A neutral-steering vehicle has the same slip in both the front and rear tires while in a turn; and as a result, the turn that's described is known as "ideal". One problem emerges here: the assertion by the sportbike rider that his bike has "neutral steering" does **not** mean that his front and rear tires develop the same slip angles in a turn! He means that he requires **zero** steering input to maintain a turn once it has started.

The use of an otherwise well-known and defined term like "neutral steering" to mean something other than its formal definition is at least confusing, but we know from the context of the argument what he actually means.

There are only three degrees of movement freedom for a motorcycle when traveling on a flat surface:

- Pitch (where the bike's front-end gets higher or lower than its rear-end);

- Roll (where the bike leans to the left or right); and

- Yaw (where the bike's front-end turns to the left or right relative to its rear-end).

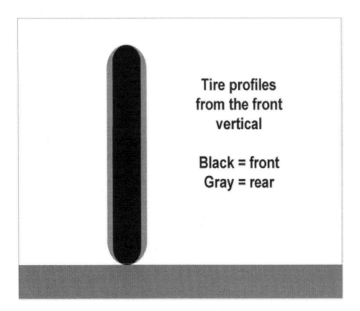

Figure 40: Tire profile

These are **not** independent of each other. For example, when a motorcycle rolls (leans) to the right, because the front tire is narrower than its rear tire, there's an automatic **yaw** of the bike **clockwise**!

Figure 40 is a graphic showing the front and rear tires of a typical bike from the front with the bike absolutely vertical and with zero steering angle. Note that the centers of the contact patches for the tires are dead center on each tire.

Now we roll (lean) the bike over to its right by 30 degrees and maintain a zero angle steering input. Observe in Figure 41 that the contact patch centers have **shifted** relative to each other as a result of the lean. Who would have believed that merely by leaning a motorcycle to its right, that motorcycle would veer to the slightly counter-clockwise, given that its steering angle remained zero? But that's a fact! By leaning it to its right, the bike automatically yaws counter-clockwise. Clearly, determining a motorcycle's dynamics (how it behaves) is not at all simple. One cannot simply assert that leaning a bike to the right results in a turn to the right.

When a bike leans to the right as a result of a counter-steering input attempting to turn the handlebar to the left, what immediately follows is an automatic turn of the front wheel to the right, because of the "restoring moment" generated by trail. As a result of that steering input, the bike begins to move in a new path—to the right of where it was pointing when the counter-steering began. So here's the problem: how do we maintain that directional change?

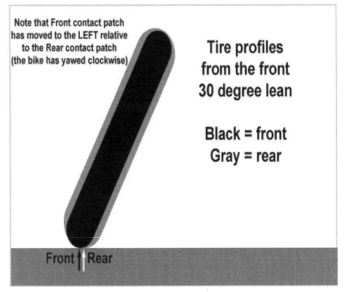

Figure 41: Profile when leaning at 30 degrees

Assume you're riding in a perfectly circular path that has a radius of 78.7 feet, as shown in Figure 42. (That size was chosen to make this easier to understand.) You may do this at an infinite number of different speeds, of course, though not faster than when a hard part firmly strikes the ground.

So how do the bike's dynamics differ when you maintain a turn radius from what happens when you just vary the speed?

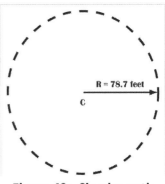

Figure 42: Circular path

We certainly know that the bike's lean angle is different. The faster you go in that turn, the greater the lean angle will be.

We also know that the faster you go in that turn, the higher the lateral (centrifugal) force will be. That, in fact, is why the lean angle is greater. But that also means that the amount of tire slippage on the front and rear tires changes (gets larger). Do they get larger in equal proportion?

It turns out, as most riders know, that the faster you go in a turn, the smaller your steering angle needs to be to result in a desired turn. At highway speeds, your steering angle never reaches a significant size, compared to parking lot practice at lower speeds.

Along with greater lean angles, greater lateral force, and greater slip angles, there's a smaller steering angle.

That means that the amount of out-tracking done by the front tire (essentially its slip angle) is **not** simply larger than it is at slower speeds. The faster you go in that turn, the **less** negative torque (forward pressure on the inside grip) is required to maintain a turn!

Indeed, based on the geometry of the front-end as well as the length of the bike's wheelbase, there can be as little as **zero** torque required to maintain that turn; and if you increase speed even more, you will begin to need a positive torque on the steering stem to maintain it.

Thus, there are tuning points for any bike where the speed and radius of a turn result in what our sportbike rider claims is "neutral steering". The vast majority of speeds used to ride that turn **require** a counter-steering pressure to maintain it.

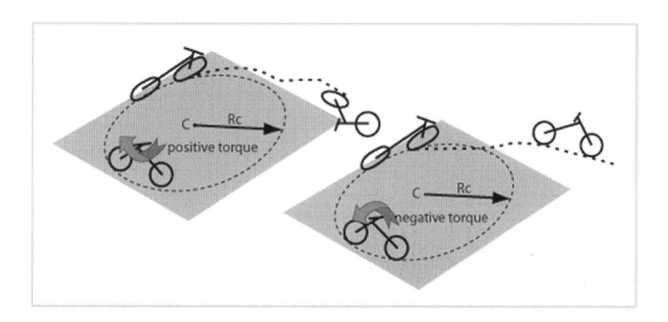

Figure 43: Positive and negative steering torque

Notice what happens to the bike's path when you remove your hands from the grips if positive torque is required or if negative torque is required. The effect of this is shown in Figure 43.

Where negative torque is required, the path suddenly gets tighter as a result of the "restoring moment", which acts as a counter-steering input to widen the path and straighten the bike up to vertical.

But in the case where a positive torque is required, removing your hands from the grips results in the path opening up. The bike becomes unstable and **falls over**.

What our sportbike rider declares is that "neutral steering" results in no change in the path of the bike if he removes his hands from the grips. Look closely at Figure 44 where we have used feet and MPH for radius and speed measurements to see why this could be true.

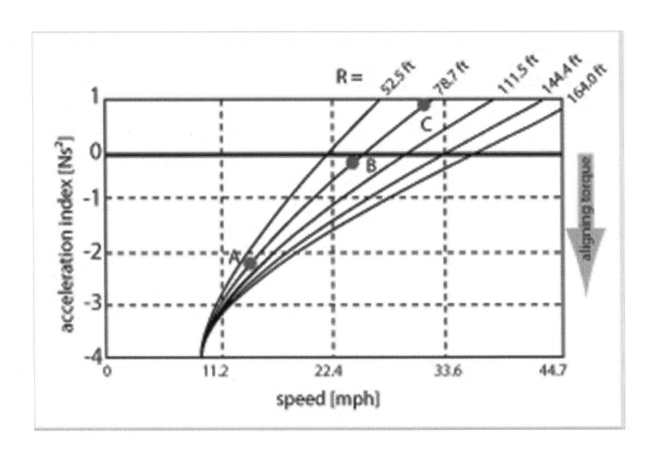

Figure 44: Acceleration indexed speed

Along the left axis is what's called the Acceleration Index. That is the amount of torque required, divided by the amount of lateral force.

When that number is negative, it means a negative steering torque is required to maintain a turn; when it is positive, a positive steering torque is required (and the bike becomes unstable if you stop providing it). Finally, if it's zero, then the bike is in what our sportbike rider claims to be a state of "neutral steering", where **no** steering torque is required to maintain the turn.

Along the bottom of the graph is the speed at which the turn is being made; and along the top we see the radius of the turn being made.

A very interesting part of this chart is that for this bike (a sportbike, by the way), counter-steering appears to start at just less than 9 MPH!

Anyway, each of the curves on the chart represents a set of measurements of the steering torque required to maintain a turn of a given radius.[9] For example, the second curve from the left shows the measurements of steering torque required to maintain a path on a circle with radius of 78.7 feet, at speeds from about 9 mph to as high as about 30 MPH.

Notice that as speed increases, the amount of negative steering torque decreases until you finally get to a point where the bike requires "neutral steering"; and that at any speed above that point, the bike requires positive steering torque (and is unstable).

Three of the test measurements made for the 78.7 foot radius curve are highlighted to make this clear.

---

[9]Measurements described in Vittore Cossalter's book **MOTORCYCLE DYNAMICS,** Race Dynamics, Inc. (2002), p. 316. ISBN 0-972051406.

Dot 'A' shows that if you are moving at a speed of only about 13 MPH, you **must** employ a forward pressure on your inside grip of magnitude greater than **two**. (The bike will have a lean angle of about eight degrees.)

Dot 'B' shows the effect of increasing your speed to about 25 MPH (and maintaining the 78.7 foot radius), where you will be very close to having "neutral steering", and the bike will have a lean angle of about 28 degrees.

Increasing your speed to about 30 MPH, as shown by Dot 'C', results in your having to provide a **positive** steering torque (pushing forward on the **outside** grip) with a magnitude of nearly one. Your bike will be unstable, and it will be leaning about 37 degrees.

Touring bikes and cruisers have curves that are wider than sportbikes so that you rarely, if ever, can find a tuning point with them where you can experience "neutral steering". Even at high speeds in a turn, the amount of friction from any steering damper isn't a significant factor in offsetting the restoring moment, so you must maintain some forward pressure on the inside grip to maintain your course with these bikes.

It seems reasonable that, because the faster you go in a turn, the greater will be the lean angle and the lesser will be the amount of negative steering torque required, many of us find it very difficult to lean a bike over far enough to scrape a peg; the steering input simply feels "strange" (weak) the closer you get to that point.

Clearly both arguments are valid and demonstrably correct.

D. Braking in a curve is counter-steering

The reason a motorcycle **tends** to go wide in a curve when you brake is because <u>braking is a counter-steering input,</u> as a result of weight transfer.

As the bike's front-end dives, its forks point more directly toward the ground. Thus, its steering becomes more efficient. (That is, less of its steering angle is being used to lean the wheel instead of to change its direction).

If your forks pointed straight down, 100% of your steering angle would be used to change direction and zero would be used to lean the wheel.

The greater the rake angle, the slower (the more inefficient) your steering is.

Braking causes an increased steering efficiency (**without** changing your steering angle); which means that as weight transfer occurs, your front tire is out-tracking too little to sustain the given course. Counter-steering being what it is, the bike leans **less** toward the inside of the curve (i.e., it stands up) as it changes directions to open up the curve.

Said differently, braking in a **left** turn is the equivalent of pushing forward on your **right** grip.

E. Tire pressure is temperature-sensitive

Some riders live in an environment that gets quite cold at certain times during the year. The discussion that follows is an important reminder about tire pressures and the effect of temperature on them; for pressure is more temperature-sensitive than you may think.

Stamped on the outside of many motorcycle tires is a recommended tire pressure range. (At least an upper limit appears on the tire.) For longest tire life, you should strive to keep them at the higher limit of those recommendations (regardless of what your motorcycle owner's manual might say to the contrary).

Further, this pressure should be determined while the tires are cold; meaning, they haven't been used for a couple of hours before you measure their pressure.

Time and outside temperature affect the pressure within your tires. With respect to time, it's **normal** for a tire to lose about one pound per square inch (psi) per month. Outside temperatures affect your tire pressure far more profoundly, however. A tire's pressure can change by one psi for every 10 degrees Fahrenheit of temperature change. As temperature goes, so goes tire pressure.

For example, if a tire's found to have 38 psi on an 80-degree mid-summer day, it could lose enough air to have an inflation pressure of 26 psi on a 20-degree day six months later. This represents a loss of six psi over six months, and an additional loss of six psi due to the 60-degree temperature reduction.

At 26 psi, a tire is severely under-inflated and dangerous!

There's nothing wrong with a tire if it behaves like this, of course. What's being illustrated here is that a rider **must** check his or her tire pressure on a regular basis (about once a week is reasonable) and must be particularly aware of it on cold days.

F. Slow-speed counter-steering? No way!

A series of videos can be found on YouTube that appears to provide reasonable descriptions of how a motorcycle steers at slow speeds—until you get down to the reality of it.

See http://www.youtube.com/watch?v=OLzB5oriblk for one such video. (A YouTube video can disappear at any time.)

The **only** way to properly steer a motorcycle at normal riding speeds, indeed at any speed over about 10 MPH, is via counter-steering. The **only** way to steer a motorcycle going at very slow speeds is via direct-steering.

Yet this video makes a compelling case that counter-steering can be accomplished at very slow speeds. <u>**It's wrong**</u>.

The fundamental mistake in the presentation is the speaker's definition of counter-steering. He maintains that it's the process whereby, when you turn the handlebar in one direction, the motorcycle will lean in the other direction, and therefore move in that other direction. It sounds pretty good, but it's actually a definition crafted to support his contention rather than fact.

Counter-steering or direct-steering result in a change of direction, not lean. <u>**A change of direction results in a lean. A lean does not result in a change of direction**</u>.

Some riders have become convinced after watching that video that counter-steering works at any speed; and they refer to that video as "proof."

In fact, what that video demonstrates is what some of us call the "**dip maneuver**", which is no more nor less than direct-steering in one direction followed by direct-steering in the opposite direction (at very slow speeds); or by counter-steering in one direction followed by counter-steering in the opposite direction at higher speeds.

Figure 45 is a set of diagrams to make this clear.

The video is an example of what has been described as doing a "dip" at slow speed. It's **similar** to counter-steering in terms of results, but it's actually direct-steering in one direction, followed immediately by direct-steering in the opposite direction. It's **not** necessary to do a "dip" before actually steering through a turn at slow speeds. And at higher speeds,

there's nothing optional about steering: you **must** use counter-steering and **cannot** steer directly.

A "dip" causes a lean of the bike without your having to lean your body in support of the turn. You can simply turn the handlebar (direct-steer) at slow speed to accomplish the same thing, while you use your body to maintain bike balance. This is what virtually every rider actually does.

A "dip" at the start of a slow-speed turn provides one valuable advantage over simply direct-steering: it allows you to start your turn on a tighter radius. That is, it gets you leaned over sooner in the turn. In essence, it allows you to begin the turn from farther outside of the radius, because the "dip" forces you to track wide to begin with.

There's no doubt that centrifugal force exists at very slow speeds. However, it's trivial compared to what exists when riding a curved path at normal speeds. Thus, when you're making very slow-speed turns, you **cannot** simply maintain the counter-steer pressure and expect to move in any direction other than that to which the front wheel points. The announcer in the video makes it clear that "doing it wrong" can make the bike fall over. What he means is that if you maintain a "counter-steer pressure" at very slow speeds, unless you immediately **direct-steer** in the direction you want to go, you'll fall down, for gravity cannot be denied.

The YouTube video demonstrates the "dip", not counter-steering, despite what the announcer calls it. Maybe another picture or two will make the "dip" more obvious.

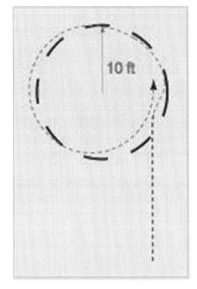 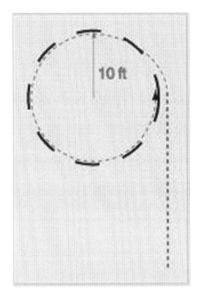

Figure 45: Starting on and starting outside the desired path

Assume that a particular motorcycle can, at best, do a 360-degree turn that has a 10 foot radius at 10 MPH. (Remember the 20-foot box in the Basic Rider Course?)

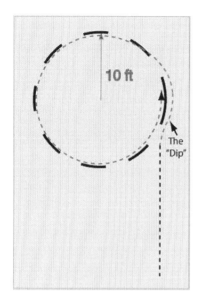

Figure 46: The "dip"

The rider would like to demonstrate the bike's ability, so he lays out a target with some chalk. It turns out, however, that he finds it impossible to keep his wheels inside the chalk marks all the way around the target.

Why is that? Because a bike can't change from a straight line into a full, tight turn instantly. For some period of time, the transition period, it's carving a **decreasing radius** turn. The part of the turn that just follows the arrow in Figure 46 is that transition period.

What this means is that it's **impossible** to start the 10-foot radius turn anywhere on the circle or inside the circumference of the circle. In other words, you **must** start that turn **outside** the circle at some distance.

An **alternative** is to do the "dip" from any point approaching the circumference of the circle. (This means the rider first **turns away from path, then turns toward it.**)

One rider has asked if the "dip" is actually a direct-steer, followed by another direct-steer maneuver. If so, then it isn't really counter-steering at all, is it? The answer: Nope. If this were a counter-steering maneuver, then you would need only **one steering input** to accomplish the turn, not two.

What's the practical value of this discussion? Most riders will be confronted with having to make a U-turn at some point in their riding career, if not many. Since lanes are usually 11- or 12-feet wide, that means you would normally make the U-turn using two opposing lanes, as shown in the diagram on the left in Figure 47, assuming you were riding the particular bike used in this example.

However, using intelligent lane positioning and the "dip" maneuver, you could make that U-turn using just one opposing lane, as shown in the diagram on the right. Note that by doing this, your bike remains entirely in-lane, as it's always leaning away from the center line.

Riders who are traveling in a group should form a single file when the group leader signals for a U-turn (and on some rides, the lead bike will joke that there will be a "mandatory U-turn" somewhere on the trip). This allows each of them to approach the side of the lane in which the group is riding, in order to make the "dip" safely. Each rider should also slow down and watch extremely carefully so as not to hit the rider in front of them while he's making his U-turn.

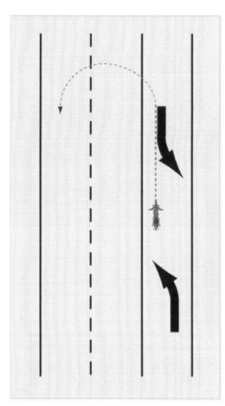
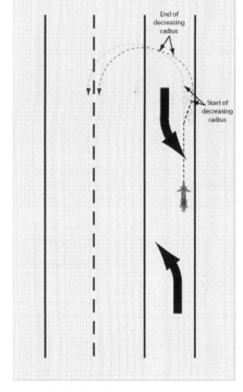

Figure 47: Making a U-turn with the "dip"

G. Spreadsheets and other tools
1. Deceleration rate calculator

This chart allows you quickly to determine the average deceleration rate achieved during a quick-stop exercise during parking lot practice. **N**ote that here the stopping distance of 36 feet is less than 40 feet but is greater than 35 feet, so the deceleration rate is between 0.7g's and 0.8g's.

Here, a close approximation can visually be determined to be about 0.78g's (the location of the 'X').

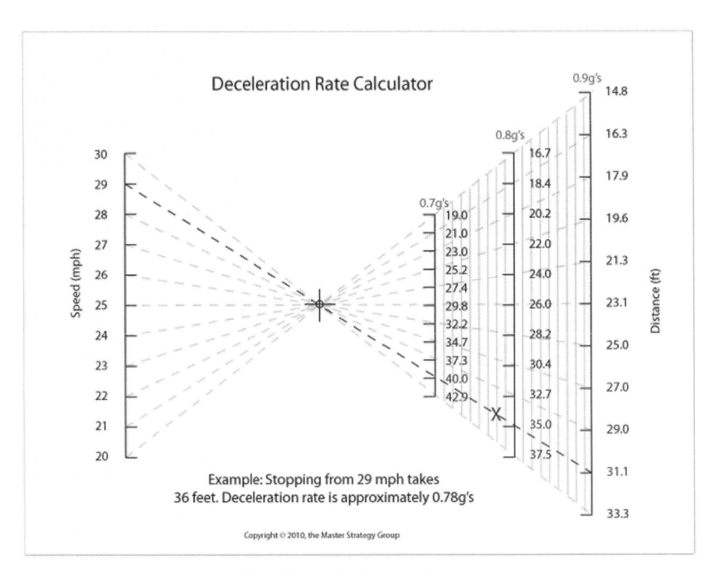

Figure 48: Deceleration rate calculator

2. Deceleration rate from speed and distance

This Excel spreadsheet calculates both the time to stop and the average deceleration rate achieved during a stop given the speed a vehicle was moving when braking began and the distance required to stop. Additionally, the spreadsheet graphs the vehicle's speed throughout its stopping distance.

This spreadsheet can be downloaded from our website at http://www.msgroup.org/forums/mtt/topic.asp?TOPIC_ID=12263.

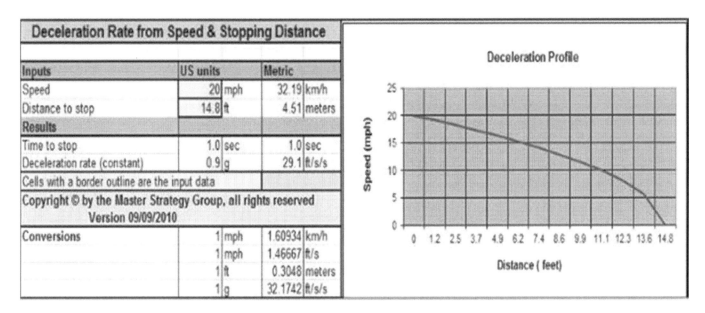

Figure 49: Deceleration rate from speed and distance

3. Stopping distance from speed and deceleration rate

This Excel spreadsheet calculates the stopping distance and time to stop, given the speed at which braking began and the average deceleration rate achieved. Additionally, this spreadsheet graphs speed throughout the vehicle's stopping distance. It can be downloaded from our website at http://www.msgroup.org/forums/mtt/topic.asp?TOPIC_ID=12264.

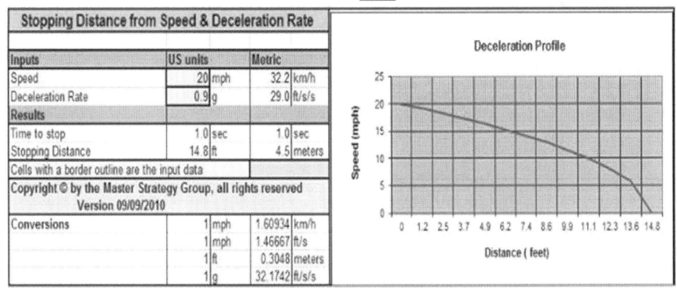

Figure 50: Stopping distance from speed and deceleration rate

4. Speed calculated from stopping distance

This Excel spreadsheet calculates the speed at which braking began, given the stopping distance, the Coefficient of Friction, the braking efficiency, and the PDR time (if any).

This spreadsheet can be downloaded at this link: http://www.msgroup.org/forums/mtt/topic.asp?TOPIC_ID=7878.

Motorcycle Speed From Stopping Distance Calculator		
Inputs	US units	Metric
Total Stopping Distance	300 ft	91.44 m
Coefficient of Friction (static)	0.86	
Braking Efficiency	100 %	
PDR time	0 sec	
Outputs		
Speed	87.98 mph	141.6 km/h
Cells with a border outline are the input data		
Copyright © by the Master Strategy Group, all rights reserved Version 04/17/2009		
If you know the total stopping distance, you can use this model to calculate the speed at the start of that distance. Note that if this distance begins at the start of a skid mark, then the PDR (Perception-Decision-Reaction) time is ZERO.		

Figure 51: Speed from stopping distance

5. Critical speed

This Excel spreadsheet calculates the speed and lean angle at which a motorcycle will lose traction, given the Coefficient of Friction, bank angle, and radius of a turn. It also converts the bank angle from degrees to a percentage. This spreadsheet can be downloaded by linking to our website at http://www.msgroup.org/forums/mtt/topic.asp?TOPIC_ID=7660.

Critical Speed Calculator			
Inputs	US units	Metric	
Coefficient of Friction	0.9		
Bank Angle	6 degrees		
Radius	40 ft	12.19	meters
Outputs			
Bank Angle %	10.5 %		
Speed	24.48 mph	35.90	ft/sec
Lean Angle	42.0 degrees		
Copyright © by the Master Strategy Group, all rights reserved Version 03/22/2010			
Conversions	1 ft	0.3048	meters
	1 mph	1.4667	ft/sec

Figure 52: Critical speed calculator

6. Speed scrubbed during a skid

This Excel spreadsheet calculates the speed scrubbed during a skid, given the starting speed, the length of the skid, the amount of roadway grade, the Coefficient of Friction, and the vehicle's braking efficiency during the skid.

This fascinating model does not require that the vehicle come to a stop at the end of the skid. It calculates the Energy Equivalent Speed Scrubbed during the skid.

The Energy Equivalent Speed Scrubbed shown here is the starting speed that would result in this skid mark length and with the vehicle coming to a stop at the end. It's **not** the speed during the skid, but rather the energy transformed and expressed as a speed. For example, if you enter a starting speed of 22.63 MPH, then the skid mark would be 36 feet long, and the vehicle would come to a stop at the end of that skid (the vehicle's Ending Speed would be 0 MPH).

The Energy Equivalent Speed is not affected by the vehicle's starting speed as the skid begins. The only change from an increase or decrease in starting speed is the time required to make that skid mark and to transform the energy represented by the Energy Equivalent Speed. Download this at http://www.msgroup.org/forums/mtt/topic.asp?TOPIC_ID=11203.

Speed Scrubbed During Skid				
Inputs	**US units**		**Metric**	
Starting speed	45	mph	72.42	km/h
Skid length	36	ft	10.97	meters
Grade % (+ or -)	0	%	0	%
Coefficient of Friction (sliding)	0.79		0.79	
Braking efficiency (%)	60	%	60	%
Results				
Energy Equivalent Speed Scrubbed	22.63	mph	36.41	km/h
Ending Speed	38.90	mph	62.60	km/h
Speed Scrubbed During Skid	6.10	mph	9.82	km/h
Drag factor	0.474		0.474	
Cells with a border outline are the input data				
Copyright © by the Master Strategy Group, all rights reserved Version 12/13/2009				
Conversions	**US units**		**Metric**	
	1	mph	1.60934	km/h
	1	ft	0.3048	meters
Typical static Coeff of Friction values	**Low**		**High**	**Wet**
Concrete (textured)	0.55		1.2	-20%
Asphalt	0.5		0.9	-20%
Gravel	0.4		0.8	-20%
Ice	0.1		0.25	-20%
Snow	0.1		0.55	-20%

Figure 53: Speed scrubbed during a skid

7. Distance traveled and speed

This Excel spreadsheet calculates the distance traveled and speed of a vehicle given the starting speed, deceleration rate, and time since braking began.

This spreadsheet can be downloaded at this link: http://www.msgroup.org/forums/mtt/topic.asp?TOPIC_ID=12367

Distance Traveled While Braking		
Inputs	**US units**	**Metric**
Speed	60 mph	96.56 km/h
Time from start	1.6 sec	1.60 sec
Deceleration rate (constant)	0.9 g	28.96 ft/s/s
Results		
Distance traveled	103.7 ft	31.62 meters
Speed at time from start	28.4 mph	45.72 km/h
Cells with a border outline are the input data		Optional input
Copyright © by the Master Strategy Group, all rights reserved Version 02/18/2011		
Conversions	1 mph	1.60934 km/h
	1 mph	1.46667 ft/s
	1 ft	0.3048 meters
	1 g	32.1742 ft/s/s

Figure 54: Distance traveled and speed while braking

8. Lateral acceleration and lean angle

This Excel spreadsheet calculates the lateral acceleration and lean angle of a motorcycle, given its speed and the radius of the curve it is riding.

This spreadsheet can be downloaded at this link: http://www.msgroup.org/forums/mtt/topic.asp?TOPIC_ID=7659

Lateral Acceleration & Lean Calculator		
Inputs	**US units**	**Metric**
Speed	23 mph	33.73 ft/sec
Radius	40 ft	12.19 meters
Outputs		
Lateral Acceleration	0.88 g	28.45 ft/s/s
Lean Angle	41.5 degree	
Copyright © by the Master Strategy Group, all rights reserved Version 06/17/2009		
Conversions	1 ft	0.3048 meters
	1 mph	1.4667 ft/sec
	1 g	32.1742 ft/s/s

Figure 55: Lateral acceleration and lean angle

9. Quadratic equation solver

Whenever you can reduce an equation so that it takes on the standard form for a quadratic equation, then you can use this tool to solve it. That form is as follows:

$$Ax^2 + Bx + C = 0$$

Note, there are **always** two correct solutions for x. This spreadsheet can be downloaded from our website at http://www.msgroup.org/forums/mtt/topic.asp?TOPIC_ID=7663.

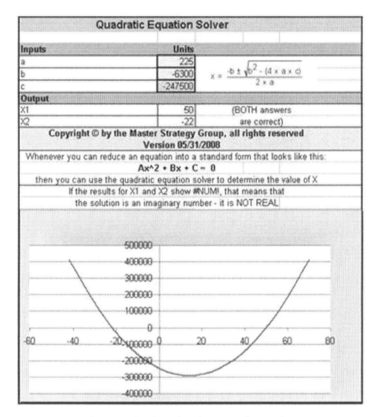

Figure 56: Quadratic equation solver

10. Radius calculator

This Excel spreadsheet calculates the radius of a circle given the length of any chord and middle ordinate.

To download this spreadsheet, link to our website at: http://www.msgroup.org/forums/mtt/topic.asp?TOPIC_ID=7657.

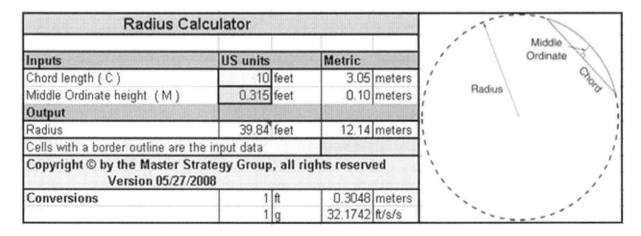

Figure 57: Radius calculator

11. Skid distance to a stop

This Excel spreadsheet calculates the skid distance a motorcycle takes to come to a stop, given its speed at the time skidding begins, road grade, Coefficient of Friction, braking efficiency, and whether the roadway is wet.

To download this spreadsheet, link to our website at: http://www.msgroup.org/forums/mtt/topic.asp?TOPIC_ID=11201.

Skid Distance To Stop Analyzer				
Inputs	US units		Metric	
Speed	30	mph	48.28	km/h
Grade % (+ or -)	0	%	0	%
Coefficient of Friction (sliding)	0.79		0.79	
Braking efficiency (%)	50	%	50	%
Wet pavement? (1=Yes, 0=No)	0			
Results				
Skid Distance To Stop	75.95	ft	23.15	meters
Drag factor	0.395		0.395	
Cells with a border outline are the input data				
Copyright © by the Master Strategy Group, all rights reserved Version 12/13/2009				
Conversions	US units		Metric	
	1	mph	1.60934	km/h
	1	ft	0.3048	meters
Typical static Coeff of Friction values		Low	High	Wet
Concrete (textured)		0.55	1.2	-20%
Asphalt		0.5	0.9	-20%
Gravel		0.4	0.8	-20%
Ice		0.1	0.25	-20%
Snow		0.1	0.55	-20%

Figure 58: Skid distance to a stop

12. Center of Gravity

This Excel spreadsheet calculates the location of your bike's Center of Gravity (CG), given as input the measured results of lifting the rear wheel off the ground.

To download this spreadsheet, link to our website at: http://www.msgroup.org/forums/mtt/topic.asp?TOPIC_ID=4675.

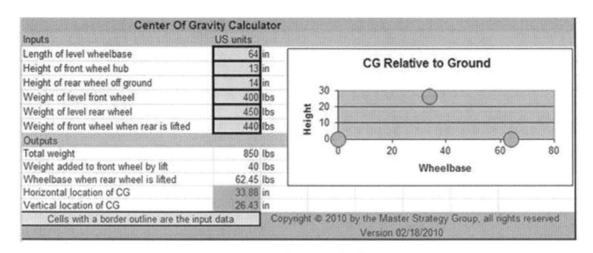

Figure 59: Center of Gravity (CG) calculator

13. Vault speed

This Excel spreadsheet calculates the speed at which an object (such as a motorcyclist) is launched from the bike (in other words, the motorcyclist's speed at time of impact), given a known distance for how far it is thrown, the difference in height between launch point and impact point, and the launch angle. You can download this spreadsheet at: http://www.msgroup.org/forums/mtt/topic.asp?TOPIC_ID=7867.

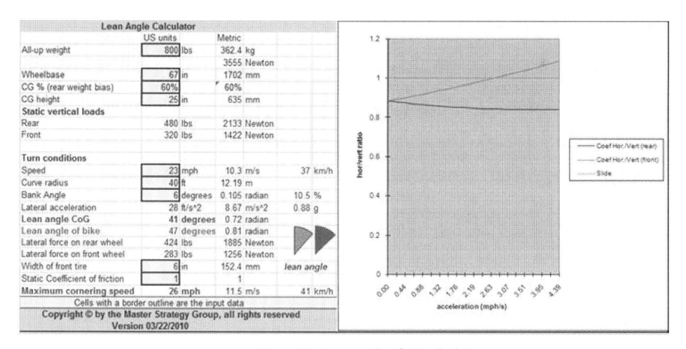

Figure 60: Vault speed calculator

14. Lean angle of CG

This Excel spreadsheet calculates the lean angle of the CG of your bike and the lean angle of the combined rider and bike CG, given nine different input specifications. It also provides a graph of lateral forces divided by vertical loads based on acceleration rates (if any), so that you can estimate when traction would be lost. You can download it at: http://www.msgroup.org/forums/mtt/topic.asp?TOPIC_ID=4676.

Figure 61: Lean angle of CG calculator

15. Skid mark analyzer

This Excel spreadsheet calculates the minimum speed that must have existed when skidding began and the Energy Equivalent Speed scrubbed during a skid, given a collision speed (or zero if none), skid length, grade, Coefficient of Friction, braking efficiency, whether the pavement was wet or not, and Transient Braking Time (which the user may set to zero).

Energy Equivalent Speed is the speed the vehicle must be traveling when a skid begins, if that skid ends with the vehicle moving at zero MPH. The vehicle could have been traveling faster than that when the skid began, in which case it was still moving at the end of the skid, but it could not have been traveling slower than that speed at the start of the skid.

This is **not** the minimum speed the vehicle was traveling when it began to skid, nor is it the speed scrubbed by the skid (unless it happened to be the speed the vehicle was moving when the skid began). It's the **maximum** amount of speed that could have been scrubbed by the skid.

This calculator can be downloaded at our website at: http://www.msgroup.org/forums/mtt/topic.asp?TOPIC_ID=4671.

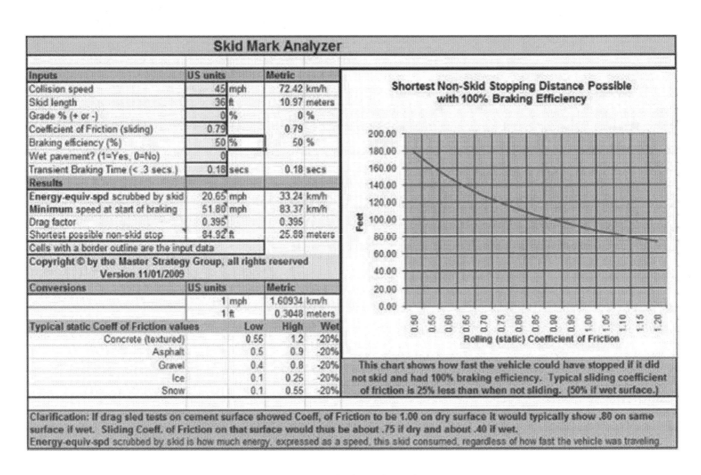

Figure 62: Skid mark analyzer

16. Speed by gear

This simple Excel spreadsheet calculates your motorcycle speed given the rear tire radius, final gear ratio, and engine RPM.

Although you have to input seven values with this model, if you combine this model with two others (Rear Wheel Radius and Gearing), you won't need to enter anything.

This calculator can be downloaded at our website at: http://www.msgroup.org/forums/mtt/topic.asp?TOPIC_ID=4695.

Speed Calculator				Wheel Radius ->		12.24 in	
Final Gear Ratio (A) ->	10.3127	7.8766	7.0990	5.5641	5.0052	4.6367
Speed			MPH				
RPM	1st	2nd	3rd	4th	5th	6th
2500	17.7	23.1	25.7	32.7	36.4	39.3
3000	21.2	27.7	30.8	39.3	43.7	47.1
3500	24.7	32.4	35.9	45.8	50.9	55.0
4000	28.3	37.0	41.1	52.4	58.2	62.9
4500	31.8	41.6	46.2	58.9	65.5	70.7
5000	35.3	46.2	51.3	65.5	72.8	78.6
5500	38.9	50.9	56.4	72.0	80.1	86.4
6000	42.4	55.5	61.6	78.6	87.3	94.3
6500	45.9	60.1	66.7	85.1	94.6	102.1
7000	49.5	64.7	71.8	91.7	101.9	110.0
7500	53.0	69.4	77.0	98.2	109.2	117.8
8000	56.5	74.0	82.1	104.8	116.5	125.7
8500	60.1	78.6	87.2	111.3	123.7	133.6
9000	63.6	83.2	92.4	117.8	131.0	141.4
9500	67.1	87.9	97.5	124.4	138.3	149.3
10000	70.6	92.5	102.6	130.9	145.6	157.1
10500	74.2	97.1	107.8	137.5	152.8	165.0
11000	77.7	101.7	112.9	144.0	160.1	172.8
11500	81.2	106.4	118.0	150.6	167.4	180.7
12000	84.8	111.0	123.2	157.1	174.7	188.6
12500	88.3	115.6	128.3	163.7	182.0	196.4
13000	91.8	120.2	133.4	170.2	189.2	204.3

Cells with a border outline are input
Copyright © by the Master Strategy Group, all rights reserved
Version 02/04/2007

Figure 63: Speed by gear calculator

17. Rear wheel radius

This Excel spreadsheet calculates the rear wheel radius, given as input the bead width, profile height, and rim diameter information coded on the rear tire's sidewall. It's at http://www.msgroup.org/forums/mtt/topic.asp?TOPIC_ID=4692.

Rear Wheel Radius Calculator				
Tire Specification				
Example: 190/50-ZR-17				
Bead Width	190	mm	7.48	in
Profile height	50	%	3.74	in
Rim Diameter	17	in.	17	in
Wheel Radius			12.24	in
Conversions	**Metric**		**US units**	
	1	mm	0.03937	in
Cells with a border outline are input				
Copyright © by the Master Strategy Group, all rights reserved				
Version 08/30/2010				

Figure 64: Rear wheel radius calculator

18. Gearing ratios

This Excel spreadsheet calculates the gear ratios based on the number of teeth found on both drive and driven gears in the transmission. These ratios are required in order to calculate torque delivered to the rear wheel when in each gear.

This calculator can be downloaded at our website at: http://www.msgroup.org/forums/mtt/topic.asp?TOPIC_ID=4686.

Gearing Calculator	Teeth (driven)	Teeth (drive)	Ratio
Primary Drive (to transmission)	73	47	1.5532
1st	43	16	2.6875
2nd	39	19	2.0526
3rd	37	20	1.8500
4th	29	20	1.4500
5th	30	23	1.3043
6th (or 1 if non-existent)	29	24	1.2083
Final Drive (shaft/chain/belt)	42	17	2.4706
Final Gear Ratios (A)			**Ratio**
1st			10.3127
2nd			7.8766
3rd			7.0990
4th			5.5641
5th			5.0052
6th			4.6367
Drive Gear Ratios (B)			**Ratio**
1st			4.1742
2nd			3.1881
3rd			2.8734
4th			2.2521
5th			2.0259
6th			1.8768
Cells with a border outline are the input data			
Copyright © by the Master Strategy Group, all rights reserved			
Version 02/03/2007			

You use the Final Gear Ratio (A) when computing the speed of the motorcycle using engine RPM.

You use the Drive Gear Ratio (B) when computing Torque to the rear wheel for acceleration.

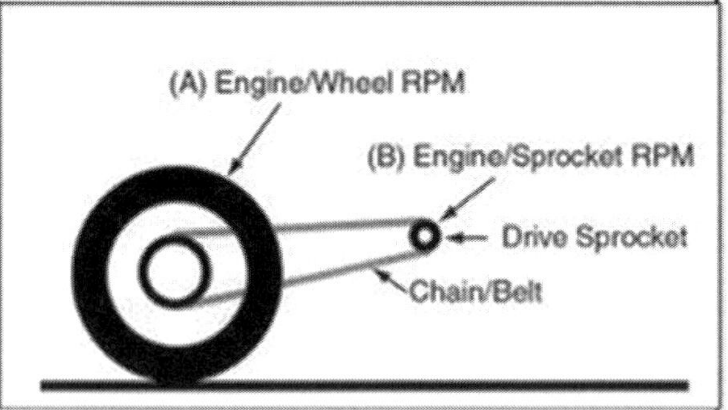

Figure 65: Gearing ratios calculator

19. Horsepower from torque

This Excel spreadsheet simply converts torque and rpm inputs into horsepower.

It may be downloaded from our website using this link: http://www.msgroup.org/forums/mtt/topic.asp?TOPIC_ID=4687.

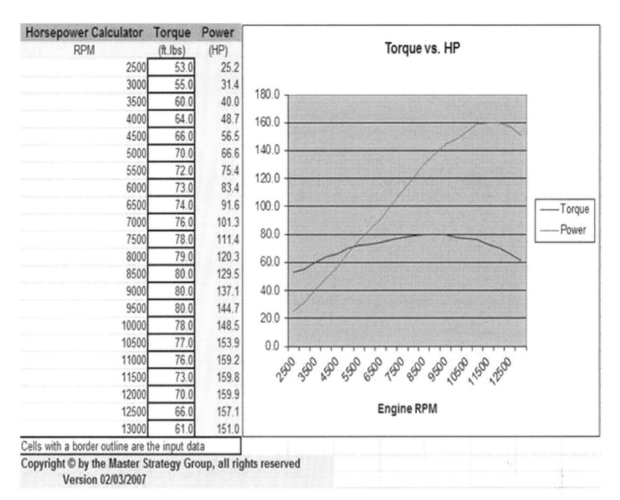

Figure 66: Horsepower from torque calculator

20. Drag and lift

This Excel spreadsheet calculates the weight on the front and rear tires resulting from virtually all variables that could affect them in a dynamic state. The user provides static state configuration information, then adds such variables as Latitude, Altitude, Wind speed, and Temperature.

This is by far the most complicated set of calculations available to you from our website. It calculates a motorcycle's weight at any point on earth, given its longitude, latitude, and altitude. It will also determine the weight on each tire based on wind speed, temperature, and altitude. Finally, it also calculates aerodynamic effects (Drag and Lift) based on speed.

You may download this calculator from our website at: http://www.msgroup.org/forums/mtt/topic.asp?TOPIC_ID=4674.

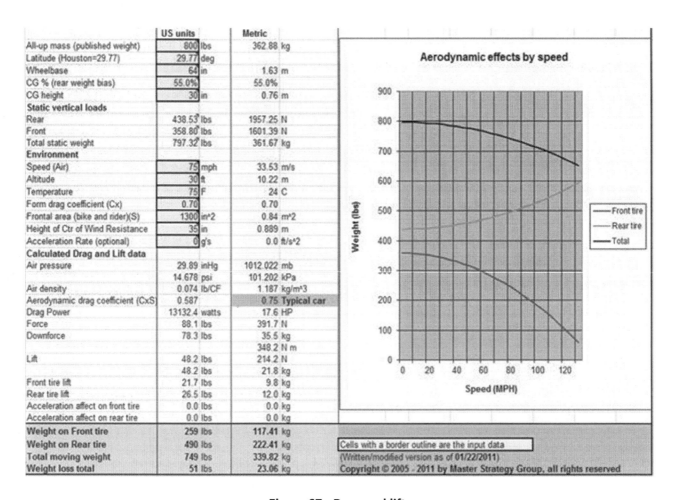

Figure 67: Drag and lift

Phase 3

I. Mature

You've arrived! The vast majority of your learning and skill development is behind you. You've accumulated a wealth of experience on two wheels, made the serious mistakes you're going to make, and are unlikely to make any more. But all of that does not mean that you've made riding motorcycles a riskless endeavor.

Motorcycling isn't safe, and no matter how long you've been doing it, it never can be. However, at this phase of your riding career, if an accident occurs when you're out riding, it's probably not going to be your fault. You're not likely to be "contributing" rider errors. Instead, you are always in control of your motorcycle and yourself. It's likely that somebody else will have made those errors, or it will truly be "an accident" instead of a planned, deliberate event, except for the crash.

Although the probabilities of **causing** a crash are somewhat lower for the mature rider, the problem with this kind of thinking is that it leads him to believe that his odds of being involved in an accident are approaching zero. That's absolutely not true.

Indeed, there have been many studies to determine the value of training and experience in reducing the odds of a rider being involved in an accident. The conclusions reached by these studies vary in the particulars, but they found a most curious result: training and experience had essentially **no effect** on accident rates.

Experience, whether measured in years or even in decades, is illusory. The experience gained by a motorcyclist who averages 50 miles per month on two wheels is certainly not as valuable as the experience gained over the same length of time by a rider who averages 1,000 per month. And even if the miles ridden are high, it takes time to accomplish those trips. Working against all riders is the fact that experience also denotes a gradual aging of the motorcyclist.

To give you a feel for the significance of aging, consider the findings of a recent study[10] derived from police crash reports of 18,225 motorcycle operators in the state of Indiana, where the riders were involved in collisions between 2003 and 2008, including those who died within 30 days of their accident. This study found that **the average age of riders who perished was almost two years older than those who survived.** It's true that this finding was inconsistent with certain studies done in other countries. Still, according to this study, <u>the odds of dying as a result of a motorcycle collision increase by about 1.5% for each year of aging</u>.

Note, this isn't the same as saying that the older you are, the more likely you will be involved in a motorcycle collision. Instead, it says that **if** you are involved in such a collision, your odds of dying increases 1.5% for each year of your age.

Formal rider training was found to have, for the six-month period following it, a modestly positive impact on accident rates. Thereafter, however, motorcycle riders had almost exactly the same odds of being involved in an accident whether trained or not. In fact, there's even some evidence that being a trained rider leads to an **increase** in accidents.

In January 2009, Wendy Moon, a well-known researcher and a colleague, wrote a blog article providing documented details of 23 studies regarding rider training. That blog article is reproduced at the end of this volume, in the Appendix section; it omits only a discussion exclusively about rider training in Australia.

See **APPENDIX I – Twenty-three Studies Documenting Ineffectiveness of Training**.

Training and experience lead to more frequent rides, longer rides, and the rider's willingness to ride in different and somewhat more dangerous environmental conditions, such as rain, heat, cold, and unfamiliar roads.

A. It's a matter of exposure

Once you get past the learning phase of an activity, then the more often you do it, the more likely you are to encounter even the least likely outcome. For example, from a positive

---

[10] Dr. Samuel Nunn, Professor of the School of Public and Environmental Affairs and Director of the Center for Criminal Justice Research, "Death by Motorcycle: Background, Behavioral, and Situational Correlates of Fatal Motorcycle Collisions," **Journal of Forensic Science,** March 2011, pp. 429-437.

point of view, if you buy enough Lotto tickets, your odds of finally winning something increases; but from a negative point of view, if you ride even a familiar stretch of country road enough times, your odds of encountering a deer in your headlight increase. Further, with experience and confidence, a rider's more likely to be willing to ride in environments that a less trained, less experienced rider simply will avoid.

Additionally, some consequences of riding motorcycles will certainly occur with greater exposure as compared to less—for example, sun and wind damage to skin, and hearing loss.

B. Aging and disabilities

Many sports and hobbies that active people engage in, such as baseball, football, track, tennis, basketball, and dance, are for athletes. To participate, even casually, you need a strong heart, good lungs, quick reflexes, conditioned muscles, and endurance.

Motorcycle riding, however, is usually much more mental than physical. While some forms of motorcycle riding involve pure athleticism, such as motocross or even dirt bike riding (which is substantially physical as opposed to mental), typical riding is much more a mental endeavor than it is a physical one. Even canyon carving looks more physical than it actually is. As riders on a machine, we let it do the work while we're along for the ride. Our involvement in the sport of motorcycling is one of control rather than exertion. We control the behavior or our motorcycles and ourselves.

But that doesn't mean that aging and disabilities are of no importance in our ability to continue to enjoy this endeavor.

The aging process changes our bodies. Our strength diminishes, our joints become arthritic or otherwise sensitive, our hearing and eyesight become less sensitive, our bones become brittle, and our endurance generally tends to diminish. Similarly, our reaction times increase, and it sometimes takes longer to make decisions—our minds slow down, or worse, we lose focus and ignore relevant facts. These are only the natural consequences of age.

Additionally, diseases and other traumas can disfigure us, can significantly affect our mobility, and can utterly destroy our endurance.

Generally, the colder it gets, the more difficult it is for an older rider to handle that cold. The same safety gear that was perfectly satisfactory for comfort at this temperature only a few years ago is no longer adequate. Yes, an additional layer of clothes can solve that problem—but it is a problem.

Similarly, older riders don't have the energy level of just a few years ago. Insuring that they have a cup of coffee and an adequate breakfast before taking off to ride in the early morning may be enough to jumpstart them now; but they can recall that only a few years earlier, they were perfectly happy to get out on two wheels and wait until the first rest stop to have that coffee and breakfast.

One solution may be to have a riding buddy who expects to make a particular ride. Putting a smile on your face and joining your riding buddy with a positive attitude is easier than admitting one's age.

And it's not just the cold and energy levels. Before every ride, most riders check the air pressure on their tires. That means getting at least one knee on the ground. But sometimes in order to reach a valve stem that's in an awkward position, it's necessary to put the rest of your body on the ground, too. Here, the problem is getting back up. It takes more and more time and effort as the years roll on to do these basic safety checks. There's really no cure for this, as electing to not bother to check your tires' air pressure is **not** an option.

For many older riders, being on their motorcycles has never resulted in any kind of serious pain in exchange for the pleasure. They haven't ever had to contend with the kinds of pains and damage caused by a crash. But mature, competent riders are still aware that terrible pain, disability, and worse could easily result from a motorcycle accident. Despite all of this, most senior riders continue to ride.

1. Hearing loss

As mentioned above, hearing loss is one consequence of long years of riding. A helmet is an inadequate defense against it.

While it's true that loud pipes will result in faster and more profound hearing damage, motorcycle sounds aren't the principal cause of that damage. Indeed, even if a motorcycle were to make no sound at all, long-distance, long-duration motorcycling will impair your hearing, because it's **wind noise** that does the most damage.

Wind noise is constant, loud, and very difficult to get away from. At highway speeds, it's well over 100 decibels (db), even when the rider's wearing a helmet!

Wearing a helmet cuts the noise by only about 3 db, and then only if it's at least a three-quarter shell and properly fitted. (An improperly fitted helmet actually **increases** wind noise!) **One hour** of exposure to 110 db will damage your hearing. At 115 db it takes only 15 **minutes**. The damage to your ears is relentless, irreversible, and **cumulative**.

How can a rider protect his hearing from wind noise? First, he makes sure to wear a helmet; that it's at least a three-quarter shell in style; and that it fits properly. A properly fitted helmet has a lining that presses against the skin on the rider's cheeks as well as across his or her forehead. Not only does this helmet not shift around on a rider's head, but it cuts wind noise from reaching his ears.

Second, riders can wear earplugs. Unfortunately, there are some problems associated with doing this, notwithstanding the fact that in some states it's illegal to do so. (In such states, you can legally drive a motorcycle if you are deaf, but not if you're wearing earplugs—if you can imagine that.) Aside from the law, many people simply cannot stand (or get used to) wearing them. And, if they are improperly inserted, they provide very little noise reduction benefit and will cause pain in no time at all.

Earplugs are cheap. Good quality earplugs can be purchased by the dozens, and their cost will be less than $1 a pair when you buy in quantity. (Don't even consider buying only one pair and reusing them day after day—this is a foolish way to save a penny. They will change in shape and protective value over time, and they will no longer be clean.) If earplugs are not for you, then try small pieces of cotton. They're more comfortable for many people, though not nearly as effective; and you certainly won't reuse them just to save money.

Wearing earplugs of any kind is not productive at speeds below about 40 MPH. But if you ride highways for any distance at all, you will **certainly** be better off for having worn them (and, by the way, you will actually be able to hear better with them in your ear than not, at those speeds).

Just because your hearing's already a "little" damaged from wind noise, you should not think it can't get worse. Riding a motorcycle at highway speeds is a **guaranteed** way to damage your hearing, and in a potentially profound way. The majority of our hearing needs involve frequencies below 16 kilohertz (KHz). These sounds are what we use when we talk and listen. These also happen to be the frequencies most affected by wind noise hearing damage.

If you'd rather ignore this advice, you should practice saying "Huh?" But don't get used to that, expecting this minor inconvenience to work forever. Your hearing will get worse.

For perspective, a noisy restaurant produces about 80 db of noise. A subway produces about 90 db of noise. A rock band generates about 110 db, a car horn about 115 db, and a gunshot about 140 db. You can see that the noise produced by highway riding falls at the high end of that range.

2. Vision changes

Along with age comes a deterioration of one's eyesight. Usually, older riders compensate by wearing prescription glasses, and that works just fine. Some also develop cataracts, which require surgical treatment but which has a very high success rate. Modern medicine also provides the option of implanted lenses, which can drastically improve vision for older riders.

But a significant requirement for avoiding trouble or dealing with unexpected threats on a motorcycle is situational awareness; and that means much more than seeing and knowing what's happening in your immediate vicinity.

Knowing you should scan 10 or 12 seconds ahead is useless if you're unable to see that far, or if you can't determine what you're seeing. Cataracts, near-sightedness, or not being able mentally to translate images seen in low-light into understandable representations of reality makes a long distance scan an exercise in futility.

Of course any sensible person would quit riding if he were totally blind. But if a rider can handle a 10-second scan distance but not more, should he quit riding? Possibly. That's a decision each older rider must make for himself. But if you can't handle even a 10-second scan distance and know exactly what lies ahead, you're already riding on borrowed time.

Also, some people have a problem with low-light situations. When riding around dusk, their distance vision becomes marginal. Night-time riding, except when on a tour and involving well-lit super-slab freeways, is no longer part of the schedule for many older riders, as it involves unacceptably low early-warning visual input.

For riding in a group, where the principal responsibility is merely station-keeping, they would probably be fine. Even for riding drag, they would still probably be fine. But such a rider should disqualify himself from ever accepting the lead rider position.

3. Strength

Very little strength is involved in riding motorcycles on public roads. Even handling a 1,000-pound motorcycle like a Gold Wing (packed or with a passenger) is virtually effortless—so long as you keep its weight on its tires. Experienced riders on big touring bikes always put two feet down on the pavement when the bike's stopped. But there are times when the rider must use only his left leg to hold the bike up, such as when it's stopped on a sloping road. Again, this isn't a particularly strenuous effort for a normally healthy senior. Similarly, lifting the bike off its side-stand when starting from a parked position involves far less 'lifting' than it does straightening out the left leg, pushing against the tank with the left thigh, and pushing slightly forward on the grips.

There are times, however, when strength comes in handy. Picking up a Gold wing after dumping it might still be manageable, but if a senior rider runs out of gas, pushing it two blocks to a gas station is probably **far beyond** his abilities.

4. Endurance, tolerance, acuity

Strength is usually associated with muscles and their ability to perform work. Aging tends to diminish a person's strength, generally, and it also manifests in weakening in general. An older person has less endurance, less tolerance, and a diminished overall physical and mental acuity. A 200-mile day trip may become difficult, not because of the lack of tone in certain muscles, but because the entire body reacts badly to prolonged stresses and to the effort to remain intensely focused on the many tasks required, including a hyper-awareness of the rider's situation.

Some older riders continue to do relatively long day rides. A 150- or 200-mile day trip is not unusual, but that's because they are normal for such riders. For many older people, however, a 50-mile day trip is about their limit in terms of being comfortable when the trip's done.

For older riders, touring is now a different matter. If they expect to do between 300 and 400 miles per day, it may require far more conditioning than it used to. It's advisable to work up to a 300-mile per day trip over a series of several weeks of increasingly long rides before taking off on it.

Even that conditioning process requires some changes in their non-riding lives to help them endure and tolerate the difficult demands imposed. Getting additional sleep before a conditioning ride is smart. Don't plan chores that make heavy muscular demands on you or schedule mentally challenging work or activities for when you return from such a ride. In fact, it's a good idea to disengage from the world completely for some number of hours or for most of a day after returning from a conditioning ride. A long nap can help the recovery process, too.

5. Disabilities

Diseases, non-motorcycle related accidents, and even sometimes self-inflicted health problems (such as being 50 to 100 pounds heavier than when the rider was younger) are evidenced in the older riding population, as well as among younger riders who have unhealthy habits, or who have met with misfortune, or who have congenital handicaps. A rider who's lost sight in one eye, one who's essentially deaf, and many who are almost too heavy for their bike's maximum load-carrying capacity are among older riders we know who still ride. Many riders haven't let common, and even uncommon, disabilities stop them from motorcycling.

Certain after-market companies specialize in providing motorcycle modifications to assist riders who have unique physical disabilities. In the extreme, at least one such company builds sidecars with ramps for wheelchair-bound riders to use, along with a special set of hand-operated controls to enable them to ride their motorcycles from there. Many riders with prosthetic devices have made adjustments to their controls that permit them to continue to ride. Much more often, a rider who has lost a leg or who cannot control his leg muscles will stop riding motorcycles altogether, but not a small number of them will elect to ride a trike instead of a typical two-wheeled motorcycle.

6. Medications

Few older riders are "drug-free" when they ride. They aren't using illegal drugs or smoking funny green cigarettes, but they're taking a thyroid or heart or diabetic medication, or an anti-depressant, or an anti-spasmodic drug; and they do so every single day of their lives without any loss of function.

But drugs, by definition, affect a person's body and mind. All prescription drugs are provided with a list of potential side effects. Riders should study the warnings that pertain to their medications; and if they have any doubts, check with their care providers to see if any of them may interact and cause them to lose balance, to affect their situational awareness, or to cause any other condition that would put them or others in danger because they are impaired.

6. Fragility

Fatality statistics show two groups of riders who are over-represented: the very young and the very old.

Very young riders die from any number of causes, but chief among them are their mistakes, dangerous behaviors, and an inappropriate choice of motorcycle. (Not all "rider errors" fall exclusively on the shoulders of the rider: a manufacturer of motorcycles who builds and sells street-legal machines capable of attaining 100 MPH in first gear and nearly 200 MPH on the top end is not blameless, despite what trade organizations such as the Motorcycle Safety Foundation would have you believe.) Researchers now believe that teen-agers, in particular, lack the brain development that would permit them to realize the consequences of their actions.[11]

Older riders are over-represented primarily because <u>they break more easily</u> than younger riders. A bruising come-off for a 25-year-old can easily become a fatal incident for a 60-year-old.

C. Modifications, lighter motorcycles, trikes, sidecars, and scooters

Sooner or later, riders reach a time when they find their current motorcycle is no longer appropriate for them. Unlike the newbie, who invariably wants a bigger, faster or different style of bike for an upgrade, older riders who have matured in their riding careers often want a new bike that's more comfortable, lighter, more agile, or simply more stable than their current ride. Ultimately, of course, instead of changing motorcycles, they will elect to hang up their saddle and exit the motorcycle scene; but there are a few riders who continue to enjoy the sport well into what others would once have considered their dotage.

Assuming that it's time to change from your current motorcycle to one that's more appropriate for your needs, you have at least the following five obvious alternatives to explore, and more are being developed all the time.

---

[11] Giedd, J., Blumenthal, J., Jeffries, N., Castellanos, F., Liu, H., Zijdenbos, A., Paus, T., Evans, A., and Rapoport, J. *Brain development during childhood and adolescence: A longitudinal MRI study*. **Nature Neuroscience**, 2-10 (1999), pp.861-863.

1. Modifications

The simplest modifications are often enough. Adding a larger windscreen and wind deflectors in front of the grips can significantly reduce wind chill and buffeting problems. Cutting down the height of the seat can allow a rider to flat-foot when holding up the bike. If the bike's electrical system is strong enough, grip warmers and seat warmers can be added to increase comfort in cold weather.

2. Lighter motorcycles

A lighter bike is often chosen to replace a heavier one, as aging tends to weaken riders. Sometimes this alternative is taken simply because a rider who once enjoyed touring finds that longer multi-day trips are no longer appropriate. Handling an 800- or 900-pound motorcycle on short trips is simply not so easy, as larger touring bikes can be difficult to maneuver at slow speeds. For whatever reason, it seems that this downsizing alternative often constitutes the last motorcycle purchase of a rider.

3. Trikes

If balance becomes a problem, as is particularly true for older riders, exchanging a traditional motorcycle for a trike is a popular solution that allows minimal changes to the kind of riding enjoyed by riders. Trikes are sometimes considered to be safer than a traditional two-wheeled motorcycle, because they are very stable, do not lean over and fall down when brought to a stop, and have three brakes instead of two.

On the other hand, because they do not lean, a trike cannot be counter-steered; and many riders experience significant centrifugal force when riding in turns. Trikes are also very expensive, usually adding more than 50% to the cost of the basic motorcycle from which it's built.

4. Sidecars

Adding a sidecar to a traditional motorcycle converts it into what's known as a "hack." Again, a hack may be purchased to deal with an older rider's balance problems, but sometimes they're bought just to facilitate carrying cargo and young family members.

Like a trike, the sidecar provides a third wheel; but unlike a trike, that third wheel is almost never equipped with a brake. That results in relatively difficult handling and a sense of instability whenever the rider accelerates or brakes.

When braking, for example, a hack tends to yaw counter-clockwise; and when accelerating, it tends to yaw clockwise.

More significantly, however, extreme turns can result in loss of control as the sidecar or rear wheel is lifted off the ground. Riders of these motorcycles report some difficulty (or at least some inconsistency) in steering a sidecar, based on speed of travel. For these reasons, adding a sidecar to a traditional motorcycle is probably the least appropriate way to deal with riding problems for a senior rider. It makes no sense simply to change the kind of problems that must be dealt with, when other solutions actually resolve some problems without adding new ones.

5. Scooters

It turns out that moving from a traditional motorcycle to a scooter is an excellent exchange for many older riders. They are simpler to handle, have no clutch lever to deal with, have a much larger cargo capacity (except as compared to a touring bike), and are lighter and more agile generally.

The maxi-scooters now on the market can easily handle hundreds of miles of freeway travel.

II. Constructive contributions

A rider who reaches the maturity phase in his riding career has done so because of superior judgment and knowledge, coupled with good to excellent riding skills. Luck plays no role in becoming a mature rider.

Further, a mature rider probably didn't attain that status on his own—others helped. Sometimes the help arrived passively when the rider mimicked good role models. Sometimes one or more of these sources actively contributed help in the form of mentoring, or writing, or as a certified instructor / RiderCoach. Those who helped were invariably already mature riders.

A mature rider usually wants to contribute constructively to the motorcycle community. Not only because we are all "family", but because riders enhance their own safety while on the road by increasing the odds that any other motorcyclist out there also behaves in as safe and as controlled a manner as possible.

Here are some suggestions of how you might wish to contribute to the motorcycling community if you're now a mature rider yourself.

A. Mentoring

A serious issue for many riders is, "Where do you get information as you grow into a seasoned rider?" Though there are many sources, most are not good ones; and many are actually very poor. Newbies and even competent riders are constantly looking for good role models: **mentors**. You could become such a person. Indeed, you could actively seek out such people and adopt a few into your flock.

1. Angels or demons?

Which voices should you heed?

When a rider's new at the sport of motorcycling, advice seems to come from all directions. It comes in overwhelming quantity and detail about subjects the newbie has never heard of before, concerning problems he can't even imagine.

Whether it's a new rider or a more experienced one, he may have a friend or family member who once owned a motorcycle who decides to be an authority. Riders also often join clubs to find others whose advice is reliable. But is it?

Like other information available in today's complex world, it's easy to reach a point where you want to put your hands over your ears and shout, "Stop! Information overload!"

This problem is one of the best reasons to take a structured training course when starting to ride. The information's provided in tiny units; and overall, only a limited amount of what you need to know is presented, but it will come in fairly manageable chunks.

In structured training programs, the instructors or Rider Coaches have watched many, many riders learn to operate a motorcycle under their supervision. If a rider doesn't understand something, he can ask for a time-out and request clarification. These courses also provide access to a live human being who should be able to answer questions and offer at least a brief explanation, enough to get the rider through the immediate situation or to help him figure out how to improve the skill in question, because the instructor has watched him personally and has been alerted to the issue.

After basic rider training, most motorcyclists are on their own. This is when the individual rider's judgment and reason for taking up motorcycling comes into play. After you know how to operate the bike, then to whom do you listen, in order to learn how to survive out there? Is it possible to find a good mentor? Must you learn everything else by yourself?

Riders who want to learn more about a particular bike and others of its marque often seek out a brand-related club and go to a few meetings. Some of these meetings may not be your cup of tea, offering nothing about what you want to learn and taking place in a social setting that isn't friendly or comfortable, and nothing like safety-oriented.

Meetings that are held in bars, or in restaurants where drinking alcohol during a meal before or during the gathering is accepted, aren't going to help you find appropriate mentors. Most riders come on their motorcycles to such meetings, so that any indulgence in alcohol means that they will be riding home at least somewhat impaired. Even one alcoholic beverage affects a rider's judgment and skill.

But some clubs are full of sharp people with a great deal of experience on the very bike you ride, and you would do well to listen to their stories if they have had problems in common. ("With that model, your bike's ignition will often turn over but the engine won't start. And you may get a big boom when the ignition boot blows off. Expect it several times a month – just put it back on.") Often, they can tell you how to solve them or who to call if your bike needs repairs.

A rider can also find useful information in the workplace. If you bought your bike to commute, you'll want to pre-drive the route for your daily travel a time or two in your car, looking with "new eyes" at signs, signals, road conditions and traffic threats, before your first ride to work on your motorcycle. Then you'll talk to other riders at your office or job about commuting: where to park, what to do with your bike in bad weather, which protective gear you can wear over a suit or a uniform.

If you just want to ride around town with a few buddies on the weekend, your route may be undetermined; but during stops and at the end of the trip, you'll probably spend time off the bike with your friends as you all "kick tires".

You'll definitely get advice from them, but can you believe it? If so, how much of it is reliable and useful?

Even competent riders should take a good look at those buddies with "new eyes" and listen to them with "new ears" before you ride with them or take their opinions as gospel.

There's a lot of foolishness out there. A rider you admire, one who looks like a Motorcycle God today, may lose his luster when you take a closer, more rational look.

Are your riding buddies relatives or old friends? Are you prone to try to one-up them, to impress them, to compete under any condition or situation, whenever one of them throws a dare? Do you think they're experts because they've been riding a few years, or because they ride a bigger bike than yours? Do you tend to listen to the guy who has the biggest mouth, because everyone else does?

In many social settings, one loudmouth will offer opinions on every subject. The reaction of others in the group may be something like this: "It's easier just to go along with him—nobody wants to get in his face," or "He's not as good as he thinks, but nobody wants to hurt his feelings. Just ride your own ride. But keep your head up around him on the road!"

Some riders have nasty tempers, some even have old brain injuries, and more riders than you can imagine are on drugs. People notice, but people don't always act as if they did. Will you have the presence of mind to say "No thanks, I'll ride alone," when you find yourself on the road with one of these people who claims to know it all? Do you have enough of a sense of self-preservation to leave a meeting or a ride where you don't think it's in your best interest to stay?

In some rider groups, you'll hear discussions like this: "Wear a helmet? Nobody else in the group does, it's proven to be more dangerous than riding without one." Or, "Wear long sleeves, even leathers, on a hot day? My brother said he got a heat stroke riding in leather. Man, take it off!" A group of peers can sound like authorities if you forget to be skeptical.

In other words, "question authority."

2. Making an irrational choice

In **Predictably Irrational**, MIT professor Dan Ariely discusses why people do irrational things (like take a dare or listen to stupid advice or ignore warning signs in other people).[12] Human beings make decisions against their own self-interest every day, and it's very hard to convince them to do otherwise once this becomes a habit of mind.

For example, when something is seen as "free," whether it has any real worth is no longer important (and this includes advice). At some point, many people accept a premise based on its perceived value, quality, or availability, not its real one.

---

[12] Ariely, D. **PREDICTABLY IRRATIONAL**: The Hidden Forces that Shape Our Decisions, Harper Collins. (2008). ISBN 978-0061353239.

Strong emotions also have the potential to cause people to accept greater risks when making decisions, especially to undertake an action they will not normally consider. Faced with certain options, they will consistently make the wrong choice. They will have a rationale, but it's a devilish one that makes no sense when you really look at it hard, unless you're willing to accept a certain logic to illogic.

According to Professor Ariely, our irrational behaviors are neither random nor senseless—they are systematic. We all make the same types of mistakes over and over, failing to recognize that they are errors despite the results.

For example, researchers asked people to estimate what proportion of African nations were members of the U.N. This sounds like a pretty neutral test question, right? But they discovered that they could influence the answer those subjects gave just by spinning a "Wheel of Fortune" in front of them to generate a random number. When it was a big number, the estimates were big. Smaller number, smaller estimate. How rational is this?

This may seem far afield from motorcycle safety, but it shows that human beings are programmed to take shortcuts in their thinking at times; and sometimes those shortcuts result in decisions that simply don't make sense in terms of protecting themselves. The results can be unfortunate because these shortcuts may seem rational when they really aren't.

When you're a rider, this desire to avoid making an effort can include giving other people authority to influence your behavior—and change your life. It can mean surrendering your common sense, not listening to your own "inner voice", or failing to **challenge** your inner voice when it's talking nonsense. It can mean developing sloppy habits or making assumptions, even though you've been warned not to do that.

A number of riders have received tips or analyses like the ones included in this volume and then gotten the opposite advice from a buddy. Sometimes, later, they come back and report, "Boy, did I find out which one of you was right!" after the fact. This may fall in the category of experimenting with two hypotheses, but unless you're in a controlled environment, those experiments are best taken in baby steps when you're involved in a hazardous sport. (If you're on a closed track, take your best shot, if that's how you want to learn.)

Before you decide to try some stunt that a friend is doing—or claims to have done—you might consider whether you could be making an irrational decision even though you already know it isn't very smart and is probably against your best interests. If in doubt, **stop**! Then bring it to a forum of riders who have demonstrated good judgment and a safety consciousness, like the one you're trying to acquire.

In the marketplace of ideas and information, it's finally up to each rider to decide what to believe. Still, riders don't have to learn everything they need to know by trial-and-error, especially when an error on the road can cost so much.

Consider what choice is best for **you**. Try to gain an understanding of the facts for yourself, and use the collective wisdom of other riders. Seek out mentors whose opinions seem to have served them well. If the advice you've been given elsewhere is stupid, you'll probably find out soon enough from them.

B. Becoming a RiderCoach or instructor

One of the most satisfying contributions you can make to the motorcycling community is to become a certified MSF RiderCoach or an instructor in a similar program in states where the MSF isn't the state-approved program. Certainly there is an element of status involved, but by far the most rewarding aspect of becoming a RiderCoach or instructor is witnessing your personal efforts turn wannabes into newbies. Your students graduate from basic rider training with an understanding of motorcycle riding fundamentals, and they have gained that understanding in a relatively safe environment with the help you provided, combined with a standardized curriculum.

The work may be largely repetitive; it consumes some of your weekends; it involves standing on your feet for long hours on hot asphalt, or in cold weather, or in rain, and riding very small motorcycles to demonstrate the proper way to perform various range exercises. On the range, you must make critical decisions about the performance of your students, including whether to permit them to continue the course. The pay is trivial; but your efforts will make a difference in the future lives of your students.

The process of applying for and preparing to become a certified MSF RiderCoach is described below for those of you who are curious or seriously considering doing the same. Here's a history of one rider's experience:

"I had taken the beginner's course, MSF Riding and Street Strategies (RSS), which was the precursor to today's Basic

RiderCourse (BRC), about five years before deciding to become an instructor (what RiderCoaches used to be called). I took that course after I had been successfully riding motorcycles for over 30 years. I learned many things during that class; most notably, that I had been doing a few things wrong for years. I had, frankly, expected to be bored out of my skull. I had expected to be talked down to. I had expected trivialities.

"Instead, I was provided with a massive quantity of well-considered and absolutely gospel information that I could not fault in any way. People entering this class without any prior motorcycle experience whatsoever were able to ride a motorcycle (at least on a parking lot) confidently and competently when they left the class. In short, I was impressed.

"Over the next couple of years, I also attended three Experienced Rider Courses (ERCs) because I wanted to be certain that my skills were appropriate using my own bike (a large Gold Wing) instead of the small training bikes used in the beginner's class. I was satisfied with the value of the classes but did not feel that I actually learned anything new in the process.

"However, during several of those ERC classes, I was told by MSF Instructors that I should consider becoming an instructor myself. After five years of that kind of feedback, I decided to look into it.

"The odds are good that if you are interested in becoming an instructor or RiderCoach, it's because one or more of the riders who are already certified to teach has told you that you were good enough to do it.

"The process started with a phone call to the State DPS facility responsible for staffing and conducting the MSF classes. During that phone call I was interviewed about my qualifications. It was clear that the interviewer was attempting to discourage would-be candidates. For example, it was made clear that I had to have completed the basic class (RSS) within 12 months of entering the instructor training curriculum, regardless of any previous basic rider course or even ERC training that I might already have completed.

"I would also have to volunteer at least four weekends as a range aide—meaning I was unable to teach any part of the class or to perform any demonstrations to the class, but I would have to be present and on the range all the time while the class was in that part of the course.

"Additionally, I was told that there would be pre-instructor-training homework that could take as long as 30 days to complete.

"The next Instructor Prep class would not be held until the following spring, at a location over a hundred miles from my home. It would be conducted over two weekends, and not consecutive ones at that. (Occasionally the MSF will teach one over eight consecutive days.)

"Finally, I was told that before I would be invited to enroll as an instructor candidate, the DPS would search my prior driving record looking for tickets, accidents, and any evidence whatsoever of infractions involving alcohol or drugs.

"It's no mystery that the reason for all of these requirements is two-fold:

- To discourage the casually interested, and

- To increase the odds that when a student completes the Instructor Prep class, he or she is highly likely subsequently to teach classes, not to consider it merely a status symbol or personal achievement.

"If you've read this far, you may well wish to become an instructor / RiderCoach. Rather than tell you all about the endless hours of classroom and range exercise the candidates had to deal with, let me just assure you that it was professional, detailed, complete, and **exhausting**. Some class days were over 14 hours in length. All candidates had to perform the demonstrations **perfectly**. And every day that I was on the range doing exercises (playing student) or teaching real students under supervision, it was **hot**!

"Also, no matter how skilled the candidates were before entering the class, each of us felt that he or she might not be good enough to graduate. By comparing ourselves to the other candidates, it was clear that at least one of them was better at some aspect of motorcycle riding (or teaching methods) than all the others. It should come as no surprise to learn that some of those instructor candidates **failed to graduate**. It was humbling, to say the least."

If you believe yourself to be more than competent—if you're now a mature motorcyclist—then becoming an instructor or RiderCoach may be exactly what will enable you to give back to the riding community and to stimulate a renewed interest in this sport for yourself.

C. Safety officer

Most riding clubs and even loosely organized groups of riders have a safety officer position within them. This is a person who's responsible for safety training and safety rules for group rides. This person is usually called upon at each club or group meeting to host a brief safety presentation, to prepare the club's riding rules, and to designate or work with the group's Road Captain for all group rides.

In other words, this is the person who's most likely to establish the group's safety attitude and practices.

An active and well-motivated safety officer will take on the following responsibilities:

- Insure that safety rules exist in written form and that all members have access to them;
- Make safety oriented presentations to the group;
- Organize First Aid training sessions and invite appropriate trainers;
- Organize group parking lot practice sessions and encourage all members to participate, even if they do so on their own away from the group;
- Organize the group's mentoring program, establish how it works, and how mentors become qualified;
- Insure that all field events conducted by the group are safely organized and that all members behave properly during the events;
- Designate a list of qualified Road Captains for the group or work with the Road Captain to train new group leaders and drag bikes; and
- Write or arrange for others to write a safety article for each issue of the group's newsletter.

This is an ideal position to accept when a rider has matured in his riding career, and especially so when that rider is recognized as possessing that maturity and having an excellent safety record.

D. Writing

While giving presentations to a live audience is usually an effective way to convey safety information, it pales by comparison to the effect of a written message. The written word, especially if it contains graphics and pictures to augment its message, can be reproduced and distributed to tens of thousands of readers.

Becoming a published writer has never been easier than it is today. First, no media has ever been better suited to the sharing of information than the Internet. Blogs, message boards, even to some extent the various social media, provide platforms upon which to stand and share your thoughts—and to have those thoughts remain available for the benefit of future readers, essentially forever.

If you decide to delve more deeply into some aspect of motorcycling and rider safety, the ability to publish your findings has also become far simpler and less expensive than it was in the past. You will want to determine, first, that you really have something to offer that's different and valuable to other riders; and you should be aware that undertaking to publish articles or even books requires a major investment in time and effort, as well as opening your work up to criticism.

In the long run, this can only improve the body of knowledge available to riders, as well as debunking myths and clarifying principles that will make riding safer for us all.

E. Ambassadorial influence

A certain segment of U.S. society, mostly older people, still recall the "Easy Rider" image of motorcyclists portrayed in vintage movies, though that segment is diminishing now. Today, most of the non-riding public sees motorcycling as a dangerous sport and holds that motorcyclists tend to be "thrill-seekers" or worse. The smallest group of the non-riders who have an opinion are somewhat tolerant of motorcycles and motorcyclists, or are truly indifferent.

To which of those opinion segments do you want a police officer to belong?

Children are naturally curious and impressed with motorcycles and their riders. They constitute tomorrow's riders, if their opinions are not damaged by viewing unsafe and arrogant motorcyclist behavior, or accidents, or by having a family member hurt or killed while riding a motorcycle.

A mature rider who's well past having to prove anything to anybody about riding is an ideal candidate to affect the public's attitude about our sport. He can do that by example, by appearance, by how he discusses the sport and what is said, and by making an effort to educate the public, especially those children who show curiosity about what we do.

If a rider's son or daughter has a show-and-tell event at school, the rider can help the student prepare an informative and entertaining presentation by lending them some safety gear, discussing how a motorcycle is different from an automobile, and even role-playing a brief ride off the bike. That presentation, especially if the rider's invited to participate, would be remembered for life by the students, and certainly by the son or daughter.

When you're out riding, wave at all children who appear interested, at all police officers who are on their feet (they are working), and at all other riders. No matter what marque or style of bike another rider has chosen, in the big picture, all riders are "family" and should treat other motorcyclists with respect.

Go out of your way to make visits to the club meetings of motorcycle groups in your area if they are open to the public. Guests are often given an opportunity to say a few words. Use that opportunity to compliment what you see, especially the bikes in the parking lot, and to plant a seed with the group about a pet safety subject or two. You will also want to meet the group's safety officer, or if there is none, help the group create such a position. Encourage rider groups to seek appropriate publicity for their events, and suggest that, unlike some organizations which plan big events that bring newspaper photographers or television crews, they wear all their safety gear when being photographed.

At rest stops, talk to the locals. No matter what you actually talk about, you're conveying the idea that motorcyclists are human beings, real people who come from many backgrounds and locations, and who have chosen to ride for many reasons. We are much more than what movies, books, or other media have stereotyped motorcyclists to be.

Many of us participate in charity events, support disabled motorcyclists, and even visit groups of veterans and retired seniors at assisted living centers and nursing homes, sharing stories and pictures of our rides, inviting them to inspect our shiny machines, and occasionally triggering wonderful memories for riders of long ago.

To the extent that you improve the public perception of motorcyclists and motorcycling, you improve your own safety out on the road, and the safety of all of us who ride. And to the extent that you encourage other motorcyclists to adopt a safety mindset, you have enhanced and improved both their safety and your own.

Ride safe, keep learning, and we'll see you on the road.

Glossary

1%er / One-percenter

A pejorative referring to bikers who demonstrate a "gangsta" image in the way they dress and their lawless behavior.

Two-second rule

This is the **minimum** distance you maintain between your motorcycle and the bike immediately ahead of you (in the same track as you are in). When riding in staggered formation this means that you would maintain a minimum of one-second spacing between your motorcycle and the next bike in the group ahead of you.

'Two seconds" becomes a distance when you measure how far your motorcycle moves in that amount of time. Thus, no matter what speed you are riding at, the minimum following distance automatically "adjusts" by using this concept.

ABS

An acronym: **A**nti-lock **B**raking **S**ystem

Computer-controlled brakes that use sensors to determine when a tire on a wheel is starting to skid and respond by very quickly **removing** braking pressure on the affected wheel, then restoring that pressure in an effort to keep stopping power at its maximum (just prior to a skid). ABS responds to imminent brake lock caused by **either** excessive braking pressure or sudden loss of tire traction. Tests have shown that extremely skilled racers can brake slightly more effectively without ABS, but that the vast majority of motorcyclists are incapable of braking as effectively without ABS as they can with it. The fundamental safety advantage of an ABS is not that a motorcycle stops more quickly with it than without, but that it virtually eliminates rear-brake lock in panic situations.

Acceleration rate

See **g's**.

Air horns

Used as a replacement or supplement for the traditionally weak "toot" or "bleep" sound of stock motorcycle horns. These usually come as a pair of horns, one providing a "C" note and the other providing a "D" note. These sounds react with each other and make the horn noticeably louder.

Alt-MOST

An acronym: **A**lternate **M**otorcycle **O**perator **S**kill **T**est.

This is a test designed by the MSF in collaboration with the National Public Service Research Institute (now called the PSRI, for Public Service Research Institute). It's used in at least 29 states to determine whether an applicant is minimally qualified to obtain a motorcycle operator endorsement on his or her driver's license.

The test consists of seven elements:

1. Left Turn
2. Controlled Stop
3. Right Hand U-Turn
4. Quick Stop
5. Obstacle Swerve
6. Stalling

The first six are usually combined into four test runs. "Stalling" is not actually a test, but the applicant is observed to see if he can control his motorcycle without stalling it.

AMA

An acronym: **A**merican **M**otorcyclist **A**ssociation

Anti-dive

A front-end design that tends to reduce the diving of a motorcycle while under heavy braking conditions, often by stiffening the suspension. Once popular, it's rarely found on contemporary bikes.

The problem with anti-dive is that it results in a higher Center of Gravity during heavy braking than would be true if the front suspension were allowed to compress more fully. That, in turn, results in **more weight transfer** rather than less.

Especially relative to sportbikes, it's easier to do a stoppie on a bike with an anti-dive front-end than on one without it.

Ape-hangers

A handlebar designed in such a way that when holding onto the grips, your hands will be substantially higher than your shoulders. A shorter version is known as "baby apes."

Apex

Usually refers to the midpoint of a turn, but as it relates to driving a vehicle, the meaning has become "the point on your driving line which touches, or comes closest to, the inner radius of a curve." Thus, "late apex" certainly refers to a point later than its midpoint.

Armored jacket

A textile, synthetic mesh, or leather riding jacket which has reinforcements in the back, shoulders, arms, elbows and other areas to protect the rider from road rash and modest bruising in the event of an accident.

ATGATT

An acronym meaning: **A**ll **T**he **G**ear, **A**ll **T**he **T**ime

A safety attitude which presumes that safety gear should **always** be worn when riding a motorcycle, regardless of temperature, distance to be ridden, or peer pressures that might discourage doing so.

Bagger

Like "dresser", this refers to a motorcycle which has luggage the offers cargo capacity, including at least a pair of saddlebags. It may also be outfitted with a top box or trunk, a pillion bag, tank bags, etc.

Body-steering

The practice of using a shift of the rider's weight or leaning the shoulder on the side into which the rider wishes to turn, instead of using direct handlebar input to cause a change of direction in his path of travel.

This is a very imprecise and limited means of controlling the bike's direction of travel and is typically employed by riders who are not formally trained in the proper way to ride motorcycles and who don't understand how counter-steering works when traveling above about 10 MPH.

Bore

In reference to an engine, its bore refers to a cylinder's diameter. A cylinder's bore and stroke define the engine's displacement.

BRC

An acronym: **B**asic (Beginner's) **R**ider **C**ourse

The MSF entry-level motorcycle riding class. Participants need no experience other than the ability to ride a bicycle.

Bullet bike

Sportbikes come in various models that range from beginner models with relatively low power and speed potential to models with awesomely powerful engines capable of attaining top speeds well in excess of 170 MPH.

The medium- to higher-powered sportbikes are often called "crotch rockets". The most powerful of these models are known as "bullet bikes". Examples of two popular bullet bikes are the Suzuki GSX-R600 and the Kawasaki ZX9R.

Gear	Maximum speed
1st	75 MPH
2nd	102 MPH
3rd	125 MPH
4th	145 MPH
5th	161 MPH
6th	178 MPH

Table 2: GSX-R600 Potential Speeds

Gear	Maximum speed
1st	76.5 MPH
2nd	101.3 MPH
3rd	126.4 MPH
4th	147.6 MPH
5th	163.9 MPH
6th	179.6 MPH

Table 3: ZX9R Potential Speeds

Both motorcycles can attain or exceed the speed limit of any road in the United States **while in first gear**.

Bungee cord

Sometimes called "shock cords", these are general-purpose elastic restraining devices with metal or plastic hooks on both ends.

They are used to secure luggage or small items to your motorcycle to prevent their falling off while traveling. They're very popular because the hooks eliminate the need to tie and untie these restraints. They can also be very dangerous if they break (usually the result of being cut, not because they were stretched too tightly) or if they manage to get entangled in your wheel or rear drive train. The most common injury to a rider from their use is severe bruising, but the loss of an eye is not unheard of.

Cage

Just about any passenger vehicle with more than three wheels. A Porsche 911sc, a Yugo, and a Jeep Wagoneer are all cages, as are pickup trucks. "Cager" refers to the driver.

California stop

Phrase often used by motorcyclists meaning to stop, typically at an intersection, without putting a foot down.

While they are probably legal virtually everywhere in the United States, some police officers will write you a citation for "failure to make a complete stop" if they observe that you do not put at least one foot down at an intersection. In some states, if you make a California Stop while taking a motorcycle riding test to obtain a motorcycle endorsement, you may fail it.

This term usually has the definition just provided; but it may be used to describe an intersection "stop" that's not actually a stop. That is, if the bike is very nearly brought to a stop (really a pause), regardless of whether a foot is used to touch the ground, and then the rider accelerates through an intersection, that's also called a "California Stop" and is illegal virtually everywhere in the United States.

Canyon carving

A euphemism that means to ride aggressively on twisty roads to experience the unique thrill provided to all single-track vehicles riders: leaning the bike at speed.

Camber thrust

When a bike is traveling in other than a straight line, it's leaned over. That changes the location of the contact patch of the tires from the middle of the tire to the side.

Because the motorcycle tire's profile is a curve, the distance from the inner and outer edges of that new contact patch to the center of the wheel axle is different. That difference causes the tire to generate what's called a "camber thrust'—meaning an attempt to make the bike turn in a tighter radius than it is currently traveling in. (The outer edge of the contact patch **is** traveling faster than the inner edge.)

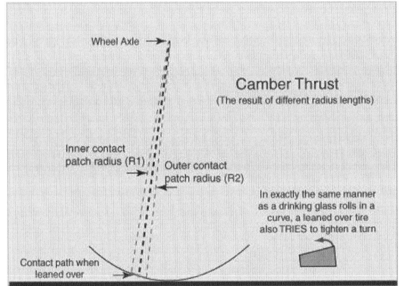

Figure 68: Camber thrust

Case guards

See **Engine Guards**.

Center of Gravity

Usually referred to with the abbreviation "CG", this is actually the location of the center of mass of an object. If the object were to be suspended from that point, it would have no tendency to pitch, roll, or yaw.

Center-stand

Some motorcycles have this stand to support the parked bike, some do not. On motorcycles that have this item, it's located under the frame of the motorcycle; when lowered, it generally raises the rear tire off of the ground for maintenance purposes. Parking a bike on the center stand requires level ground.

The center-stand should not be used during windy conditions or when the bike is parked and covered, as the motorcycle is not as stable on the center-stand as it is on the side-stand.

Centrifugal force

A reactive force responding to centripetal force. It is an inertial force and is used in discussions of rotating objects. It's sometimes called a "fictitious" force, in that it feels as though it is pushing a mass outward from the center of rotation, but an inertial force (momentum) actually tries to maintain a direction of travel. This force acts on the body that is moving in a circular motion. It is zero when the rate of rotation of the reference frame is zero.

Centripetal force

A force that pushes a mass along a curved path. This force is always orthogonal to the instantaneous direction of travel, toward the center of rotation and contributes to keeping the body in circular motion.

Chicken strips

Chicken strips are the part of a tire that has never been worn against the pavement. Chicken strips only appear on tires that have never been leaned over very far (leading to the presumption that the rider is "chicken", or fearful of riding with the bike leaned). Once a bike is ridden while in a lean, the tire will no longer have chicken strips.

A front tire may have a "chicken strip" even after its corresponding rear tire has none, because the tire profiles are different, with the front tire requiring a bigger lean angle to wear it toward its edges.

Chopper

Usually a custom-designed motorcycle with an extended rake angle, ape-hangers, a stretched appearance, a custom paint job, custom chrome components, and often an over-sized rear tire.

Originally, "chopper" referred to a motorcycle that had all unnecessary parts removed in order to enhance its speed through weight reduction or merely to make it look "tough".

Chopping a throttle

This refers to rapidly closing, rolling off, or backing off the throttle to reduce speed. It is a phrase that seems to be unique to motorcycle usage, possibly with its origin in racing.

Closing the door

An expression that describes what a "drag' / 'sweep' / 'tail-gunner" in a group ride does when he recognizes that a lane is about to be lost.

Specifically, the last rider in a group will move alone into the lane that's about to be lost, in order to prevent a vehicle traveling behind the group from trying to pass it, so that the vehicle won't run out of lane and have to cut into the group of motorcycles.

Coefficient of Friction (μ)

A value representing the ratio of force of friction between two bodies and the force pressing them together. As calculated, it is the tangential force (F)(driving, centrifugal, or braking) required to produce sliding, divided by the Normal force between the surfaces (N) (weight) That is, $\mu = F/N$.

Static or Rolling Coefficient of Friction describes when the two solid objects are not sliding, while Dynamic or Sliding Coefficient of Friction describes when they are already sliding.

The Dynamic or Sliding Coefficient of Friction is almost always lower than the Static or Rolling Coefficient of Friction, often by about 25%.

Colors

A vest or jacket with insignia attached that identifies the rider as being affiliated with a particular organization. Alternatively, "flying your colors" refers to the display of a flag on your motorcycle.

Contact patch

The part of a tire which is touching the ground. This is the only part of a tire that is flat, and it exists only because of gravity.

The contact patch provides traction to keep the tire from skidding or sliding.

Cool collar; also, "Kool Kollar"

A wrap worn around the neck to provide significant cooling to a rider in very hot weather.

This object is a cloth tube that either contains a bead-like material that swells when immersed in cold water and then dries slowly; or it contains an inner plastic tube which, in turn, contains ice and / or ice water.

Whichever design the cool collar takes, it works first as a result of being chilled and secondarily by evaporation of the moisture it contains.

Counter-steering

The **only** way a single-track vehicle, like a motorcycle, can be directed to change its direction of travel when it's traveling at speeds faster than a person can run, or about 10 MPH.

Counter-steering usually involves pressing forward on the handlebar grip on the side **toward** which you wish to turn. Often described as "Push Right, Go Right" or "Push Left, Go Left". However, by merely shifting your weight on the motorcycle ("body-steering") you can cause small amounts of counter-steering to occur. Weight shifting to change the direction of travel of a motorcycle is imprecise and usually results in only slight amounts of direction change, whereas use of forward pressure on the handlebar grips is highly efficient and precise, and it can cause any amount of direction change with little effort.

At slower speeds, a rider must use direct-steering, wherein he turns the handlebar in the direction he wishes to go.

There's no choice in how to steer. Depending on speed and the geometry of the front-end of a motorcycle, physics determines whether the rider must use direct-steering or counter-steering.

Crash bars

See **Engine Guards**.

Crotch rocket

A sportbike. Crotch rockets are fast, agile, and powerful, which makes it easy for a rider to lose control and get in over his head. Hence the term "rocket.' These bikes have a relatively short wheelbase as compared to the height of their Center of Gravity, so that weight transfer during braking and acceleration is significant.

Cruise control

An electronic version of the simpler mechanical device known as a "throttle lock", used to maintain a rider's speed automatically. These are located on or near the right grip and provide the ability to lock in a particular speed, increase or decrease that speed, and disengage (turn off) the feature.

Application of either brake also automatically disengages cruise control—which, because mechanical versions do not respond to braking, is the single most important deficiency of a "throttle lock".

It is dangerous to use cruise control when riding on wet pavement.

Deceleration rate

See **g's**.

Decreasing radius turn

A turn in which the rider is required to use an increasing steering angle, or decreasing speed, as he progresses through it. Frequently, this is a turn where the arc gets sharper as you progress through the curve.

A decreasing radius turn is dangerous. Such a turn that does **not** have a decreasing radius is even more dangerous, because it isn't obvious. Only a literalist should think that a "decreasing radius curve" necessarily involves a decreasing radius. The problem with a decreasing radius turn is that you can find yourself going too fast to exit it safely, even though you were not going too fast for the first part of the curve.

Unlike a constant radius turn, there's no one smooth line through this kind of curve which has a single apex to it allowing you to pick a single stable speed and maintain it through the turn with the same lean angle.

Three scenarios individually or if combined result in a curve that must be treated as if it is decreasing radius:

1. The early part of the curve provides a more positive camber (leans inward) than does the latter part of the curve;
2. There's a rising elevation in the early part of the curve and a falling elevation towards its end; and

3. The traction in the early part of the curve is better than towards the end.

Though each of the curves described above has a constant radius, they must be treated in the same way as a decreasing radius curve in order to negotiate them safely.

What this should tell you is that on any unfamiliar road, you should avoid trying to take the curves as fast as appears possible. Further, always plan to exit a curve some distance away from its outside edge, so that you have some ability to "overshoot" your line **when** the unexpected happens.

Delta-V

This stands for "change in velocity", otherwise known as acceleration. Note that velocity is speed in a particular **direction**; it is not simply speed.

Thus, if you change speed **or** you change direction, you are creating a Delta-V. You are accelerating. Why is that important to know? Because acceleration consumes traction.

Direct-steering

The **only** way a single-track vehicle, like a motorcycle, can be directed to change its direction of travel when it's traveling at slow speeds (slower than a person can run). Sometimes called "caster-steering" (referring to casters like those on a vehicle such as a grocery cart), direct-steering involves turning the handlebar in the direction you wish to go. Even "body-steering" is direct-steering at slow speeds.

At higher speeds, the **only** way a single-track vehicle, like a motorcycle, can be made to change its direction of travel is by using counter-steering, wherein you press forward on the handlebar grip on the side **toward** which you wish to turn (often described as "Push Right, Go Right" or "Push Left, Go Left").

There's no choice in how you steer. Depending on your speed and the geometry of the front-end of your motorcycle, physics determines whether you use direct-steering or counter-steering.

Do-rag / Skull cap

Do-rags are cloth coverings used to cover a rider's hair and forehead in an effort to keep sweat from dripping into the eyes or being absorbed by the helmet liner, and in order to avoid "helmet hair" (disarray caused by sweat or static).

For most riders who don't wear a helmet, these are *de rigueur*. They help prevent a rider's hair from being whipped into his eyes by the wind.

Do-rags are tied at the rear of the head. They can be worn under a helmet as well and, like skull caps, provide modest comfort. Far more importantly, they provide a measure of sanitation improvement—especially when wearing someone else's helmet or a loaner helmet at a training center, because they can be washed after use.

Skull caps usually are smaller than do-rags and do not cover any part of the forehead. These are specifically worn under a helmet. They cannot be worn without a helmet, as they're not tied to the head.

Drag / Sweep/ Tail Gunner

Each of these terms refers to the last rider in a group of motorcycles who are riding with discipline, as opposed to a number of riders who happen to be going in the same direction and in proximity.

This rider is typically responsible for acquiring a new lane when the group changes lanes, rendering assistance to any rider who must leave the group, assessing the skill level of new riders to the group, and communicating with the lead bike rider about traffic conditions behind the group. This rider is often the "safety officer" for that group.

This rider is specifically selected for the position by the lead bike (the group leader), who may also be the Road Captain for the group. The drag bike has authority within the group second only to the group leader.

Dresser

A touring bike; or a standard or cruiser motorcycle which has been enhanced through add-ons to make it more comfortable for longer rides.

Add-ons that make a motorcycle a dresser include windscreen, backrest, good-time radio, CB radio, and saddlebags. After attaching these add-ons to a motorcycle, that bike is said to be "fully dressed" (or a "dresser").

Drive / front sprocket

A motorcycle chain is driven by a toothed gear, called a drive sprocket. The chain, in turn, drives a wheel (or driven) sprocket.

The drive sprocket is the smaller of the two sprockets and is often called the front sprocket, while the larger driven sprocket is often called the rear sprocket and is attached to the rear wheel hub.

Duck-walking

The process of moving your motorcycle while straddling the saddle, using your legs for power instead of the engine.

Dumping a bike

Similar to a "low-side", but not the result of loss of traction and occurring, usually, at a speed of **zero** MPH.

A bike is dumped when the rider applies brakes while in a very slow turn, or is trying to get his bike up onto (or off) its center-stand, or is walking the bike and it gets away from him, or forgets to put the side-stand down and tries to get off the bike, or any of dozens of other "dumb" things that lead to losing control of the bike such that it falls over onto the ground.

Note that when someone says he "laid it down,"' he's not talking about dumping his bike—instead, he's most likely saving face by trying to explain what happened when he locked his rear brake, lost control, and crashed.

Dyno / Dynamometer

An instrument used to measure and document power. In particular, these devices may be found at some motorcycle dealerships and are used to determine the performance characteristics of individual motorcycles.

The fundamental output of a dyno run is a graph which shows engine torque and horsepower throughout its rpm range and, sometimes, a chart showing potential land speeds that the motorcycle can attain (discounting wind resistance) in each of its transmission gears.

Edge traps

Any uneven roadway surface that can "capture" your tire when you attempt to cross over it, causing you to lose control of your motorcycle and end up eating asphalt.

Any surface that's at least one inch higher than the roadway on which you are riding can trap your tires.

This difference in height isn't always between lanes.

For example, a curb is an edge trap. (If your tires are placed against a curb, you **cannot** simply drive away without leaning the bike substantially and duck-walking it.)

If you must cross over an edge trap, do so with as large an attack angle as possible. Turn away from the edge, and then turn toward it before crossing over.

EFI

An acronym: **E**lectronic **F**uel **In**jection.

Refers to a computer-controlled fuel injection system that replaces carburetors in order to manage fuel / air mixtures with precision. An EFI eliminates the need for the choke on a motorcycle, as well as replacing its carburetors.

Engine guards

Also called "case guards" or "crash bars". A set of sturdy tubular bars (usually chromed, and often with highway pegs attached), designed to protect the engine if the motorcycle falls over. They offer minimal protection to the rider during an accident, but may prevent broken cooling fins or scratched engine cases if the kickstand sinks into soft asphalt, and the cycle topples.

Engine guards protect the bike. Leathers protect the rider's legs. On touring bikes, they may prevent the motorcycle from falling completely on its side to a horizontal position.

ERC

An acronym: **E**xperienced **R**ider **C**ourse.

A second-level motorcycle training hosted by the MSF. In this class the rider must provide his own motorcycle, as one is not provided by the program.

A rider is expected to have had at least six months of street-riding experience before taking this class.

Fairing

A plastic cowling affixed to the front of a motorcycle. These are designed to improve the aerodynamics of the bike and provide the rider more comfort by shielding him or her from wind buffeting. A fairing usually includes a clear windscreen. Fairings are either mounted directly to the frame of the motorcycle or to its front fork assembly.

If attached to the front forks, the fairing turns with the handlebar; while if attached to the frame, the fairing remains rigidly in place regardless of handlebar movement.

Naturally, fairings attached to the front forks result in more wind-affected steering input than those that are frame-mounted.

The interior surface of many fairings, as it faces the rider, often performs the same function as a car's dashboard: instrumentation, radios, travel computers, speakers, etc., are mounted there. This is particularly true of "dressers".

Family

A group of riders is known as a "family" instead of a "herd" or a "flock." When a group of such riders who have been temporarily separated regroup, it's normal for the drag bike to announce that fact to the group leader via his CB by saying: "We're family."

Final drive

The mechanical components which transfer power from a motorcycle's transmission to its rear wheel (driven wheel).

The most common final drive consists of a chain and sprockets. Some motorcycles employ a drive shaft similar to that of a rear-wheel-drive car. Late-model Harley-Davidson and Boss Hoss motorcycles use a reinforced rubber belt and sprockets.

Floorboards

Used instead of pegs on many cruisers and touring motorcycles, these are pivoting plates upon which a rider may place his foot flat as he rides. Because floorboards make it almost impossible to get under a gear shift lever in order to up-shift, bikes that are equipped with floorboards are usually also equipped with heel-toe shifters.

Foot

A flat rock, wood, plastic, or metal object placed between the side-stand and hot asphalt.

When temperatures exceed about 90 degrees, it's dangerous to leave a bike on asphalt with only a side-stand holding it up. The surface area of the side-stand is so small that, as the asphalt warms up, the side-stand will sink into it, and the bike will fall over on its side. If you are going to park on asphalt on a hot day you should put a foot under that side-stand. If you are not carrying a foot with you, it's easy enough to make one by crushing an empty can.

Force

Any influence that causes a free body to change speed, direction of travel, or shape. A force has both magnitude and direction. Thus, it is a vector quantity.

Newton's second law can be expressed as **F = ma** where "F" is Force, "m" is mass and "a" is acceleration. That demonstrates that **weight is a force;** specifically, weight is the **force** generated by the gravitational attraction of one object on another object. Weight equals mass times gravitational acceleration.

Forward controls

When the gear shift lever and rear-brake pedal are in front of a vertical line from the rider's knees, they are referred to as forward controls. Their position makes it virtually impossible to stand on the foot pegs.

Friction zone

That part of the clutch lever travel from the area where the clutch just starts to engage until it's fully engaged.

g's

The acceleration rate at which an object will fall if it's in a vacuum and close to the earth. Gravity is an acceleration. Objects close to the earth in a vacuum will increase their speed at the rate of 32.17 feet per second every second.

This rate is sometimes described as "feet per second per second" or "feet per second squared", and it's usually expressed as an abbreviated and rounded number: 32.2 ft/sec^2.

Any other acceleration or deceleration rate can be specified as a percentage of gravity.

Thus, for example, a deceleration rate of 0.8g's means that an object is slowing down at 80% of the rate of gravity. Since gravity (or "g") is 32.17 ft/sec^2, this object is decelerating at a rate of 25.74 ft/sec^2. (That's 17.55 MPH per second.)

GPS

An acronym: **G**lobal **P**ositioning **S**ystem.

A satellite-oriented system, including computers and receivers, which provides for the determination of a very precise location (latitude, longitude, and height) of an object.

Over time, if the device being tracked is moving, the system also provides for the determination of its precise speed and direction of travel.

More and more touring motorcycles are being built with a GPS navigation system built in, and add-on devices are available for any other motorcycle.

These navigation systems provide color graphic screen presentations of street maps, and both planned as well as actual travel itineraries. Some can even announce the turns that should be made in order to follow a planned itinerary.

Gravity

An acceleration that, near the earth, attempts to increase the speed of a falling object in a vacuum by 32.17 feet per second per second.

Group riding "Prime Directive"

Never hit the bike in front of you.

GWRRA

An acronym: **G**old **W**ing **R**oad **R**iders **A**ssociation.

An international association of Honda Gold Wing owners.

Hack

A relatively ancient term for a motorcycle's sidecar.

Sometimes, a motorcycle that has a sidecar is improperly called a "hack" as opposed to a "rig".

Note that a motorcycle that has been converted into a trike by replacing its rear-end with the two-wheeled rear-end from a car is **not** known as a hack.

Handlebar

Generally, a tubular piece of pipe, available in various lengths and angles, to which the hand grips, clutch, and front-brake levers, hydraulic master cylinder, mirrors, turn signal, headlight, and engine cut-off switch controls are attached.

The handlebar attaches to the top of the triple-tree.

It's sometimes described as the sixth control on a motorcycle, because it's what is used to change the bike's direction of travel.

Hanging off

Phrase used to describe the cornering technique used by a motorcyclist who races through a curve at high speed, in which he positions his body to the extreme inside of the bike and below the normal riding position.

This decreases the bike's lean angle and allows higher speeds through the curve.

No public roads in the United States require a rider to hang off his bike if that rider is traveling at legal speeds.

In other words, if you see a rider hanging off on public roads, he's attempting to break the law on public roads.

Used on a race track, this is the only way to maximize speed through a turn. When used on public roads, this is a sure indication of a squid pretending to be a racer.

Heel-toe shifter

Instead of a normal gear shift lever, bikes equipped with floorboards are usually also equipped with a heel-toe shifter.

Down-shifting is accomplished by pressing down on the forward lever with the toe of the rider's foot, while up-shifting is accomplished by pressing down on the rearward lever with the heel of the foot.

Helmet hair

The condition of your hair after you remove your helmet.

It will be partially matted and partially sticking out at odd angles. Sweat has had its way with you.

High-side

When a motorcycle rider gets launched into the air and over the bike, instead of simply falling down alongside a falling bike (see low-side). The motorcycle will almost always be thrown into the air following that rider and may fall on him.

This usually happens as a result of losing traction on the rear tire, then suddenly regaining it after the rear of the motorcycle has slid sideways a meaningful distance.

If there's only a momentary loss of rear-wheel traction, or if the rear-end of the bike has not slid meaningfully to the side before traction is regained, loss of control of the bike usually does not occur, and the rider is **not** tossed off the bike.

Highway boards / Highway pegs

A second set of foot pegs for a rider to use for stretching his legs. The pegs are usually well forward of the normal operator's pegs and thus not a good place for one's feet when dealing with traffic or in demanding riding conditions. They are intended to serve as a way to stretch the legs when out on the open road—hence the name "highway" pegs.

HOG

An acronym: **H**arley **O**wners **G**roup. Also, H.O.G.

A manufacturer-backed organization with some 1,300 chapters around the world. Chapters are usually associated with a Harley-Davidson dealership.

Many other brands have similar organizations.

HP / Horsepower

A unit of power. US standard HP is equal to 33,000 foot-pounds per minute.

Hydroplane

When a tire is lifted off the surface of a roadway by a body of water such that all traction is lost. Hydroplaning occurs when water's depth is ¼ inch or greater and the tire is moving at speeds of about 50 MPH or greater.

Tire tread is supposed to be designed to shed water away from in front of a tire and away from the center of the tire in an effort to reduce the risk of hydroplaning. But the tread patterns on the front tire of contemporary motorcycles no longer seem designed to do this in favor of other factors.

Speed, weight per square inch on the tire's contact patch, width of the tire, depth of the water, and tread design are all factors in determining whether hydroplaning will occur.

The higher the air pressure, the narrower a tire becomes, and the more weight per square inch of contact patch. Thus, a practical anti-hydroplaning strategy is to insure that the air pressure in your tires is near the maximum rating printed on the tire's sidewall.

Integrated / linked braking

When the front and rear brakes of a motorcycle are not individually and uniquely activated by only one control each.

For example, when applying the rear-brake pedal causes full activation of the rear brake along with partial activation of the front brake; or when applying the front-brake lever causes full activation of the front brake and partial activation of the rear brake.

Iron Butt Ride

A ride encompassing 1,000 miles to be completed within 24 hours in an event sanctioned by the Iron Butt Association. The IBA is a US-based organization dedicated to safe, long-distance, endurance motorcycle riding with over 20,000 members world-wide.

The concepts of "safe", "long distance", and "endurance" are mutually exclusive in the eyes of many experienced riders and some state legislatures, which have outlawed these events on public roads as illegal tests of endurance.

Kickstand

See **Side-stand**.

Kinetic energy

The energy possessed by an object resulting from its motion.

Energy cannot be destroyed, but it does change form. The energy contained in gasoline changes into heat energy when it's burned, for example. The energy used to change your bike's speed from zero to 60 MPH becomes your bike's kinetic energy at that speed.

Exactly the same amount of energy is changed to some other form (usually heat) when you reduce your bike's speed from 60 MPH to zero.

Note, kinetic energy increases at the square of an object's change of speed.

Thus, **doubling** your bike's speed from 30 MPH to 60 MPH results in a **quadrupling** of its kinetic energy. That's why it takes four times as much distance to stop from 60 MPH as it does to stop from 30 MPH.

$E_K = (1/2)mV^2$

Laid it down

This is how some riders describe what has happened when a rider locks the rear wheel of a bike with excessive braking, whereupon it yaws out from under him, resulting in a low-side. In other words, it's an excuse designed to save face. (That's what helmets are intended to do.)

Lane-splitting

The act of riding between the lanes of a roadway, typically faster than surrounding traffic.

In several countries, this is perfectly legal (often called "filtering"), while in the United States it is illegal in all states other than California, where it is not illegal if done in a safe manner and within the limits imposed by its traffic laws.

Late apex

One of various terms used to describe a path through a curve that is not simply "the smoothest".

While "late apex" is a popular term, "delayed start" seems more appropriate.

Late apexing has several advantages:

- You are less likely to run wide.
- You have better visibility into the corner.
- There's more margin for error if you make a mistake, for example if the corner turns out to have a decreasing radius.

To determine whether your apexes are too early, you should be able to unwind the steering and add throttle at the apex and beyond. If you can't add throttle, or you still have to add more counter-steering after the apex, you've turned too early for the corner.

Leathers

Collectively, the various pieces of leather apparel a rider wears for protection. May include chaps, jackets, and pants.

While the most obvious advantage of leathers is preventing road rash, another key function is to minimize the effects of being struck by bugs and debris. Leathers may be custom tailored or "off the rack." They may also have armor in critical locations, such as over the spine. They're part of what is referred to as ATGATT.

LEO

An acronym: **L**aw **E**nforcement **O**fficer.

Might be a state trooper, provincial police officer, local police officer, or a representative of some other jurisdiction.

Low-side

When a motorcycle falls down because of insufficient speed while in a turn or because it loses traction—indeed, for any reason at all—and the motorcyclist falls along with the bike. This is far less dangerous than a "high-side", where the rider is launched into the air over the bike. Note that even if a "fall down" starts as a "low-side", if some portion of that bike "hooks up" or "catches" the ground while sliding before the rider exits the bike, it can become a high-side. This is **the** reason you must leave the bike when or before it hits the ground. "Holding on" or "riding the tank" when a bike falls down is good advice only in science fiction movies.

Maxi-scooter

Though most scooters are used for practical surface-street commuter vehicles, they are insufficiently powered for usage on highways and freeways. Scooters with engines of 500cc's or larger are quite adequate for sustained highway riding and are called maxi-scooters.

MIC

An acronym: **M**otorcycle **I**ndustry **C**ouncil.

This is a not-for-profit (501)(c)(6) (**industry trade group**) organization which is the principal lobbying arm for manufacturers and distributors in the motorcycle industry.

MOM

An Acronym: **M**otorcycle **O**wner's **M**anual.

"Ask MOM" means "look in the manual".

Momentum

Represented by the symbol p, this is an inertial characteristic of a moving mass that attempts to keep that mass moving at the same speed and direction; that is, it opposes any drag forces. Momentum is calculated as the product of mass and velocity ($p = mv$). Momentum is always calculated from the observer's point of view.

An 800-pound motorcycle traveling due north at 50 MPH has a momentum of 40,000 lbs. MPH traveling due north from an observer standing on the ground, but it has a velocity and momentum of zero from the rider's perspective.

Note how similar momentum is to force. Indeed, Aristotle claimed that **F** = m**v** before Newton showed that **F** = m**a**.

MSF

An acronym: **M**otorcycle **S**afety **F**oundation.

The Motorcycle Safety Foundation is a national, not-for-profit organization formed in 1973 and "sponsored" by the U.S. manufacturers and distributors of BMW, Ducati, Harley-Davidson, Honda, Kawasaki, KTM, Piaggio / Vespa, Suzuki, Triumph, Victory, and Yamaha motorcycles. While many think that it is a 501 (c)(3) not-for-profit organization, **it is not**. The 501 (c)(3) designation is reserved for education and charitable organizations.

The MSF is a 501 (c)(6) non-profit which is specifically **a trade group organization,** the sole purpose of which is to promote the well-being of the group's members, **not** the safety of students. Its goal is often thought to be to promote safe motorcycle operation in the U.S. Instead, its goal is essentially **only** to promote the business interests (motorcycle sales) of its "sponsors" (read: owners).

Other countries may have their own version of MSF.

Newbie / Newby / Noob

Usually, anyone who's just started riding motorcycles. Newbie can also apply to a state of mind that may linger for quite some time. A person may consider himself a newbie, even though he or she has been riding for years. Newbies are (hopefully) building skill and confidence. A smart newbie knows his limits.

Offset

When referring to your motorcycle's front-end geometry, this is the distance between a line through the center of your steering stem and a similarly angled line drawn through the front wheel hub.

The offset is primarily determined by the width of your triple-tree but can also be affected by how your forks attach to the hub of your front wheel.

Offset is designed to produce the desired trail in cooperation with the rake angle and diameter of your front wheel.

Orthogonal

Perpendicular. This term is used especially when discussing forces and vectors.

Out-tracking

When in a turn, a bike's front wheel is instantaneously traveling in one direction, while it's actually pointing toward the outside of that direction (relative to the curve). This is because of the "restoring force", a slight torque of the steering stem toward the inside of that turn. In other words, it's the bike's way of trying to align the direction its front wheel points and its actual instantaneous direction of travel.

The result is that the motorcycle attempts to go in a straight line; and the rider must, in almost all cases, **maintain** counter-steering pressure on the inside grip in order to continue along your chosen path.

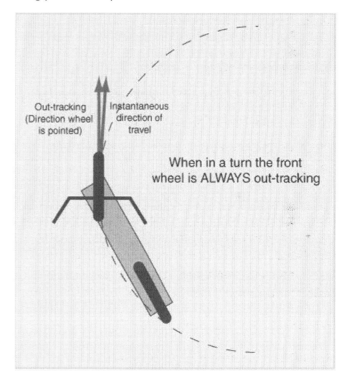

Figure 69: Out-tracking

PDR

An acronym: **P**erception, **D**ecision, **R**eaction.

This is the amount of time a person takes to perceive a threat, then decide what to do about it, and then actually react to a threat.

139

It has been shown that 70% of all drivers have a PDR of 1.6 seconds or less when confronted with an **unexpected** threat, such as if the car ahead of them slams on its brakes.

It has also been shown that when the threat is expected—for example, when a rider sees a green light turning yellow—PDR times are at least one full second shorter.

Motorcyclists have PDR times slightly faster than automobile drivers, because it takes less time to react (move fingers to the front-brake lever, instead of the foot to the brake pedal). By simply covering the front-brake lever, PDR time is further reduced by a tenth of a second.

Pillion

This is a passenger "seat" on a motorcycle—usually just an extension of the rider's seat—and is located directly over the rear wheel axle of the bike.

Sometimes, improperly, a motorcycle passenger is referred to as a pillion.

Unless there's a backrest or "sissy bar" on the pillion, it should **not** be used to carry a passenger! Instead of being a "seat", these pillions are merely soft platforms for carrying strapped-on luggage.

PLP

An acronym: **P**arking **L**ot **P**ractice.

Practice in performance of slow-speed maneuvers.

PM

An acronym: **P**reventative **M**aintenance.

Refers to doing work on the bike (such as changing its oil) **before** wear or damage occurs.

PMS

An acronym: **P**arked **M**otorcycle **S**yndrome.

Refers to a certain anxiety caused by an extended period of poor weather, such as winter in many parts of the country.

Poker run

This is a traditional motorcycle event used to raise money for charity (usually). These are legal in most states but not all.

The event starts at a registration table and usually involves a fee to participate.

The winner of the event is usually awarded 50% of the collected fees, while the other half of those fees is donated to a charity (or used to support the sponsoring organization).

At the registration desk participants are given a map of the event course. On it are designated stopping points at which each rider receives a playing card (randomly drawn). There are five stopping points along the way so that riders who complete the course will have a poker hand. A frequent alternative to this methodology involves getting buttons or other unique items at each stop and then trading these items for cards drawn at the conclusion of the ride.

At the end of the run, riders go back to the registration desk and either present a poker hand or trade the items acquired on the ride for cards to form a poker hand. Then, depending on the group's rules, they may be able to throw away one or two cards and draw replacements (for an additional fee).

Each poker hand is recorded along. When the event is over, the winning hand will be announced and the winner presented with part of the collected fees, usually half.

Poseur

A pretend biker.

For someone who is into image, not riding, it is far cheaper to buy the clothes for looks than to buy the bike and ride it.

Precession

All spinning objects evidence this phenomenon, a term usually referring to a spinning wheel.

When a torque is applied to a spinning wheel, such as when you change direction of travel, precession tries to lean that wheel in a perpendicular direction relative to that torque.

For example, turning a moving motorcycle to the right results in the front wheel of the motorcycle trying to lean to the left, in part, as a result of precession.

Precession accounts for only about one tenth of the force trying to lean the front wheel. It's often, though incorrectly, assumed that "gyroscopic" precession accounts for a motorcycle's lean during its turns.

In fact, precession is only one of the reasons that counter-steering is essentially effortless and smooth. (Out-tracking and centrifugal force causes the lean.) Tests have been performed on motorcycles in which the front wheel was replaced with a ski. Counter-steering remained in effect.

Primary drive

This is the mechanism that transfers power from the engine to the transmission via its clutch.

PTT

An acronym: **P**ush **T**o **T**alk.

Refers to the button or switch lever used to activate the microphone and transmitter functions of a CB or HAM radio.

Rake angle

The angle formed by the bike's front forks relative to vertical. A typical rake angle is 30 degrees. The rake angle determines the bike's steering efficiency. A small angle makes for "quick steering" (sometimes called "twitchy"), while a larger angle makes for "slow steering".

Rake angle is a fundamental component in determining trail.

Redline

Refers to the start of a red area marked on a tachometer which designates an engine rpm speed beyond which the engine will begin to lose power–and ultimately self-destruct if the engine is allowed to run even faster or for a prolonged period of time.

Restoring force

This is the force created as a result of how long the trail of a bike's front-end geometry is, the speed it's traveling, and the weight being carried by its front tire.

The restoring force tries to keep the bike's front wheel pointing in the same direction as that pointed to by the body of the bike. In other words, if a rider is in a turn, it is the restoring force that tries to correct his steering input and cause the bike to quit the turn.

This is not an academic idea! It's the reason that, if you remove your hands from your handlebar, the bike will try to find a way to drive in a straight line with a vertical posture.

NOTE: There are times when your bike's front-end will generate a **negative restoring force**! (Especially when surmounting an obstacle or bump in the road.) In that case, the force generated will try to cause any out-of-straight alignment to accentuate. The result is the bike's being dumped when crossing a railroad track.

Road rash

What happens when exposed skin meets pavement. This is the reason to wear all the gear, all the time. Skin can be worn off all the way down to bone in a motorcycle crash.

Roll on / Roll off the throttle

Change the engine speed by turning the throttle. Roll on the throttle means "give it more gas", while roll off the throttle means "reduce engine speed".

Scoot

Slang for a motorcycle or motor scooter.

Scooter / Motor scooter

A two-wheeled, motor-driven cycle which has two unique characteristics: an engine that's attached directly to the rear wheel (as an integral part of the swing arm assembly), and smaller diameter wheels. By not having the engine attached to the frame, a scooter requires far fewer parts to convey engine power to the rear wheel. Thus, it's typically much lighter than a typical motorcycle. The engine placement on a scooter frees up a great deal of space under the rider's seat which becomes cargo space.

Most scooters, though not all, employ an automatic transmission so that there's no need for a clutch lever. Instead, on the left grip is a brake lever. It controls the rear brake, while the right lever continues to control the front brake, according to standards. (Some scooters reverse this configuration.) Modern scooters no longer use a rear-brake pedal. Because of this, all scooters manufactured in the U.S. must have applied for and received a waiver of design regulations which stipulate that the right foot must be provided a rear-brake pedal. Scooters are very practical surface-street commuter vehicles but tend not to be adequately powered for use on major highways. Scooters with larger engines (typically 500cc's or bigger) are called maxi-scooters and are capable of sustained highway usage.

Short-legging

Refers to the situation where a rider attempts to put down a foot on pavement or solid ground when stopping a motorcycle but finds that no pavement exists where it was expected.

For example, if you stop near a puddle of water and put a foot down into it, you may short-leg if your foot doesn't stop where you thought it would because the ground is farther below the water's surface than you expected. This causes your bike to lean over farther in that direction, as if your leg were actually "shorter" on that side than you thought. Riders can also short-leg a bike on an unexpected slope or drop-off, such as a ditch concealed by trash or leaves.

Side-stand

Used on all street-legal motorcycles to hold the bike securely in a modest lean to the left whenever there's no rider on it. These are sometimes called "kickstands" or "jiffy stands".

Sissy bar

Any vertical extension at the rear of a motorcycle, usually padded and shaped like a backrest, that helps keep the passenger from falling off the rear-end.

Skid

When a tire loses traction (usually because of excessive brake usage) and the tire is dragged by the bike forward in a straight line, thus wearing off rubber and leaving a skid mark. A slide, on the other hand, is when a tire moves to either side instead of straight ahead.

Slab / Super-slab

A multi-lane, divided highway, usually featuring limited access via merging ramps. Other names include: freeway, tollway, turnpike, autobahn, or expressway.

Slabs usually have high-speed, high-density traffic with many drivers intent on getting somewhere fast.

Slide

Similar to a skid, but refers to a tire that has lost traction, typically in a curve, and is moving laterally (to the side) rather than in-line with the body of the bike. A tire can skid and slide at the same time.

A slide does not necessarily result from excessive brake usage, though it certainly can. More often, however, a slide is the result of encountering a low-traction roadway surface (such as sand or wet leaves) or of excessive acceleration.

Slip angle

The angular difference between the direction in which the contact patch is pointing and that of the wheel itself. The contact patch always points in the direction of actual travel.

Slow ride

A common on-bike competition, often seen at rallies or safety events.

Participants compete by riding their own bikes down a designated straight line while being timed. The rider who takes the longest time to complete the course wins. Any rider who puts a foot down during the event, or who rides outside the course, is eliminated.

Extremely good riders can be seen at such events beginning their leg of the competition by riding down the course, then stopping mid-course without putting a foot down. They will rest like that long enough for all the other riders to finish the race, then come in last and win.

A version of the "slow ride" may also be included in some safety classes or in parking lot practice, to enhance a rider's balance and slow-speed control.

Smoky / Smokey

A slang term for a law enforcement officer (LEO) which has been derived from the cartoon character "Smokey the Bear," who represents fire dangers. The character wears a hat that is similar to the hat worn by many LEOs, especially state troopers.

In a group ride, the hand signal for a "Smokey" is a series of repeated taps on the top of the helmet from the lead rider. This can mean that the group should slow down, but it can also mean that the group should anticipate a lane change to accommodate a patrol car that has stopped another vehicle.

In Texas and many other jurisdictions, when an LEO has pulled a vehicle over on the side of the road, the traffic passing by is required either to change lanes to reduce the danger to the officer; or if this is impossible, to reduce speed.

In Texas and certain other states, the law requires a driver either to vacate the lane closest to the stopped emergency vehicle, if the road has multiple lanes traveling in the same direction, or else slow down **20 MPH below the speed limit**. (If the speed limit is below 25 MPH, the driver must slow down to 5 MPH.)

Note: this means dropping your speed **not** to 20 MPH below the speed you were going when you spotted the Smokey at the side of the road or next to your lane, but 20 MPH below the posted limit.

Sprocket

A gear specifically designed with teeth made to engage chain links or belt cogs.

See **Drive Sprocket**.

Squeezing both levers

Pulling in on both the clutch and brake levers in a rapid and controlled manner. It's the desired automatic "panic reaction", especially for newbies, whenever a rider finds that the bike is out of control. It may not "save" a bad situation in all cases, but is far preferable to freezing at the controls, which is what most new riders tend to do.

Note that the word "squeezing" is significant! "Grabbing a handful" of the brake lever is specifically inappropriate—as it implies extremely aggressive behavior which can result in worsening an already bad situation.

New riders are advised that if they do not know what else to do, or are faced with making too many decisions to handle immediately, "Squeeze both Levers" should become their automatic and immediate response.

Squid

A motorcyclist who does absurdly unsafe things, including (but not limited to) weaving in and out of traffic, speeding, pulling wheelies or doing stoppies, passing in places where visibility is limited, or hanging off while riding curves on public roadways.

Stoppie

Bringing a motorcycle's rear wheel off the ground as a result of hard braking.

Figure 70: A stoppie

Stroke

When talking about an engine, stroke refers to the distance its pistons travel within a cylinder. An engine's bore and stroke define the engine's displacement.

Sweep / Drag / Tail gunner

See **Drag / Sweep / Tail gunner**.

Swing arm

The part on (most) motorcycles to which the rear tire (and many times the shocks, brakes etc.) are mounted. It connects these components to the frame of the motorcycle.

This arm moves or "swings" in an up and down (or vertical) fashion, over road bumps or imperfections, hence the name.

Tail Gunner / Drag / Sweep

See **Drag / Sweep / Tail gunner**.

Tank slapper

A description of what happens when a motorcycle's front-end goes unstable, resulting in the handlebar's rapid and uncontrollable swinging between a full-stop right and full-stop left movement, usually ending up with a crash of the motorcycle.

In many motorcycles this can actually cause dents in the gas tank, thus the name. It can happen at any speed.

This is caused by harmonic feedback that's insufficiently damped by a steering damper, or by loose or improperly torqued head bearings. The harmonic feedback is usually caused by roadway imperfections. Though not necessary to cause a tank slapper, a broken shock absorber can do so, as well as mismatched shock settings.

Target fixation

People tend to go where they're looking. The risk is that if a rider is looking at the grill of an on-coming semi or at the curb, he's likely to hit it. What's more, if one focuses his attention so narrowly, it's likely there will be another threat that will appear as a rude surprise (maybe a parked car, or another corner) just a bit further up the road.

The best way to avoid target fixation is to look where you **want** to go. To break your attention from this condition, look not at the threat, but at the escape route.

Throttle lock

A mechanical device that permits locking the position of the throttle to maintain a particular speed. These should **never** be used if the roadway is wet!

The electronic version is called "cruise control".

Threshold braking

This describes a rider who achieves a deceleration rate in excess of the deceleration rate that results from skidding without locking the brake(s) on his motorcycle. It's called threshold braking because it approaches the rate at which tire slip is so great that the tire begins to skid. A close analogy would be braking a non-ABS-equipped motorcycle and achieving a deceleration rate equal to or greater than the rate an ABS-equipped motorcycle can achieve with that system actively working.

Since the maximum deceleration rate that can be achieved depends largely on the roadway material, the condition of that roadway, and the condition of a tire's rubber, there's no specific deceleration rate that represents threshold braking.

If a bike's tires and a roadway can produce a sliding (dynamic) Coefficient of Friction of 0.9, then any deceleration rate greater than 0.9g's would properly be called threshold braking. Since on modern freeways, the rolling (static) Coefficient of Friction can be over 1.2, while on typical asphalt roads it's closer to 1.0, these represent the maximum deceleration rates achievable before skidding occurs.

Very skilled riders can **sometimes** achieve deceleration rates from 0.1 to 0.2g's greater than ABS-equipped bikes can achieve when utilized by less skilled riders.

Throttle rocker

An attachment to the throttle that extends under the palm of the right hand and allows the rider to control the throttle (thus, speed) without having to use a firm grip with the thumb.

In other words, the attachment is used to ease wrist and hand stress and to diminish incidents of thumb cramps.

'Throttle rocker" is one of many terms for this device. "Wrist rest" is another term that means the same thing.

Topbox / Top box

A cargo-carrying space located behind the pillion—analogous to an automobile trunk—usually sufficiently large to hold one or two full-face helmets.

Torque

A twisting force. Torque, more properly called "moment", causes rotational movement (known as angular velocity).

In other words, torque (not horsepower) is what causes your motorcycle to accelerate by turning your rear wheel.

Tourer

A motorcycle specifically designed for long distance travel.

Typically, these bikes have substantial "creature comfort" add-ons such as a good-time radio, a CB, and a fairing and windscreen. They always have softer seats (including pillion), luggage "bags" and a "top box", larger gas tanks, and are designed with an upright posture with the foot pegs directly below the rider, instead of "forward".

These bikes are larger and heavier than cruisers and as such are not nearly as easy to handle at slow speeds or for local, short distance, rides.

Track / Left track / Right track

A logical division of a public roadway lane wherein the lane is divided into three equal parts: left, right, and middle. (A bike's handlebar, at approximately 30 inches wide, is just under one-third of a lane wide.)

This is usually associated with group riding rules where the individual motorcycles tend to restrict their riding to either the left or right tracks, usually in a staggered formation. Motorcycles are almost never ridden in the center of the lane because of poor traction conditions caused by accumulated oil on the roadway there.

Trail

When talking about the front-end of a motorcycle, this refers to the distance (on the ground) between the center of the front tire's contact patch and the point on the ground to which the "steering stem" points.

This is the component of your motorcycle's front-end geometry that provides steering stability. More importantly, it causes your motorcycle automatically to try to steer in a straight line via the restoring force. The greater the trail, the more stable your steering will be, the more difficult it will be to change directions, and the stronger the restoring force will be at any given speed. Trail is a function of rake angle, offset, and the diameter of your front wheel.

Trike

A motorcycle converted into a three-wheeled vehicle by replacing its rear-end with the two-wheeled rear-end of a car. Note that a motorcycle which has a sidecar added is **not** known as a trike.

Triple-tree

The part of the motorcycle's front-end that connects the two forks and the steering stem to the motorcycle frame.

Vernier

A secondary adjustment device providing the ability to perform "fine tuning".

Wear indicator

For tires, a wear indicator is cast as part of the tire. It's a small narrow "bar" which usually goes across the tread. When the tire tread wears to a point in which this "bar" or wear indicator becomes visible, the tire must be replaced.

Weight transfer

Upon acceleration or deceleration, weight is transferred from one wheel to the other. On acceleration, weight is transferred from the front to the rear wheel. When braking, it's transferred from the rear to the front wheel. The amount of weight transferred is a function of the acceleration / deceleration rate and the ratio of the wheelbase length to the height of the bike's Center of Gravity.

Wheel traps

See **Edge Traps.**

Wheelie

Bringing a motorcycle's front wheel off the ground as a result of hard acceleration.

Figure 71: A wheelie

Wobble

Annoying and potentially dangerous vibration. Front end wobble may be caused by an unbalanced or out of round wheel / tire, rain grooves in the pavement, unequal damping due to unequal fluid levels in the front shocks, or loose windscreen attachments (among other things). Rear end wobble may be caused by an axle out of perpendicular to the swing arm, improperly secured or unbalanced load, or an unbalanced or out of round wheel / tire (among other things). Also sometimes called "shimmy".

Wrist rest

See **Throttle rocker.**

APPENDIX A – Engine guards

Some people call them "crash bars", some "case guards", still others call them "engine guards"—but, until recently, no one "officially" has called them "leg guards" or "leg protectors".

No motorcyclist would argue that they are not a good thing to have on a motorcycle, and quite a few riders have added them to their motorcycles if they did not come stock.

Thus, the following facts may be surprising:

- There's a genuine dispute in the scientific community as to whether leg guards do more harm than good.
- No government or agency thereof has ever required them.
- No independent testing or professional organization recommended them, until recently.
- The motorcycle industry as a whole categorically rejects the need for leg guards.
- Honda's testing on their use reached no definitive conclusions.

How can this be?

On May 30, 1995 in the United States Court of Appeals, Fifth Circuit, the case of **James Satcher versus Honda Motor Company** (No. 94-60492) was heard on appeal. In the written opinion handed down by that court is a summary which listed those facts.

An interesting read, the opinion describes the situation in which Satcher lost a leg in a motorcycle accident and sued Honda, claiming that since Honda made the motorcycle without leg guards, they made a product that was defective and unreasonably dangerous in a crash.

Following are two paragraphs from that opinion that should cause you to wonder:

> Honda presented two well-qualified experts, John Snider and Warner Riley, who opined that leg guards should not be used because their safety benefits are outweighed by their safety disadvantages, including the possibility of greater upper body injuries. For example, Riley explained that the problem with unpadded robust bars is that they can cause the cyclist to leave the motorcycle and land upside down, and that padded crash bars increase in-flight whiplash, which can result in a broken neck. They were also of the view that in this particular accident, Satcher would not have benefitted from crash bars. There is a disagreement in the scientific community as to whether head impact increases when crash bars are used.
>
> Honda itself conducted certain crash tests in the 1960's. One report concluded that at certain speeds crash bars are effective at reducing leg impact in an angled collision. However, it found that in broadside collisions "there seems to be an indication that each of the various body area impacts is greater in the case of motorcycles equipped with crash bars than in the case of those which are not," and that a commercially available crash bar "has no protective effect or it has a possible reverse effect in broadside collision[s]." This conclusion was disputed by Ezra as not supported by Honda's own experimental data. The report also noted that it was far from definitive.*fn4 A Honda chief engineer testified that "thus far we have created, tested, evaluated various experimental devices; however, we have yet to come up with a ... practical as well as effective device that would protect the leg."

So, the question is presented in good faith: Since most riders don't believe that guards are a bad idea, how is it that the facts presented to the court suggest otherwise? How could our perceptions be so wrong or misguided? Or are they?

[Several motorcyclists have stated that their perception has always been that these guards are to protect the motorcycle, not the rider. They advise that "only non-riders" think they are any good at protecting rider or passenger.]

It's clear that at least on the Honda Gold Wings, the case guards (that wrap around the engine heads) provide very little in the way of leg protection. Motorcycles that have larger / wider guards (where the rider often mounts highway pegs), therefore, must do something more. At least one thing they do is provide a measure of leg protection. Rear guards are designed to protect the bags, but they are obviously capable of providing some measure of protection to the passenger's legs as well.

On many motorcycles none of these guards exist at all. Engine guards could easily be added that tend to protect the engine, but most riders who add them obtain guards wide enough so that if the bike is on its side, the leg is not crushed.

Obviously, none of these guards provide much in the way of leg protection in the event of an accident (at least from impact damage), but if they keep a laid-down bike from crushing a leg, surely riders would agree that's a good thing?

That same court case discussed "leg guards" and "crash bars" on police motorcycles:

> Police crash bars are used in part to hold lights or other accessories needed on police vehicles. Their efficacy as a safety device is the subject of disagreement. Kenneth Harms, a former Miami police chief with experience on the motorcycle patrol and in investigating motorcycles accidents, believes that police crash guards, particularly those used on Harley-Davidson motorcycles, are effective in reducing injuries. Harms conceded that he had no scientific or engineering expertise in motorcycle design. Harley-Davidson has expressly recommended against the use of crash bars on its police motorcycles.

Once again there's a difference of opinion. A police chief says they reduce injuries, particularly on Harley Davidson's, while Harley Davidson recommends against using them. Odd, no?

Some riders are prone to argue that testimony heard in court consists of lies and misrepresentations, designed to benefit one side or the other. But perhaps neither side is telling lies. Rather, the manufacturers may be so frightened of litigation that they are forced to take the position that engine guards are not necessary / important in protecting legs from injury lest they be sued by owners of all their products that were sold without them. They are slanting their evidence, in good faith, with facts and opinions that will minimize their liability.

That's a far cry from being unbiased and telling all there is to tell. But the parties have no obligation to do either, in court.

Not all motorcyclists believe it's better to have crash bars than not. The famous Harry Hurt study, for example, states:

> Crash bars are not an effective injury countermeasure; the reduction of injury to the ankle-foot is balanced by increase of injury to the thigh-upper leg, knee, and lower leg.

Note that this was one finding of a study of some 900 **reported** accidents. Had the study included all instances of leg injury caused from a motorcycle crashing on its side, the conclusion would have been different. On the other hand, a relatively current study (February 1995) performed in England by the Transport Research Laboratory (TRL) had very different conclusions:

> Our research shows that properly designed leg protectors could reduce the severity of, or even eliminate, at least 25% of leg injuries without increasing injuries to other parts of the body. In some cases, they could save lives.

Contrary to the arguments of the major motorcycle manufacturers cited earlier, TRL went on to say:

> An important factor in this research has been to ensure that if leg protection is to be of benefit not only must leg injuries be reduced, but the potential for injuries to other parts of the body, particularly the head, must not be increased. In all the tests the potential for leg injuries and head injuries has been carefully analyzed. At no time has leg protection worsened the potential for head injury, or injury to other parts of the body, and in some instances there has been a significant reduction in this potential.

Further, the British government has proposed a European Commission (EC) Initiative that may someday result in a requirement for these devices.

APPENDIX B – Path of travel

When a rider is moving in a straight line, or when he's travelling in a curve at very slow speeds, the path the bike travels is perfectly obvious. But when he's in a turn at higher speeds, that path is not at all obvious.

This discussion pulls together concepts that have been discussed in other parts of this book, such as traction, centrifugal force, Center of Gravity (CG), steering angle, slip angle, under- and over-steering, tire pressure, and load. Individually, these are easy to visualize and understand; but in a dynamic world, it's often hard to put the set of them together into a meaningful understanding of an issue.

A discussion of "path of travel" will help you do just that.

First, a quick review. Tires are flexible. Even containing the maximum air pressure they can safely be inflated to, they flex. As a result of that flexing, when you are in a turn at any reasonable speed, there is a difference between the direction the wheel is pointing and the direction the tire's contact patch is pointed.

See APPENDIX C – Slip Angles.

In addition, whenever you input a steering angle other than straight ahead, the contact patch slips a little as it assumes a direction. That is, a percentage of the contact patch is literally sliding across the pavement, not just rolling on it.

This slippage results in what's known as a *slip angle,* which is the difference in the direction to which the tire is pointed and the direction of travel. There **must be** a slip angle, or you could not change the direction your motorcycle is traveling.

Combined, the flexing of the tire and the slippage of the contact patch result in a slip angle. That's the difference between the actual direction of travel and the steering angle used. This is called "drift", because your vehicle is drifting slightly toward the outside of the path you told it to move in via the steering angle you input.

Look at Figure 72, which shows a view of a motorcycle from overhead while it's making a turn at **very slow speed:** the motorcycle is assumed to be standing absolutely vertical, and both tires of a single bike are shown. (Of course, if the bike is moving in a curve, no matter how slowly, there will be a lean angle. The effect of a lean angle is ignored here; it will be discussed later.) The dark arrowhead represents the instantaneous direction of travel of the front tire.

By drawing a perpendicular line through the axle of each tire on the bike to the point that they meet, you can derive the Origin (O) of the radius of the turn being ridden. Understand that the dashed circle is **not** the path of travel of the motorcycle. Rather, it shows a constant relationship between the **two** radii in a turn, the relationship that defines **neutral** steering (more about that soon). The length of the vertical dashed line shows the radius described by the rear tire, and the length of the angled dashed line shows the radius described by the front tire.

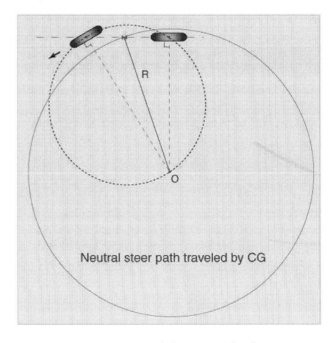

Figure 73: Neutral steer path of CG

Because the radius for the rear tire is **always** shorter than that of the front tire, the rear tire **always** turns **inside** the circular path described by the front tire.

(This is easy to demonstrate: think about trying to avoid hitting a cone with your rear tire during a cone weave during your parking lot practice, after your front tire has turned and cleared it.)

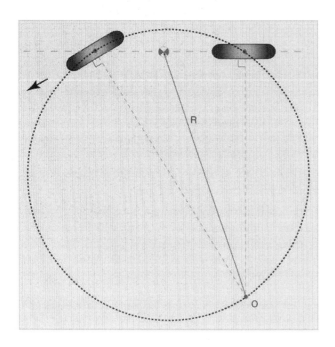

Figure 72: Radius of CG path of travel

These preliminary comments will become clearer.

Let's add the location of the bike's CG and connect that to the origin of the circle, as well. The new line is marked "R", as it's the **actual radius** of the turn described by the CG.

If that were all there is to it, this would be a short lesson. But when that motorcycle is traveling at any meaningful **speed**, that dark black arrowhead no longer points in the direction the front tire is moving at that instant.

Instead, because of tire flex and slip, both tires have an instantaneous velocity (V) pointing to the **outside** of the actual path of travel. Drift, remember?

Furthermore, the bike is no longer vertical. It's leaning toward the inside of the turn. The result of that lean is that the wheelbase gets longer. (We will ignore that minor fact in the diagrams that follow, but realize that, as the wheelbase is longer, the radius of the actual path of travel becomes very modestly longer.)

If we assume that the slip angle for both tires is essentially equal (say, 10 degrees), then we can draw a new picture showing how to locate the origin of the actual path traveled, as follows:

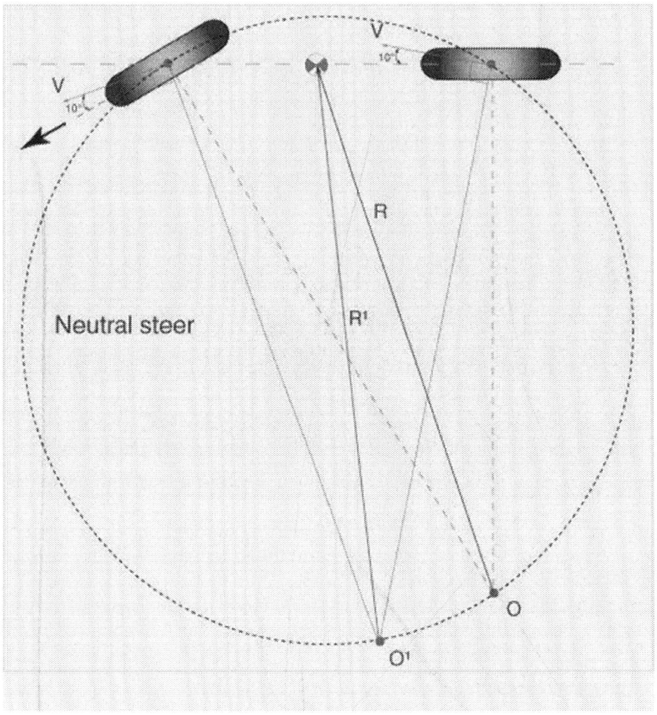

Figure 74: Identical slip angles on both tires

When the slip angles are identical, as shown in Figure 74, you can see that the new radius "R1" is **almost** identical in length to the original radius "R"; but more obvious is that the new origin "O1" is almost exactly riding on that relationship circle.

These won't be exactly the same, but because the length of the wheelbase is so much smaller than the length of the radius, and the placement of the CG is very close to the midway point between the contact patches, that difference is trivial. But the slip angles for the front and rear tires are usually **not** the same. The greater the load carried by a tire and the lower the tire pressure inflating that tire, the larger its slip angle will be.

This explains why, after your tires warm up, your bike won't drift as much as it does when the tires are cold. Furthermore, the greater the longitudinal forces exerted on the tires (acceleration and braking), the greater the slip angle will be.

Remember, automobiles tend to be **under-steer** vehicles, while motorcycles tend to be **over-steer** vehicles. In a car, where the engine and transmission are both in the front, you see an extreme example of this. Motorcycles, with the rider in place, tend to have more weight on the rear tire than the front, and that bias toward the rear is substantially increased when you add a passenger.

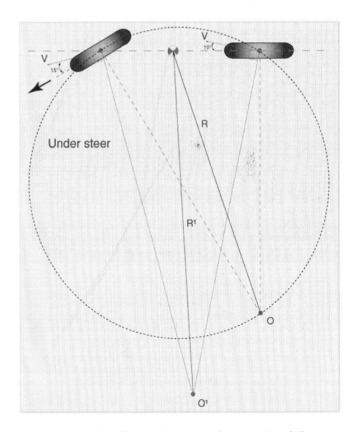

Figure 75: Slip angles on under-steering bike

Look at Figure 75, where this time we use 15 degrees for the slip angle for the front tire, while leaving a 10-degree slip angle for the rear tire. This shows the path of travel of the CG for this very unusual under-steering motorcycle. A typical over-steering motorcycle (with a greater slip angle in the rear) is shown in Figure 76.

From the last two diagrams, you see that an under-steering vehicle goes **wide** in a turn, while an over-steering vehicle cuts a tighter turn. One more thing that isn't shown but that you should be aware of is that if you take a turn too fast (beyond its critical speed) in an under-steering vehicle, the front tire loses traction first; but because most motorcycles are over-steering vehicles, their rear tires lose traction first.

This is all **very good** news, actually. From a "feel" point of view, your motorcycle handles with positive feedback—confirming that you're making the turn as desired—while a vehicle with under-steer characteristics feels less than "sure-footed"—like it's not quite doing what you ask of it.

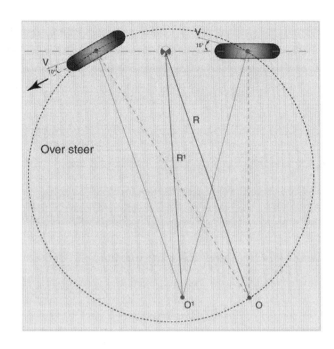

Figure 76: Slip angles on over-steering bike

APPENDIX C – Slip angles

In the discussion on counter-steering, many facts about camber thrust were presented, as well as how it helps convert the **lean** of a wheel into a **turn** of that wheel.

We will now look at the tires more closely and see that, though camber thrust helps change the direction of travel of the wheel, the fact that the tires are flexible results in phenomena that tends to fight changing direction.

Specifically, we will look at one kind of tire deformation (torsional) that accounts for under- and over-steering.

Tires can deform in four ways:

1. Radially - (from side to side) - like the bulging in the sidewall above the contact patch.
2. Circumferentially - like the way the sidewalls wrinkle in soft drag tires when accelerating.
3. Axially - a deflection that tries to pull the tire off its wheel or rim.
4. Torsionally - this is a difference in axial deflection from the front to the back of the contact patch. Think of a turn to the right. If the rim of the wheel towards the front leads the contact patch and the rim of the wheel towards the back trails the contact patch then it is clear that the rim has twisted to the right more than has the contact patch. (See the second diagram below.)

Figure 77 below is a representation of a tire as seen from the top, looking through the tire to the bottom of it.

The dark area is what the contact patch would look like if you had x-ray vision. This shows a tire that's moving in the direction in which it's pointed.

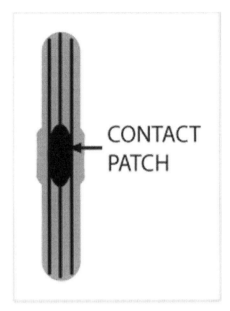

Figure 77: Contact patch

The lower the air pressure within the tire, the greater the tire's *radial deformity*.

That is, the larger the bulging will be around the contact patch, and **the larger the contact patch itself will be**.

In Figure 77, the bulging demonstrates that the sidewalls of your motorcycle tire have great flexibility. Because the tire's rubber flexes, it generates heat; but it's a poor conductor of that heat, so that if your tire pressure is too low and it flexes more than it's designed to do, then you can damage the sidewalls by riding on under-inflated tires—and a catastrophic failure can result.

To get a feeling for **torsional deformity**, sit on your motorcycle at a dead stop and turn the handlebar 20 degrees in either direction. When you let go of the handlebar, the front wheel will be pointed something between 15 and 18 degrees from where it was before you turned it—not 20 degrees.

Indeed, if you paid attention, you noticed the handlebar "springs" back part way when you let go of the grips. How can you account for this phenomenon?

Obviously, the contact patch did not turn as far as you thought it would when you turned the handlebar. Why? Because the contact patch has traction with the road surface, and the tire's sidewalls flexed (it became torsionally deformed).

The fact that there was a springing back of part of the movement of the handlebar is merely the result of the torsional deformity "unwinding" when force was removed.

Torsional deformity happens whenever you are moving in other than a straight line. Figure 78 shows a tire from the top (ignoring lean angle) on a bike that's making a right turn.

Note that the direction the wheel actually travels is determined by which way the **contact patch** is pointed, **not** the wheel itself.

Further, the diagram illustrates what happens to **both** the front and rear tires. Indeed, because of the greater camber thrust of the front tire, the discussion so far is more apt for what happens with the rear tire than of the front one.

The angular difference between the direction the contact is pointing and that of the wheel itself is called its *slip angle*. Clearly, if the slip angles for the front and rear tires were the same, the bike would steer essentially as if there was no slip angle at all. But, at least for a motorcycle, the rear tire generates a larger slip angle than does the tire in the front.

If the rear tire's slip angle is larger than the front one, you have a condition known as *over-steer*, while if the front tire's slip angle is larger, what is known as *under-steer* results.

A slip angle results from a combination of the facts that the tire's sidewalls are flexible **and** that the tire has traction. Note that if there's no traction (riding on ice, for example), then the slip angle will become essentially zero.

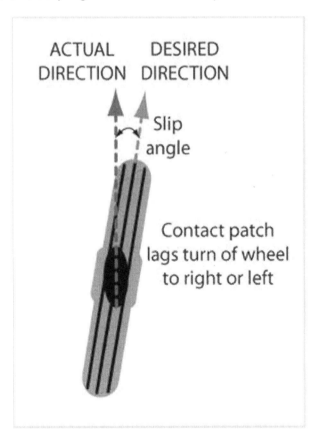

Figure 78: Contact patch lag creating slip angle

On the other hand, if a wheel travels in a direction other than the one in which its contact patch is pointing, then you have a **slide** **angle** rather than a slip angle. Slide angles and slip angles are very different.

To be clear, inertia determines the direction a bike will travel if it slides. If you lose traction, you will slide in the direction the tire was traveling at the time the slide starts. So long as you have traction, you will travel in the direction the contact patch points, not the tire. **Slide angle** is the angular difference between the direction in which inertia sends you and the direction your tires are pointing; while **slip angle** is the angular difference between the direction in which your contact patch is pointed (thus, the direction in which the tire moves) and the direction in which the tire is pointed.

Decreased traction reduces slip angles and increases slide angles!

What else affects slip angles? Acceleration and braking, tire profile size, belt wrap direction, tire camber, and traction.

- Acceleration and braking affect traction primarily because of weight transfer.

- A "low profile" tire has sidewalls that do not flex as much as normal tires. Hence, less torsional deformity (i.e., lower slip angles).

- Radial tires are belted with the belt threads running radially while standard tires are biased at an angle or circumferentially. In addition, radial tire sidewalls are constructed to strongly resist axial deformation. In other words, radial tires produce smaller slip angles than do the others. (This means that it's critically important that you NEVER have one tire be a radial and the other be standard construction. Corner handling will be almost unpredictable!)

- Compared to the rear tire, since the front tire of a motorcycle is narrower and has greater camber, its camber thrust is greater. Camber thrust attempts to turn your wheel into a turn. Thus, greater camber thrust yields smaller slip angles.

- Adding weight carried by a tire increases that tire's traction. Thus, it also increases its slip angle.

For these reasons you should expect that your rear tire is almost always generating a greater slip angle than your front tire. (i.e., your motorcycle tends to over-steer).

What changes a slip angle into a slide angle? Excessive slip angles! That is, a slip angle is so called because the part of the contact patch that's to the outside of your turn is moving faster than the wheel itself is in the direction it (the contact patch) is pointing while the part on the inside is moving more slowly. (Exactly like camber thrust.) Since the outside part is moving faster than the tire, it must be slipping. The inside part is gripping better than it would if moving in a straight line. For this reason the contact patch "walks" itself into the turn.

The greater the slip angle, the larger portion of the contact patch that's slipping. At some point there is so little part of the contact patch that is not slipping that traction is lost and the tire begins to slide. **Until shortly before sliding, traction increases**. Note, however, that traction is generally not lost all at once. Rather than a tire's experiencing an abrupt loss of traction, it tends to be lost gradually.

Now you know how it is that over-steer means that the rear tire has a greater slip angle than does the front one, thus it probably has more traction; yet despite that greater traction, it's usually the first tire to slide while in a curve.

APPENDIX D – Speed advisory signs

When a roadway has signage on it that includes the words "SPEED LIMIT", those signs represent the maximum speed that you may legally drive on that roadway. Despite some instances where people have argued in court that, since the sign didn't use the word "maximum" it could also mean that it was a minimum speed expected, the courts have ruled that these signs represent **maximum** speed limits.

Did you know that if the words "SPEED LIMIT" do not appear on those signs, then they are **usually** **not** speed limits at all? They are known as "speed advisory signs" and represent the maximum speed at which you are assumed to be able to travel **safely** on that roadway. That is, you can go that fast with essentially **zero** risk of having an accident caused by that speed—as a result of losing traction.

There may be an exception here or there, but in virtually every state across the country, you won't be cited for exceeding the speed limit if you're traveling faster than that posted speed, unless it's otherwise unsafe to do so (for example: rain, construction, fog, congestion).

In a recent court case, an expert witness in a civil suit had to explain this distinction to a jury, where the case involved two motorcyclists who suffered serious injuries after colliding with each other while riding at about 3:00 a.m. one morning on a county road that was posted with a 65 MPH **speed limit** sign. As they approached a relatively tight, right-turning curve, they saw a sign on the roadway that said: "35 M.P.H.". This was a **speed advisory** sign that warned them about the upcoming turn.

What both those attorneys (the defendant's and the plaintiff's) thought those signs meant was shocking. The defense attorney claimed (outside the presence of the jury) that there was essentially no difference between the two signs shown above: that both represented a maximum speed limit.

The plaintiff's attorney knew differently and was quick to point out the distinction in the courtroom in front of the jury. Unfortunately, he had not the slightest idea what a speed advisory sign actually meant and caused trouble for his client by exaggerating his "understanding" of the distinction in front of that jury.

Both attorneys, by the way, admitted that their clients had been speeding at the time of the accident—at somewhere between 70 and 85 MPH. So this was **not** a case about speeding. It was a civil case about who was liable to pay for the damages resulting from the accident the riders had. This discussion will cover what those speed advisory signs mean and why they exist.

Almost 80 years ago, in about 1930, when cars (and motorcycles) were far less capable than they are today, it was recognized that states had an obligation to construct and maintain roadways that were essentially safe to drive upon.

It was further recognized that despite the otherwise safe speeds you could drive on those roadways when they were basically straight lines, some curves simply had to be constructed which could not be driven on safely at the speeds the roadway was otherwise designed to support. Therefore, the states agreed to provide warnings—signs that advised of upcoming danger. These "caution-warning-danger" signs were invariably associated with tight turns.

But how did they determine what speed to post on those signs? After all, some turns were tighter than others.

Engineers collaborated with automobile manufacturers and tire manufacturers and determined that automobiles could be expected to travel safely on any road of "normal quality", provided they did not experience more than about 0.2g's of centrifugal force while making a turn. This was well below the traction capabilities of tires at the time.

Better rubber compounds and better roadway surfaces since then have made their assumptions even more conservative.

In response to this determination, test vehicles equipped with a swinging weight inside them (a metal ball) were constructed with an indicator of the angle that the weight made relative to vertical.

In other words, if a particular curve was ridden at 35 MPH, the weight would be observed to lean about 15 degrees away from vertical because of centrifugal force.

It turns out that when the weight angle was between 10 degrees and 14 degrees, then the vehicle was experiencing a sideways acceleration of very close to 0.2g's.

Based on these results, advisory speeds were established, rounded to the nearest 5 MPH, at whatever speed caused that weight to lean about 12 degrees. That, as it happens, is the same lean angle your motorcycle adopts when riding that curve at roughly that same speed.

Riders **must** understand this: You can determine **only** your motorcycle's speed and direction of travel. The lean angle you and your motorcycle adopt in a curve is **not** set by you! It is absolutely, entirely determined by your speed and the radius of the turn you're riding.

The faster you take that turn, or the tighter it is, the more your bike will lean, and the greater your lean angle will be. That's the law! (of physics).

If you try to "lean more" into a turn, you're actually changing the path of travel and thus the radius of your turn, which changes the lean angle in response to that.

Thus, speed advisory signs specify a speed at which you're virtually guaranteed that it's safe for you to ride. It's merely a "caution-warning-danger" signal, not a speed limit.

Note: at least one state finds no difference between a speed limit sign and a speed advisory sign and can successfully ticket you for exceeding the speed posted on that sign. The vast majority of states, however, recognize the difference.

But if a speed **advisory** sign is posted at 35 MPH, how fast can you actually ride through that turn with relative safety?

That's an interesting question. The plaintiff's attorney ruined his credibility in front of the jury by bragging that as a motorcyclist himself, he "knew" that with enough skill and good equipment he could "easily" handle any curve at twice the speed posted on an advisory—for example, he could easily take the turn in question that was posted with a 35 MPH advisory sign at 70 MPH. Indeed, he said, "I could do that with my car." (He was attempting to discredit the expert witness at the time.)

The jury soon heard the truth of the matter, demonstrated in the expert's calculations shown in Figures 79 and 80.

	US units		Metric		
All-up weight	700	lbs	317.1	kg	
			3111	Newton	
Wheelbase	67	in	1702	mm	
CG % (rear weight bias)	60%		60%		
CG height	21	in	533.4	mm	
Static vertical loads					
Rear	420	lbs	1866	Newton	
Front	280	lbs	1244	Newton	
Turn conditions					
Speed	35	mph	15.6	m/s	56 km/h
Curve radius	375	ft	114.3	m	
Lateral acceleration	7	ft/s^2	2.14	m/s^2	0.22 g
Lean angle CoG	12	degrees	0.21	radian	
Lean angle of bike	14	degrees	0.25	radian	
Lateral force on rear wheel	92	lbs	407	Newton	
Lateral force on front wheel	61	lbs	272	Newton	
Width of front tire	6	in	152.4	mm	*lean angle*
Coefficient of friction	1		1		
Maximum cornering speed	75	mph	33.48	m/s	121 km/h
Cells with a border outline are the input data					

Figure 79: Spreadsheet for lateral acceleration, 35 MPH

The spreadsheet examples presume the roadway is flat; it has no bank angle. The higher the bank angle, the **lower** the lateral acceleration will be and, thus, the higher the speed at which a motorcycle can travel on it without losing traction. As you can see, the spreadsheet in Figure 79 shows the data for a curve with a radius of 375 feet taken at 35 MPH.

Notice that the motorcycle would have a lean angle of 12 degrees, which means that it would be experiencing centrifugal force (lateral acceleration) of about 0.22g's. In other words, that roadway should have had a 35 MPH advisory sign posted on it, even though the rest of the roadway was posted at 65 MPH.

Now see what happens to those numbers when you take that same curve at double the speed, or 70 MPH. The bike lean angle has increased to about 41 degrees, which means it's experiencing centrifugal force (lateral acceleration) of about 0.87g's. The Coefficient of Friction of that roadway and the tires on your motorcycle is almost certainly about 0.8, meaning that if you tried that curve at 70 MPH, you would lose traction and wash out before even reaching 70 MPH!

	US units		Metric		
All-up weight	700	lbs	317.1	kg	
			3111	Newton	
Wheelbase	67	in	1702	mm	
CG % (rear weight bias)	60%		60%		
CG height	21	in	533.4	mm	
Static vertical loads					
Rear		420 lbs	1866	Newton	
Front		280 lbs	1244	Newton	
Turn conditions					
Speed	70	mph	31.3	m/s	113 km/h
Curve radius	375	ft	114.3	m	
Lateral acceleration		28 ft/s^2	8.56	m/s^2	0.87 g
Lean angle CoG		41 degrees	0.72	radian	
Lean angle of bike		47 degrees	0.83	radian	
Lateral force on rear wheel		367 lbs	1629	Newton	
Lateral force on front wheel		244 lbs	1086	Newton	
Width of front tire	6	in	152.4	mm	*lean angle*
Coefficient of friction	1		1		
Maximum cornering speed		75 mph	33.48	m/s	121 km/h
Cells with a border outline are the input data					

Figure 80: Spreadsheet for lateral acceleration, 70 MPH

Although the attorney stated that a skillful rider could take any curve at twice the speed posted on an advisory sign, now you know that that is **not true**.

If you think that the knowledge (or lack thereof) of those two attorneys should be a serious concern given the nature of the trial in which they were engaged, then you will be dumbfounded by what the other side's expert witness had to say about that curve. She's a very talented motorcycle racer who also happens to be a certified MSF RiderCoach.

In a deposition prior to the trial, she was asked if it was possible to ride a motorcycle safely on that curve at speeds greater than 35 MPH. She responded that it was certainly possible to do so. When asked if she could safely ride that curve at 50 MPH, again she responded that she could do so. She added that it was merely a matter of skill and technique.

"Really?" said the attorney. "Then could you safely drive that curve at, say, 100 MPH?" She said that she could do so. "Well, could you safely drive that curve at 150 MPH?" Again, she said that she could.

Her credibility as an expert witness fell to **zero**. At 150 MPH, her bike would be leaning over at **77 degrees,** and she would be experiencing about **4.5g's** of centrifugal force—well beyond the abilities of any motorcycle, regardless of her skill or technique.

You can take a curve posted with a 35 MPH advisory sign at 50 MPH with almost no risk of losing control, assuming no other safety issues. Many riders do it often, and you probably do, too.

But forget about listening to an "old salt" who tells you that you could "safely" handle any curve at twice its advisory speed, when that will result in a crash with virtual certainty.

There are some other things that an "old salt" may tell you that make a lot of sense in the right situation, but which can also result in your eating asphalt. For example, some would suggest that you get into the habit of always taking curves using a "late apex" approach. **Nuts**!

By definition, the late apex method involves delaying the start of your actual turn and then using a **greater** lean angle (meaning a tighter radius) than you would normally use at the beginning of the curve; then opening it up (lessening the lean angle) as you get to the apex.

Using a late apex method while trying to press speed limits at the same time is **dangerous**. Late apex turning is generally safer than a single lean angle turn, but **not** when getting near posted speed limits.

APPENDIX E – Pulling a trailer

It's generally understood that however you load your trailer, the resulting load should result in a tongue weight of approximately 10% of the total weight of the loaded trailer.

Some have argued that it is safe to pull a trailer if the tongue weight is anywhere between 10% and 20% of the total. This will show why you should ignore that advice.

Since very few trailers employ their own braking systems, it's generally thought that the tongue of a trailer cannot "dive" like the front-end of your motorcycle when you brake--that the weight of the trailer simply pushes straight ahead into the rear of the bike, and because the hitch is so low that causes essentially no handling problems for the biker. Again, don't believe it.

Finally, it's been argued that no matter how high or low the trailer hitch is relative to the rest of the trailer, handling isn't affected and the weight on the tongue of the trailer isn't affected. Total rubbish!

Why is 10% a good target weight to be found on the tongue of your trailer?

Well, let's assume that the fully loaded trailer weighs 300 pounds. That puts 30 pounds of weight on the ball of your hitch if it's loaded as recommended. That does far more than simply add weight to the rear wheel!

You have leveraged those 30 pounds because it's **far** aft of your rear-wheel hub. The consequences are that you have substantially moved the Center Of Gravity (CG) of your bike towards the rear. By placing weight aft of the rear-wheel hub you have actually reduced the weight on the front wheel as well as increased the rear-wheel weight; i.e., <u>**you have added more than 30 pounds of weight to the rear wheel and diminished weight (traction) on the front tire**</u>.

But 30 pounds is usually not so much weight that you will have control problems. On the other hand, consider that you might also have packed more in your luggage and may even be carrying a passenger for that trip. Both, like adding the tongue weight, result in moving your CG aft of where you are used to finding it. This argues that you should take it easy for a few miles as you re-familiarize yourself with the bike's now new handling characteristics.

The discussions mentioned earlier involved full awareness of the need to place your heaviest cargo directly over the wheels of your trailer.

This is to minimize tongue weight. But what was totally lacking in evidence in those discussions was a sense of the importance of managing the height of the CG of the trailer.

- Load your trailer with as close to 10% of the total weight of the trailer and cargo on the tongue as you can estimate (Obviously, it does not have to be exact.)
- Secure the trailer contents so that it cannot shift forward and aft as you accelerate or brake.
- Place your heaviest cargo at the bottom of the trailer, as close to directly over your wheels as possible.
- If you are going to place anything on top of your trailer, **make sure it is light**.
- Determine the weight distribution of your trailer while the tongue of the trailer is at the height it will be when connected to your bike.
- The longer the tongue, the less will be the weight transfer, all else being equal.
- If you are pulling a trailer, use it to store your cargo - empty your bike's luggage (saddlebags) as much as possible.
- Always take it easy for the first several miles of pulling a trailer so that you can learn the new handling characteristics of the bike.

1. Path of travel

Your trailer wheels will always travel a path that's inside the path taken by your motorcycle's rear tire when in a turn. Thus, you must provide ample clearance for that trailer whenever you change directions.

This is particularly important when you start moving, for example after having stopped to gas up your rig. Turning to the side closest to the pumps when you exit that station requires that you are well clear of crash guard posts. A slow ride through your neighborhood requires that you stay well clear of the curbs. "Cutting a corner" tightly can result in a trailer wheel jumping that curb just before it tosses your bike to the ground.

2. Securing that pulled vehicle

At a cycle accessory shop the other day, a man who was the proud owner of a new Wing and a color-coordinated trailer was polishing it mightily in preparation for a week out on the road.

He had 20 years riding experience and has "always" had a trailer, so he said.

In a discussion about handling characteristics, effects on gas mileage, tire wear (including that of the rear tire on the bike), and proper weight distribution and loading practices, it was possible to learn a lot from him. And his hitch was a beauty—all chrome. Besides having the typical ball connector, it had a swivel in it. Even the chains he used were chromed!

But upon closer examination of those chains, it was clear that the man did not have them crossed. In all his years of pulling a trailer, nobody had ever bothered to tell him to cross those chains so that they form a "catch" for the tongue should the hitch ever disconnect from the ball. (One other benefit is that when in a tight turn, crossed chains tend to prevent the length of chain on one side from being "stretched" while on the other side's being dragged on the ground.) When he left the accessory shop this time, they were crossed.

If that man's hitch had ever managed to dislodge from the ball, the tongue would have dug itself into the pavement—and a good ride would have been over!

Further, unlike losing a trailer from the back-end of a car or truck, on a bike the trailer's tongue is right in line with the motorcycle's rear tire. Even if it could not quite reach the ground should it disconnect, that tongue can certainly reach the tire if the chains are too long. All in all, bad news!

If you attach a trailer to your bike, be sure to cross a pair of chains under its tongue before connecting the chains to the hitch; and be sure that the chains are not so long that the tongue can reach your rear tire after a disconnect.

Also, don't use cheap spring clip connectors on the end of those chains. If those chains are supporting the tongue of your trailer and if you were to then stand on that tongue (as some policemen are apt to do, trying to "test" them), they **must hold**.

In most states you are required to use **two** chains when pulling a trailer, and in every state you are responsible for any damage that the trailer causes, should it get away from you.

3. Swivel hitch

Most trailer hitches connect with a ball and latch assembly. A motorcycle can lean about 35 degrees relative to the trailer without binding the latch and ball assembly. That's a greater lean angle than many Harley-Davidsons can achieve without dragging a peg or floorboard. But most other motorcycles can achieve a lean angle in excess of 45 degrees.

If the ball and latch bind, both the motorcycle and trailer frames can be damaged. Though one never expects to have his motorcycle end up on its side on the road, after an accident you can be sure that's the position the bike end up in. Obviously that means that if you drop your bike with a trailer attached, you can do serious damage to both the motorcycle and the trailer.

Most trailer hitches can be equipped with a swivel joint that allows a difference in lean angles between the bike **and** its trailer to be substantially greater than 35 degrees.

This is a relatively inexpensive way to protect your motorcycle and trailer investments.

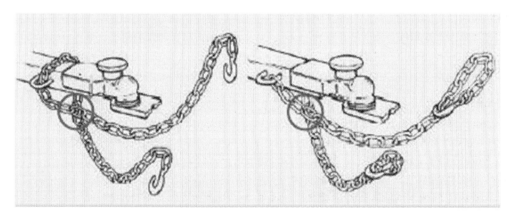

Figure 81: Crossed chains for towing a trailer

APPENDIX F – Passengers are <u>not</u> helpless

The general impression among motorcyclists is that a passenger would be totally helpless, should something happen to the rider that prevents him from maintaining control of the bike. Nonsense!

An accident occurred in Ohio some years ago when a deer attempted to jump over a motorcycle from the side and hit the rider, knocking him completely off the bike. The man's wife was a passenger at the time. She managed to lean forward, take control of the bike, and get it off to the side of the road, slowing it down so much that it simply fell over (into the grass) at a minimal speed.

There was no rider in front of her, so she was able to reach the controls to do this. But that's not the end of this story.

Even if the rider were still there—having, for example, collapsed from a heart attack—the passenger can almost always gain control of the motorcycle anyway.

Two controls that the passenger usually cannot reach are the gear shift lever and the rear brake; but the three that she can reach by grasping the grips are the clutch lever, the throttle, and the front brake. (And, not incidentally, the engine cutoff switch.)

Thus, the passenger can steer the bike as well as control its speed.

Even with a rider backrest, a passenger can stand on her pegs and lean over the rider to gain control of the bike in a flash. Cash and I have practiced this maneuver and demonstrated it to several motorcycle groups at rallies and other gatherings.

It does not take a rider (or anyone on the bike) to balance a motorcycle moving at any reasonable speed. Because of trail, all motorcycles automatically attempt to become vertical and to steer in a straight line. In other words, though there will likely be some wild gyrations of the bike as it finds its way to a stable posture, there is **time** available to the passenger to get control of that bike.

The first order of business is to slow it down. The second order of business is to stay away from surrounding traffic in order to steer it to as safe a place as possible before it falls over, because it **will** fall over. Before it does, that engine cut-off switch should be turned off.

Your passenger is certainly not helpless. Perhaps it would be a good thing to let her know it and even practice assuming control (at a dead stop, engine off, on the side-stand).

Figure 82 is a picture of Cash and me using my Gold Wing in a Co-Rider Safety Demonstration, showing her taking control of my bike even though I'm still in the rider's saddle and there's a backrest between us.

Figure 82: Passenger steering the bike

Note that she was not standing nearly as tall as she could have been, should she have needed to, if I had not been this far out of the way.

This is another reason why a person who prefers to be a passenger and never intends to ride a motorcycle by themselves should be encouraged to attend the BRC.

Note that if she lies on the rider, she also tends to keep him on the bike. A good thing if traveling at 70 MPH, no?

APPENDIX G – How the drag and lift model works

This is a very complicated piece of code. This isn't surprising, since there are many concepts that included which aren't straightforward.

There are two kinds of drag: friction and pressure. Friction drag is essentially insignificant compared to pressure drag at motorcycle speeds. This model only calculates pressure drag.

Calculating the pressure drag force is a fluid dynamics problem. Air is treated as a liquid. The computation involves a standard algorithm (used even by the Wright brothers):

Drag force = $(d * V^2 * Cx * S) / 2$

Where:
d = air density
V = velocity
Cx = Drag coefficient
S = Frontal surface area

The first thing you should notice from this is that the drag force increases with the square of your speed. By the way, in these calculations, V is the speed of the wind hitting you from directly in front of you. If you're riding at 65 MPH and there's a head wind of 10 MPH, V is set at 75.

The drag coefficient is a dimensionless number that represents, essentially, the form of the object that's being hit by the wind. A parachute would have a Cx on the order of 1.5, a ball would be more like .45, a wing would be on the order of .1 or .2, and a teardrop has a Cx of .05. Sportbikes have Cx values between .3 and .6, touring bikes have values between .4 and .9, and cars tend to have values of between .26 and .36.

The surface area presented to the wind is extremely important in this analysis. If you have a windscreen on your bike, it adds a meaningful amount of area; but note that it's only the area of the windscreen that is **outside** the profile of the bike and rider that is added to the total.

Air density is a very difficult number to come up with because it's a function of altitude, temperature, and moisture content. Air density is highest at sea level and decreases with altitude. It increases as temperature goes down. Standard air pressure assumes sea level at 59 degrees F. Moisture decreases density (as odd as that sounds). The model assumes normal dry air.

Once the drag force is calculated, all you need to do is multiply it by the velocity again and you get the amount of power involved (Power = Force * Velocity)—in other words, you can see how much Horsepower is being consumed fighting wind drag.

Torque is a force that tries to rotate an object. The amount of torque involved is measured as its "moment." That is, if you multiply the force by the length of a lever arm, you can determine how hard that force is put to use. In this analysis, the drag force is multiplied by the height of the Center of Wind Resistance (where the surface area above that height is exactly the same as the surface area below it) in order to calculate the downforce caused by the wind drag. Downforce acts as a torque. That is, all forward pointing forces are at the contact patch, and wind drag is through the Center of Wind Resistance so that, like weight transfer caused by acceleration, you know how much weight is added to the rear tire (and removed from the front one).

Pressure drag is vectored in line with the direction of the wind. Vectored at 90 degrees to the direction of the wind is another force called Lift. Lift is most difficult to calculate since it depends on a lift coefficient very similar to the drag-coefficient used to calculate drag. The lift coefficient is a dimensionless number that reflects such things as the aerodynamic shapes involved, surface texture, and the relative height of obstructions compared to the length of the body following that obstruction.

A windscreen, for example, creates a significant lift just aft of itself; while the farther back you go, the less lift is created.

Every part of the surface area, from rider's helmet to rear running lights, creates both drag and lift. The method used here to closely estimate the lift coefficient was to use the drag coefficient and multiply it by the height of the Center of Wind Resistance, then divide by the length of the wheelbase.

This number, in essence, indicates the efficiency of drag forces in the creation of lift.

As the drag coefficient already reflects the "form" of the bike, here it is used as the lift coefficient as well. Since lift could be larger or smaller than drag (for an airplane wing, it's obviously much higher; for a bike–since it stays on the ground for all reasonable speeds–it would be lower. As a reasonable approximation of lift force, here the drag force divided by the ratio of height of the Center of Wind Resistance and the wheelbase is used. An equation in Gaetano Cocco's book, **Motorcycle Design and Technology**[13], totally supports that approximation. He states that lift for a motorcycle is the downforce divided by the wheelbase. That, as it turns out, is exactly what this calculation says.

The lift formula used was as follows:

Lift force = Drag force * H / Wheelbase

Where:

H = height of the Center of Wind Resistance.

Now, application of the downforce merely shifts weight from the front tire to the rear tire. If nothing else were going on, the total weight of the motorcycle and rider would be unaffected. But there is a lift force in addition to the downforce. The question is: how should that lift be apportioned between the front and the rear tires? As an arbitrary choice here, the location of the Center of Gravity along the wheelbase is used in the same way it is used it to determine weight distribution of a stationary bike. Thus, for example, in a typical bike that has 55% of its weight on the rear tire, the model allocates 55% of the lift to the rear tire as well.

The weight on the front tire is found as follows:

Front tire weight = Static weight on front tire - Downforce - Front tire lift

And the weight on the rear tire is found as follows:

Rear tire weight = Static weight on rear tire + Downforce - Rear tire lift.

Though it has nothing to do with aerodynamics, acceleration / deceleration causes weight transfer, which directly affects the weight on each tire. Acceleration doesn't affect total weight as does aerodynamic lift, but it does affect the distribution of weight on your front and rear tires.

---

[13] **Motorcycle Design and Technology**, supra, p. 143.

APPENDIX H – An equipment and camping checklist

The odds are good that you will forget to take something when you go camping, especially the first few times. We all do that, but these checklists should minimize the problem. They start with those items that you probably want to take with you whenever you ride, whether you plant to camp or not, depending on security in the neighborhood where you're stopping and how long you plan to stay. Putting a cover on your bike and locking it with a chain helps prevent theft of both motorcycles and shiny parts anywhere, but you will especially want to cover it when you leave it parked near your campsite for any length of time. You'll see that planning to cook out dramatically increases the complexity of your packing and work. What you decide to pack from that part of the list may be reduced dramatically if you bring prepared food, but don't forget the items related to sanitation and clean-up.

1. For everyday rides

☐	Identification	☐	Magazine / paperback book
☐	Cell Phone	☐	Maps / GPS
☐	Cash and credit / debit cards	☐	Rain Gear
☐	Liability Insurance Proof Form	☐	Rope or heavy cord, 6-10' long
☐	Motorcycle registration certificate and MOM	☐	Shop rags and Wet Ones, etc.
☐	Scissors, First Aid kit, emergency aids (EpiPen, etc.)	☐	Spare bulbs
☐	Medical Insurance Card	☐	Spare fuses
☐	Medical information (MedicAlert or DownTag, etc.)	☐	Stranded wire, 10" long
☐	Contact information for relatives	☐	Sunscreen
☐	Road service or motorcycle towing cards	☐	Tire plugging kit
☐	1 Cargo Net, 2 Bungee cords	☐	Tire pressure gauge
☐	Chain Lube	☐	Toolkit and jumper cables
☐	Clean water	☐	Totes or other rainproof boots
☐	Flashlights and Emergency Flashers	☐	Windscreen cleaner
☐	Extra gloves	☐	Bike cover – optional
☐	Good-time Radio or CD player	☐	Lock and Chain – optional
☐	Swiss Army knife	☐	Air compressor - optional

2. For Camping – additional personal items and equipment

☐	Air mattress	☐	Lantern and fuel
☐	Bug repellent	☐	Lip balm, make-up, and lotion
☐	Candles / flashlight and spare batteries	☐	Matches / lighter / Fire Starter
☐	Collapsible chair	☐	Medications and equipment (BP monitor, diabetes test strips)
☐	Comb, brush, and shampoo	☐	Safe sex supplies
☐	Compass	☐	Shaving kit
☐	Dental hygiene, night guard, and storage items	☐	Sleeping bag and pillow
☐	Deodorant, soap, towels, shower shoes, and washcloths	☐	Tent, poles, stakes, rope, spade
☐	Eye glass case, cleaner, reading glasses, and sunglasses	☐	Toilet paper
☐	Kotex/tampons	☐	Trash bags

3. For Camping – additional items for cooking and picnicking

☐	Camping stove and fuel, or grill for cooking over fire	☐	Freeze-dried foods and mixes
☐	Canned foods and drinks	☐	Ice chest and ice supply
☐	Can opener	☐	Knife / fork / spoon sets
☐	Chocolate	☐	Paper plates / bowls
☐	Charcoal and charcoal lighter fluid	☐	Paper towels
☐	Coffee (appropriate for coffee pot) / tea	☐	Plastic garbage bags and gloves
☐	Coffee pot and filters	☐	Salt and pepper
☐	Condiments (Ketchup, mustard, relishes, herbs)	☐	Snacks, candy and marshmallows
☐	Cooking pots / pans / skillet	☐	Sugar and instant creamer
☐	Corkscrew	☐	Tablecloth
☐	Cups / plastic glasses	☐	Vegetables, fruits, eggs, bread, buns, meat, nuts, and dairy
☐	Dishwashing soap, scrubbing pads, drying towels and wash-cloths for hands	☐	Utensils for cooking – stirring and serving spoons, skewers, paring knife, carving tools, cutting board
☐	Dried cereal / dried fruit / granola	☐	Wine or other adult beverages

4. For Camping – extra clothing, information, and entertainment-related items

☐	"Dickey"/ balaclava / scarf	☐	Sweater(s)
☐	Hat(s)	☐	Sweat shirt(s) and pants
☐	Lighter Jacket	☐	Swim wear and beach towels
☐	Shirt(s)	☐	T-shirts, long-sleeved
☐	Shorts	☐	Tennis shoes / sandals
☐	Socks (several pairs)	☐	Underwear
☐	Books / Portable TV / CDs	☐	Paper and writing instruments
☐	Camera, memory cards, batteries, and accessories	☐	Cards / games / poker chips
☐	Plug-in modem	☐	Tickets / passes to all events
☐	Laptop computer and power cord	☐	Travel guides

APPENDIX I – Twenty-three studies documenting ineffectiveness of training

Motorcyclists believe that training is a key part of the motorcycle safety puzzle. Rider educators are particularly committed to the notion—even though they rarely know how their students perform after leaving the course. The Motorcycle Safety Foundation itself has not claimed for more than a decade that training is effective in reducing crashes. Then again, few motorcyclists are aware that rider training—and, in particular, MSF's training—has been studied over and over again.

Here's a list with summary[i] of twenty-three training and / or licensing studies that have been done over the past thirty years. Bibliographic detail is given in footnotes. Quotations are drawn either from the study or abstract itself or from "Evaluation Of Rider Training Curriculum In Victoria".[ii]

1. In **1979**, a British medical journal reported, "A **University of Salford** team tried to assess the effectiveness of training. Overall, 65% of the riders had accidents in their first three years, the untrained group faring slightly better than the trained. But the groups may not have been sufficiently comparable, Raymond pointed out; and intrinsically poor riders who would have given up without training could have affected the results."[iii]

2. In **1978**, Canadian researchers **Jonah**, et. al, evaluated the Motorcycle Operator Skill Test (MOST).[iv] "It was expected that the greater the riding experience and training, the higher would be the skill scores....skill was greater among the more experienced riders (i.e. miles ridden motorcycle)but unexpectedly it was lower among training course graduates. Further analyses revealed that course graduates had less skill than untrained riders even when experience differences were controlled."

3. A Ph.D. dissertation published in **1980** on the **South Dakota** training program[v] found that, "Survival Rate Analyses indicated that Course riders who did not pass the course were not more likely to have accidents than riders who passed. Course graduates had a higher accident rate for mileage covered before and after the course than the untrained subjects."

"This result also occurred when subjects were matched on relevant background variables. It was concluded that MSF Rider Course graduates are as likely to become involved in accidents as untrained riders."

When the MSF course scores were analyzed in conjunction with the Motorcycle Operator Skills Test (MOST), "There were no relationships found between skill test item scores and types of accidents which implied some deficiency in those skills."

4. Also in **1980**, R.S. **Satten** produced a report for the Illinois Department of Transportation[vi] based on a group of 200 riders. He found MRC riders were less likely to have had crashes or citations, but they also tended to be female and had fewer years of experience and rode less per week.

5. Another **1980** study by J.W. **Anderson** on 40,000 San Diego license-applicants at six months and a year out[vii] and found, "The improved procedures programs had significantly lower motorcycle accident rates after 6 months than the control group and the lowest rate belonged to the group with remedial training (30 minutes classroom and 2.5 hrs. skill training). After one year, riders in the group which included remedial training for those who failed had 14% fewer total fatal and injury accidents than those in the current procedures program. This was still true when controlling for riding exposure."

6. In **1981**, **Jonah**, et. al.[viii] did a study to determine whether trained riders (MTP) "were less likely to have had an accident or committed a traffic violation while riding a motorcycle compared to informally trained (IT) motorcyclists." However, they found that those who had successfully passed MOST were 42% more likely to be crash-involved than those who failed.

However, "Multivariate analyses, controlling for the differences in [sex, age, time licensed, distance travelled [sic], education and BAC] revealed that the MTP graduates and IT riders did not differ in accident likelihood but the MTP graduates were significantly less likely to have committed a traffic violation than the IT riders. Although the lower incidence of traffic violations among graduates could be attributed to the training program, it is possible that the graduates sought formal training because they were safety conscious and this attitude also influenced their riding behaviour."

7. In **1984**, in a study involving 516 trained and a control group of untrained riders over three years, Rudolf G. **Mortimer** found that, "when controlling for age and years licensed, those who took the course did not have a lower accident rate than the control group; (b) there were no differences in the violation rates between the groups; (c) the cost of damage to the motorcycles per million miles was not less for those who took the course; and (d) the estimated cost of medical treatment of injuries per million miles was not significantly less for the group which took the course."[ix]

8. There was another study done in **1984** for the Illinois Department of Transportation that "compared a group of participants in the training program with a control group of people who had a current valid motorcycle license. Some members of each group never actually rode. The trained riders rode less often, rode less powerful machines, were less likely to own a motorcycle and were less likely to hold a license. Not surprisingly, trained riders were less likely to report having been involved in an accident or obtaining a moving violation or infringement notice. They had, however, been involved in fewer accidents per mile ridden."[x]

9. A study published in **1986** comparing almost 60,000 riders who took either the **California test or Alt-MOST**[xi] and either took training (basic or remedial) or not. It found, "applicants assigned to the MOST II group had more fatal and injury motorcycle accidents and motorcycle convictions than applicants assigned to the Standard Test. When the analysis was restricted to the licensed riders, the MOST II riders had more total motorcycle accidents at the 2-year stage and more motorcycle and total convictions than the riders in the Standard Test group."

10. **Wisconsin** produced a report in **1987**.[xii] It used three-years of data involving almost 3,000 MRC graduates and about 43,000 untrained riders. When "Z" tests were applied, it found, "[T]here seem[s] to be no significant differences between the group with MRC training and the group without MRC training. Based upon this analysis, the effectiveness of the MRC program in reducing accidents among motorcyclists has been very small or not significant at all."

MRC graduates did have a significantly lower ratio of citations-but once again, the authors point out that they weren't able to control for things that might change that-and they point out that 50 percent of graduates did not go on to get their endorsements.

The study points out that the majority (56.8%) of MRC graduates were female-and that significantly affected the ratios of citations and crashes in a positive way while the control group was overwhelming male (93.4%). Women had much better safety records than males in both groups-but the disparity between men and women in the two groups did make a difference. When just male trained and untrained riders are compared, the accident ratio of all male MRC trained was 0.043 compared to 0.53 for untrained males. Trained women had a 0.10 and untrained women 0.11 ratio for crash-involvement as percentages of the whole.

11. A study on the **New York** licensing system that compared the state test with MOST[xiii] was published in **1988**. While the attrition / failure rates were similar between both groups, it found there was no difference between groups that received shorter or longer training or no training or took

one test or the other and got their license. Nor were there differences in crash severity between licensed and unlicensed groups one year later.

"Neither the skill test nor the training course was shown to be any more effective for riders who had previous riding experience compared to novice riders.

"Riders who attempted the MOST II had higher failure rates on their first attempt at a license than control group riders who attempted the current New York test. Trained riders did not do better on their first attempt at the MOST II than untrained riders. Riders in the twenty-hour training group did worse than those in the three-hour group on their first attempt at the MOST II. The untrained riders performed better than the trained riders on their first attempt at the sub-tests of the MOST II that assessed correct braking procedures and obstacle avoidance.

"Those riders who were assessed by the MOST II as showing higher skill levels were not significantly less likely to be involved in subsequent motorcycle accidents."

12. In **1988**, **Mortimer** published the results of a further 913 graduates and a control group of 500 untrained riders. Once again he found that graduates of the MRC did not have a lower violation rate, accident rate, total cost of damage to accident-involved motorcycles, a significantly lower mean cost of injury treatment per accident, or a lower total cost of injury treatment. Mortimer's study found that 30% of those who took the course did not ride afterwards. MRC graduates had more loss-of-traction crashes (gravel / low-friction pavement). Untrained riders had twice as many multi-vehicle crashes as trained riders. [xiv]

13. A dissertation published in **1989** on the **Texas** program[xv] matched trained and untrained riders and followed 988 of them. At the end of four years it found, "...the trained respondents were not significantly different from the comparison respondents."

"The trained motorcyclists had 2.4 times the rate of a motorcycle crash compared with untrained motorcyclists," and that "Most of the excess risk experienced by the trained group occurred within two years of training."

14. A **1989** study, this time by McDavid, et. al,[xvi] was done on the **British Columbia Safety Council's** 37-hour training program. It found, "Trained riders tend to have fewer accidents of all kinds (all motor vehicle accidents combined), fewer motorcycle accidents, and less severe motorcycle accidents. Although these differences are not large in a statistical sense, they suggest that when care is taken to carefully match trained and untrained riders, training is associated with a reduction in accidents.

15. In **1990**, a paper, "The promotion of motorcycle safety: training, education, and awareness"[xvii] found, "Very little support for the beneficial impact of education / training can be found in the evaluation literature." And suggested one of the reasons for that is "the need to focus more on rider motivations and attitudes than on skills...."

16. A **1990** evaluation of the **Ohio** state program with 2,000 trainees and a 6,000 licensed but untrained control group [xviii] found that, "A higher percentage of the trainees who had scored in the highest skill category had been involved in a motorcycle crash than those in all other skill test categories. However, those trainees who obtained scores above 85% on the knowledge test appeared to have a lower motorcycle crash involvement rate in 1989."

17. In **1991**, **Billheimer**, et. al., published his report on the **California program**.[xix] Overall, trained students had less crash-involvement six month after they began riding-however, most of that effect came from true novices-those who had not ridden more than 500 miles before training. Those who had more than 500 miles of experience had a slightly higher rate of crash-involvement than untrained riders, but it was not a statistically significant difference.

At one year, comparisons "show no significant differences between the accident rates of trained and untrained riders one year after training." Nor were there any differences at two years.

18. In a 1994 report to the California state legislature on the MRC:RSS published in **1995** **Wilson**, et. al,[xx] found that 44% of students failing to complete the course said they no longer rode when interviewed a year after training, compared with 24% of those who passed and of those who no longer rode, 16 percent said taking the RSS influenced their decision. "Preliminary analyses showed that accident rates for untrained riders appeared to be 10% higher than for their trained counterparts in the six months after training."

19. Though not a study on training or licensing, the European accident causation study, Motorcycle Accident In-Depth Study (MAIDS) found: "When the accident population and

the exposure population are compared, the data indicates that a similar number of riders in both groups have received no PTW training (40.1% of the accident population and 48.4% of the petrol station population). However, it is important to note that the PTW training status for 93 riders was coded as unknown. ... The data indicates that 47.2% of those riders without any type of training failed to attempt a collision avoidance maneuver. Similarly, the data indicates that 33.2% of those riders who had compulsory training also failed to attempt a collision avoidance maneuver. These results are difficult to interpret since there were many cases in which there was insufficient time available for the PTW rider to perform any kind of collision avoidance."

20. Motorcycle safety researchers at Monash University Accident Research Centre in Melbourne, Australia, produced a review of current licensing and training practices around the world[xxi] in **2005**. Assessing all the evidence in a multitude of countries (as well as their previous literature review published in 2000), the authors conclude, "There is no real evidence of particular programs or components leading to reductions in crash risk...." "Standard motorcycle training courses leading to standard motorcycle tests have not been shown to result in reductions in crash involvement."

21. Another Monash study published in **2006**[xxii] done on **older riders** found "no significant relationship between involvement in one or more crashes in the past five years and having completed a training course at some time for fully-licensed riders ... although there was a trend towards (p <.01) an association between having completed training and involvement in multiple vehicle crashes." Nor was there any relationship between trained or untrained and crash severity. Nor was there a significant relationship between how recently or distantly one took a course and crashing.

22. In **2007**, the Australians did a focus group study on 40 riders that had taken adult-centered training (various curriculum based on Q-ride).[xxiii] Participants felt / believed that training helped them avoid crashes however, in reality, there were several crashes and near misses where training didn't help. The authors suggested "This suggests either a lack of learning transfer, a decay over time of information learnt, or that other factors not addressed in training (e.g. of an attitudinal or motivational nature) influenced rider behaviour once licensed. Training is therefore arguably not enough to always keep riders safe in the traffic environment unless skills are practiced, honed and tempered with self-control."

It also found that "that the most salient information from training is that which has been subsequently experienced on-road. 1) information from training may decay unless subsequently reinforced by experience; 2) learners may be more able to integrate information from training once they have had some riding experience as opposed to the pre-license stage where there is potential for 'information overload' due to the cognitive resources required in initial skill acquisition; and 3) the information may become more personally relevant to novice riders once some experience has been gained."

23. Also in **2007**, a study was done on **Indiana** riders.[xxiv] The authors found that riders who took "beginning rider training courses are more likely to be accident involved than those that do not - and that those that take the beginning course more than once are much more likely to be accident involved."

"The Motorcycle Safety Foundation's Basic Rider Course was found to be significant with three variables in the accident model. For the first variable, those that completed the Basic Rider Course were found to be 44% more likely to be accident involved. This may reflect the ineffectiveness of the course, the fact that the course is attracting an inherently less skilled set of riders and / or the post-course skill set is being used to ride more aggressively....Commenting on the effectiveness of the material taught in the Basic Rider Course is beyond the scope of this paper. In terms of the course attracting inherently less skilled riders, we do control for a wide range of variables in our model. However, it is possible that unobservable variables that are not correlated with those included in the model are still influencing our estimates here."

The second course-related finding was that those that completed the Basic Rider Course multiple times were an additional 180% more likely to be accident involved. This finding may reflect the fact that people that take the course repeatedly are trying to improve an inherently diminished skill set (or one that changes over time) that affects their accident likelihoods. Thus, this variable may be capturing one's inherent ability to master, or the need to refresh, the relatively complex physical and mental skills necessary to operate a motorcycle. Interestingly, there was no significant age difference between people that took the Basic Rider Course once and those that took it multiple times (both roughly 45 years of age). However, those that took the course multiple times had, on average, almost 12 more years of experience. It appears that more experienced riders—perhaps those noting a decline in their skills or those having had recent experiences with near misses—are more likely to take the Basic Riding Course repeatedly.

"People that cited no need for taking the Basic Rider Course were 51% less likely to be accident involved (the average age of these riders was 24.4 years, and 85% of these riders had 5 or more years of experience). This seems to provide some supporting evidence that the people taking the beginner course may be inherently less-skilled riders. It is also interesting to note that 12% of our sample took the Motorcycle Safety Foundation's Experienced Rider Course (the sequel to the Basic Rider Course) but this did not have a statistically significant effect, positive or negative, on accident probabilities."

[i] Usually, the summaries are my own or drawn directly from the studies or abstracts of the studies. On rare occasions, I preferred to use a quote from Narelle Haworth, et. al.'s Evaluation of Rider Training Curriculum in Victoria. Monash Accident Research Centre. 2000.

[ii] Haworth, Narelle and Rob Smith, Naomi Kowadlo. Evaluation Of Rider Training Curriculum In Victoria. Monash University Accident Research Centre. 2000.

[iii] Motorcycle and Bicycle Accidents Source: The British Medical Journal, Vol. 1, No. 6155 (Jan. 6, 1979), pp. 39-41 Published by: BMJ Publishing Group. The report referred to was, Raymond, S and Tatum, S (1977). An evaluation of the effectiveness of the RAC / ACU motorcycle training scheme. A Final Report. University of Salford, Department of Civil Engineering, Road Safety Research Unit, Salford.

[iv] Jonah Brian A. and Nancy E. Dawson. Validation of the motorcycle operator skill test. Road and Motor Vehicle Traffic Safety Branch, Transport Canada. 1978.

[v] Osga, Glenn Arthur. An Investigation Of The Riding Experiences Of MSF Rider Course Participants. University of South Dakota.

[vi] Satten, R.S. Analysis and evaluation of the motorcycle rider courses in thirteen Illinois counties. Proceedings of the International Motorcycle Safety Conference, Washington DC, Vol. 1, pp. 145-193. 1980.

[vii] Anderson, J.W. The effects of motorcycling licensing and skills training on the driver records of original applicants. Proceedings of the International Motorcycle Safety Conference, Washington DC, USA, Vol. 1, pp. 381-401. 1980.

[viii] Jonah, B.A., Dawson, N.E., & Bragg, W.E.. Are formally trained motorcyclists safer? Accident Analysis and Prevention, 14(4), pp. 247-255. 1982.

[ix] Mortimer, Rudolf G. Evaluation of the motorcycle rider course. Accident Analysis & Prevention, Volume 16, Issue 1. February 1984, pp. 63-71.

[x] As reported in Evaluation of Rider Training Curriculum In Victoria. Narelle Haworth, et. al. Monash University Accident Research Centre. 2000. Lakener, E. A survey of motorcycle riders in Illinois. A report submitted to the Traffic Safety Division, Illinois Department of Transportation. 1984.

[xi] Kelsey, S.L., Liddicoat, C., & Ratz, M. Licensing novice motorcyclists: A comparison of California's standard test and the MOST II (Motorcycle Operator Skill Test) administered at centralized testing offices. Research Report of the California Department of Motor Vehicles, Research and Development Office. 1986.

[xii] Leung, Kam S. and Vernon A. Reding. Evaluation of the Wisconsin Motorcycle Rider Course. Wisconsin Department of Transportation. 1987.

[xiii] Buchanan, L.S. (1988). Motorcycle rider evaluation project. Report prepared for the US Department of Transportation, National Highway Traffic Safety Administration, Washington, DC.

[xiv] Henderson, Michael. Education, Publicity and Training in Road Safety: A Literature Review. Monash University Accident Research Study. 1991.

[xv] Lloyd, Linda Elizabeth. An evaluation of the Texas motorcycle operator training course. 1989. The University of Texas at Austin.

[xvi] McDavid, James C.; Lohrmann, Barbara A.; and Lohrmann, George. Does Motorcycle Training Reduce Accidents? Evidence for a Longitudinal Quasi-Experimental Study. Journal of Safety Research, Vol. 20, pp. 61-72, 1989.

[xvii] Simpson, M. and D. R. Mayhew. The promotion of motorcycle safety: training, education, and awareness. Oxford University Press. 1990.

[xviii] Rockwell, T.H., Kiger, S.M., & Carnot, M.J. An evaluation of the Ohio motorcyclists enrichment program, Phase II initial assessment report. Prepared for the Ohio Department of Highway Safety. 1990.

[xix] Billheimer, J.W. California Motorcyclists Safety Program; Final evaluation report. Prepared for California Highway Patrol, under contract to Crain and Associates. 1991.

[xx] Wilson, P., Dunphy, D. & Hannigan, M.J. (1995). The California Motorcyclist Safety Program: 1994 Annual Report to the State Legislature.

[xxi] Haworth, N. & Mulvihill, C. Review of motorcycle licensing and training (Report No. 240). Melbourne: Monash University Accident Research Centre. 2005.

[xxii] Haworth, Narelle and Mulvihill, Christine and Rowden, Peter. Teaching old dogs new tricks? Training and older motorcyclists. In Proceedings Australasian Road Safety Research, Policing and Education Conference, Gold Coast, Queensland.. 2006.

[xxiii] Rowden, Peter J. and Watson, Barry C. and Haworth, Narelle L. What can riders tell us about motorcycle rider training? A view from the other side of the fence. In Proceedings 2007 Australasian Road Safety Research, Policing and Education Conference, Melbourne, Australia. 2007.

[xxiv] Savolainen, Peter and Fred Mannering. Additional evidence of the effectiveness of motorcycle training and motorcyclists' risk-taking behaviour. TRB 2007 Annual Meeting CD-ROM. 2007.

Index

1

1%er / One percenter · 164

2

2-second rule · 33, 35, 164, 195, 235, 237

A

ABS · 33, 164, 202, 203
acceleration rate · 69, 108, 136, 181
Acceleration Rate · *See* g's
additives · 56
aggressive
    braking · 23, 27, 28, 29, 30, 31, 45, 54, 110, 199
    steering · 100
    stopping · 13, 28, 29, 31
    swerving · 28, 29, 30, 31
air pressure · 50, 54, 86, 115, 152, 184, 195, 208, 213, 241
All **T**he **G**ear, **A**ll **T**he **T**ime · 166, 195
Alt-MOST · 142, 165
anti-dive · 55, 110, 111, 166
apex · 100, 166, 173, 205, 220
    delayed start or late apex · 166, 186
ATGATT · *See* All The Gear, All The Time
attention · 3, 29, 58, 59, 60, 61, 66, 67, 202

B

being alert · 59, 60, 61
braking efficiency · 25, 26, 46, 129, 130, 134, 137
BRC · 102, 126, 160, 167, 240
bullet bike · 96, 167

C

California stop · 168
camber thrust · 169, 212, 213, 214
camping · 90, 91, 243
Center of Gravity · 10, 16, 18, 22, 26, 43, 96, 104, 108, 113, 114, 117, 136, 166, 169, 172, 206, 208, 221, 242
centrifugal force · *See* force:centrifugal
centripetal force · *See* force:centripetal
CG · *See* Center of Gravity
chain · 175, 179, 199
Coefficient of Friction · 15, 113, 129, 130, 131, 134, 137, 171, 203, 219
conspicuity · 61
contact patch · 8, 10, 169, 171, 184, 198, 204
control of
    motorcycle · 3, 4, 6, 29, 40, 44, 49, 53, 73, 77, 79, 81, 86, 94, 142, 165, 166, 176, 177, 183, 198, 199, 203, 207, 225, 239
    self · 3, 6, 81, 83, 94, 142
counter-steering · 1, 28, 29, 30, 81, 117, 119, 120, 122, 123, 124, 125, 127, 155, 171, 174, 186, 190, 193
cruise control · 172, 202
cupping · 54

D

dealing with threats · 6, 183
deceleration rate · 6, 7, 8, 9, 10, 11, 12, 14, 15, 16, 17, 21, 26, 28, 29, 46, 93, 96, 128, 129, 132, 181, 202, 203, 206, *See* g's
decreasing radius turn · 126, 173, 186
Delta-V · 28, 174
Dielectric · 58
dip manuever · 125, 126
direct-steering · 124, 125, 127, 172, 174
distractions · 45, 58, 60
do-rag · 174, 197
downforce · 11, 18, 19, 47, 241, 242
drag and lift · 48, 49, 140, 241
drag force · *See* force:drag
Drag / Sweep / Tail Gunner · 175
dumping · 45, 52, 153, 176, 194

E

ear plugs · 41
edge traps · 177
endurance · 40, 41, 95, 97, 151, 152, 153, 185
energy
    heat · 51, 185
    kinetic · 50, 51, 185
    spring · 50
Energy Equivalent Speed · 130, 137
Engine Guards · 178

F

flight plan · 43
following distance · 33, 34, 35, 81, 164, 195, 236
force
    centrifugal · 28, 112, 120, 125, 155, 171, 193, 208, 217, 218, 219, 220
    centripetal · 170
    drag · 240, 242
    lift · 241, 242
    momentum · 170, 188
    Normal · 106, 171
    precession · 193
    restoring · 28, 190, 194, 204
    tangential · 171
    torque (twisting) · 108, 176, 190, 192, 195, 201, 203, 241
    weight · 11, 166, 171, 179, 184, 194, 206, 214, 220, 221, 241, 242
fork seals · 52, 181
forks · 52, 178, 190, 193, 206
forward controls · 179
friction zone · 180
front-brake lever · 8, 182, 185, 189, 191

G

g's · 181
gravity · 48, 104, 106, 107, 109, 171, 181

H

hanging off · 100, 182, 199
heel-toe shifter · 179, 183
high-side · 23, 39, 183, 188
Highway Boards / Highway Pegs · 183
hydroplane · 184

I

inner voice · 156

L

laid it down · 176, 185
lane-splitting · 185
lateral acceleration · 112, 113, 114, 132, 218, 219
lift force · *See* force:lift
limits
    any · 3
    braking · 23
    load · 114
    performance · 6
    personal · 32, 35, 59, 92, 93, 102, 103, 189
    speed · 102, 215, 220
    traction · 46
low-side · 175, 183, 185, 188

M

medication · 2, 37, 42, 44, 82, 154, 227
momentum · *See* force:momentum
MSF · 2, 159, 160, 165, 167, 178, 189, 199, 200, 219

N

newbie · 3, 189, 199
Newton · 179, 188

O

offset · 52
Offset · 190, 204
orthogonal · 107, 170, 190
out-tracking · 120, 190, 193

P

PDR · 20, 129, 191
planning · 41, 74, 86
posture · 203
precession · *See* force:precession
Prime Directive · 65

R

rake angle · 115, 170, 190, 193, 204
rallies · 198
rear-brake pedal · 179, 184, 196
restoring force · *See* force:restoring
RiderCoach · 156, 159, 161, 219
risk compensation · 32, 33
risk homeostasis · 33
RSS · 142, 160

S

shock absorber · 201
situational awareness · 61, 153
skid · 8, 10, 13, 15, 16, 21, 23, 24, 50, 54, 111, 114, 130, 134, 137, 164, 171, 197, 202, 203
slide · 104, 112, 114, 118, 197, 214
slip angle · 111, 112, 115, 118, 120, 198, 208, 210, 211, 212, 214, 215
slow ride · 198
speed advisory sign · 79, 215, 216, 217, 218, 219, 220
sprung weight · 50
squeeze both levers · 199
steering damper · 201
stoppie · 166, 199
swing arm · 21, 23, 51, 54, 196, 200, 206

T

tangential force · *See* force:tangential
tank slapper · 201
target fixation · 202
threshold braking · 14, 202, 203
tire plugs · 55
torque · *See* force, torque
touring · 1
traction · 164, 171, 173, 175, 183, 184, 188, 197, 204, 205
Trail · 190, 193, 204
trail braking · 205
training · 178, 190, 200
triple-tree · 182, 190, 206

U

unexpected · 2, 3, 173, 191, 196

W

weight · *See* force:weight
weight distribution ratio · 27
weight transfer · 7, 10, 16, 18, 23, 26, 27, 28, 47, 49, 52, 53, 54, 104, 105, 106, 107, 108, 109, 111, 113, 114, 166, 172, 206, 214, 221, 241, 242
weight transfer angle · 22
weight transfer ratio · 10, 13, 108, 111, 112, 206
wheelie · 199, 206

Table of Figures

Figure 1: Using 0.5 second squeeze time 12
Figure 2: Using 0.7 second squeeze time 12
Figure 3: Using 0.3 second squeeze time 12
Figure 4: Braking force using 0.7 second squeeze time 13
Figure 5: Using 0.5 second squeeze time 14
Figure 6: Using 0.3 second squeeze tim 14
Figure 7: Using 0.3 seconds with 90% front brake 15
Figure 8: 0.3 second squeeze at 30 MPH 15
Figure 9: Impossible, but claimed stopping rate 16
Figure 10: Probable crash stop 16
Figure 11: Rear end lift during stop 17
Figure 12: 0.3 second squeeze, 90% front brake 18
Figure 13: Effect of high speed on downforce and lift 18
Figure 14: Comparing weight transfer and chain angles 20
Figure 15: Cardboard box obstacle on freeway 21
Figure 16: Rear-end compression forces 21
Figure 17: Brake and swerve choices and consequences 25
Figure 18: NHTSA chart of fatalities by age 29
Figure 19: Emergency Medical Tag 33
Figure 20: Example of a balaclava 39
Figure 21: Moving camouflage 42
Figure 22: Looming effect 42
Figure 23: Drag and lift model output 43
Figure 24: Control of weight by speed 44
Figure 25: Group lane change into slower lane 60
Figure 26: Group lane change into faster lane 61
Figure 27: Closing a gap within a group 67
Figure 28: "Closing the door" 67
Figure 29: On-ramp threat to group 72
Figure 30: Reaction blocking traffic 73
Figure 31: Suitable reaction 73
Figure 32: Cargo capacity of a non-touring bike 79
Figure 33: Effect on CG of adding a rider 88
Figure 34: At-rest forces (Weight and Normal) 89
Figure 35: Moving forces (driving and resistance) 90
Figure 36: Vectored forces 90
Figure 37: Lean Angle Calculator sample output 94
Figure 38: Slip angle 96
Figure 39: Under- and over-steer paths 96
Figure 40: Tire profile 98

Figure 41: Profile when leaning at 30 degrees 98
Figure 42: Circular path 98
Figure 43: Positive and negative steering torque 99
Figure 44: Acceleration indexed speed 100
Figure 45: Starting on and starting outside the desired path 102
Figure 46: The "dip" 103
Figure 47: Making a U-turn with the "dip" 103
Figure 48: Deceleration rate calculator 104
Figure 49: Deceleration rate from speed and distance 105
Figure 50: Stopping distance from speed and deceleration rate 105
Figure 51: Speed from stopping distance 106
Figure 52: Critical speed calculator 106
Figure 53: Speed scrubbed during a skid 107
Figure 54: Distance traveled and speed while braking 108
Figure 55: Lateral acceleration and lean angle 108
Figure 56: Quadratic equation solver 109
Figure 57: Radius calculator 109
Figure 58: Skid distance to a stop 110
Figure 59: Center of Gravity (CG) calculator 110
Figure 60: Vault speed calculator 111
Figure 61: Lean angle of CG calculator 111
Figure 62: Skid mark analyzer 112
Figure 63: Speed by gear calculator 113
Figure 64: Rear wheel radius calculator 114
Figure 65: Gearing ratios calculator 114
Figure 66: Horsepower from torque calculator 115
Figure 67: Drag and lift 116
Figure 68: Camber thrust 130
Figure 69: Out-tracking 139
Figure 70: A stoppie 143
Figure 71: A wheelie 145
Figure 72: Radius of CG path of travel 148
Figure 73: Neutral steer path of CG 148
Figure 74: Identical slip angles for both tires 149
Figure 75: Slip angles on under-steering bike 149
Figure 76: Slip angles on over-steering bike 150
Figure 77: Contact patch 151
Figure 78: Contact patch lag creating slip angle 151
Figure 79: Spreadsheet for lateral acceleration, 35 MPH 154
Figure 80: Spreadsheet for lateral acceleration, 70 MPH 155
Figure 81 Crossed chains for towing a trailer 157
Figure 82: Passenger steering the bike 158

List of Tables

Table 1: Stopping measurements..**11**
Table 2: GSX-R600 Potential Speeds **129**
Table 3: ZX9R Potential Speeds **129**

Made in the USA
San Bernardino, CA
31 January 2015